THE MACANESE CHRONICLES

A History of Luso-Asians in a Global Economy

Roy Eric Xavier, Ph.D

Far East Currents Publishing - Presented by Ponto Final Macau (Newspaper) and the Portuguese and Macanese Studies Project

Copyright © 2020 Roy Eric Xavier

All rights reserved

This is a historical work based on empirical research conducted by the author.

No part of this book may be reproduced, or stored in a retrieval system, or transmitted in any form or by any means, electronic, mechanical, photocopying, recording, or otherwise, without express written permission of the author.

ISBN: 978-0-578-71034-1

Print Version Cover design by Veronica E. Xavier

E-book Cover design by Art Painter

Library of Congress Control Number: 2018675309
Printed in the United States of America

This book is dedicated to my parents,

*Nuno Alvares Xavier
and
Josephine Eldetrudes Castro Xavier,*

*my cousin,
Margarida Alvares Marques Savant,*

My family in the United States and in many other countries,

*and to
Filhos e Filhas de Macau past, present, and future.*

READER COMMENTS

"I read (The Macanese Community of Hong Kong) with detailed interest. ... For years I had hoped someone as you would come to the fore to write on this topic, and you have now realized my expectation."
Armando M. da Silva
Emeritus Professor, Towson University, Baltimore

"I have read (The Macanese at War) with great interest ... The strong theme that comes through here is the "agency" of the Macanese under adversity."
Geoffrey C. Gunn,
Emeritus Professor, Nagasaki University

"Your article (on The Origins of Macau's culture) is just wonderful. I have read your work several times. Please, continue. We need people like you."
Lucio de Sousa
Professor, Tokyo University of Foreign Studies

"I found your meticulously researched article (on the Hongkong Printing Press) very inspiring."
Calvin Wong
Department of Chinese and History
City University of Hong Kong

"The work you are doing is extremely important. Keep going with it."
Marisa C Gaspar
Research Fellow
Universidade de Lisboa (ISCSP)

"You've certainly compiled a most important and valuable resource, one which I've used for my PhD and which I used for other projects a few years ago too."
Amelia Allsop
Senior Researcher, Kadoorie Heritage Project
Hong Kong

"I just want to say how much I appreciate your papers on the Macanese community in Hong Kong. I am a Macanese person ... my father was born in Hong Kong but migrated to Australia ..."
Sally Barnes
Monash University - Graduate Student, Education
Melbourne, Australia

"Just want to say thank you for your information. It is very useful for my study. I have interest in Shanghai Portuguese Refugees."
Jude Fong
Graduate Student, History
University of Macau, China

CONTENTS

Title Page
Copyright
Dedication
Reader Comments
Prologue
Introduction
Part 1   1
Chapter 1   2
Chapter 2   20
Chapter 3   31
Chapter 4   46
Chapter 5   55
Chapter 6   69
Part II   76
Chapter 7   77
Chapter 8   89
Chapter 9   109
Chapter 10   126
Chapter 11   139
Chapter 12   146

PROLOGUE

The people who lived on the southern tip of Imperial China, whose families fished for centuries along the shores of Guangdong and Fujian, always kept a wary eye on the horizon for signs of typhoons. In the regional lore, there is a story that while out one day near the Pearl River delta several boatmen were caught in a terrible storm. As the weather grew worse, they prayed to Neang Ma (Mazu), a Confucian sea-goddess, to save their catch and rescue them.[1] As the mounting waves and wind threatened, it was only by the grace of the goddess that their shallow boats and all aboard were saved from certain death. Soon after, everyone in the village near the great stone, where it is said the goddess lives, helped build a small temple to commemorate her kindness. Dug out of a small hillside overlooking the sea, the modest shrine would celebrate their salvation and a growing devotion to the divinity.

The year was 1488. The small shrine was called the Temple of A-Ma, the name for the goddess in the local dialect. The temple soon grew to include several more chambers built higher up the hill, then alcoves for Buddhist and Taoist deities, and became a center for religious worship in the region. And like most events outside Beijing, the capital of the Ming Empire to the north, the construction of the temple and the fortunes of the village were eventually forgotten in history.

The location of the temple, however, has long been a vantage point from which to witness the region's development. More than fifty years earlier, during the era of the Treasure Fleets under the eunuch General Zheng He, the promontory where the temple now sits was a place where the people could glimpse the sails of the great ships passing along the horizon.

Their destinations, from China to the Middle East to discover new cultures and seek trading partners, could scarcely be imagined by the villagers scratching out a living on fish and shrimp in the shallow waters between the delta's islands. Then one year the great ships were gone, without an explanation, and never returned.[2]

In the years that followed, a different excitement occurred with greater frequency. It was the terror of marauding pirates who pillaged local villages, killing those who resisted, and capturing others as slaves.[3] For seventy years in the absence of the Ming fleets, the situation along the coast where the temple was built remained unchanged. Then in 1553, the villagers heard distant explosions and saw fires on ships in the throes of battle. Then men with beards, dressed in breeches with their heads covered in the style of Arabs, took the battle to the village shores.

The pirate leader, Chang Si-Lao, was soon trapped in his stronghold not far from the temple.[4] Once captured and slain, news of his death by the bearded men was reported to the mandarins in Canton and then to the Emperor as proof of their victory. As a reward, the newcomers were allowed to trade on the islands of Shanchuan and Lampacao, where they met merchants from Canton. Later they were permitted to build a settlement on Macau.[5] A new day had come.

The A-Ma Temple still stands today in Macau, the modern gaming city that took its name from the sea-goddess. The shrine and many other structures are remnants of a past that was scarcely noticed by the Ming empire, and all that is left of the Portuguese empire that settled Macau, and the British empire that later succeeded both. The echoes of those empires are evident throughout Southeast Asia today, if only we attempt to understand their histories and listen to the stories of the people who have lived there for over a thousand years. This book is an attempt to recapture some of that history, and to understand how the Asian descendants of those first bearded soldiers settled in the region and changed the world forever.

INTRODUCTION

We begin by observing that there is little general knowledge, or documented information, about the racially mixed Portuguese from Asia, who scholars and researchers have identified as "Luso-Asians". The most visible members of this community are the Macanese (Macaense), who settled for over 400 years in the former colony of Macau. Comprised of a small group of islands in the Pearl River Delta 107 kilometers downriver from Canton, China's southern trading center, Macau served as a conduit for foreign trade into China, and a barrier used by the Imperial Court in its early relations with Portugal, England, and other western countries.

As a result of increased merchant trade, religious tolerance, and the arrival of diverse groups from India, Africa, and Southeast Asia by the late 16th century, Macau and its mestizo population transformed the city from a fishing village into an international commercial center in less than a century. Despite numerous setbacks, including a foreign invasion, dynastic changes, and wars among the powerful empires that protected Macau and benefited from its location, the diverse inhabitants developed a shared and unique culture.

This culture served as the foundation for reviving critical relations with regional sultanates from the 17th through the 18th centuries after Portugal's empire declined and China and Japan retreated from foreign contact. By preserving relations and cultural links between Europe and Asia, Macau's "clandestine" merchants navigated the backwaters of Southeast Asia to amass great fortunes, while continuing a nascent economy that contributed to the transition of Europe from agrarian economies to trade-based capitalism. The innovative practices of the Macanese extended well into the twentieth century, including the early adoption of printing to distribute commercial information through their involvement in newspaper publishing, journalism, and advertising, and the introduction of paper currencies into the Chinese banking system. Illustrating the origins of Macanese culture, and introducing the history of their exploits and influence on a new global economy will be the goals of this study.

Following the Scattered Trail

Examining the social origins of Luso-Asian settlements during Portugal's colonial period and the history of Macau is often difficult due to the irregular accounts of ancient chroniclers. Early Portuguese studies also were unable to overcome a narrow focus on initial "contacts" and "discoveries" that often neglected the impact of colonial policies on indigenous peoples over several centuries.[6] The result has been an inability among general readers and academics alike to recognize the early role of the Portuguese as initiators of exchanges and relationships with diverse peoples, as well as instances of religious and colonial persecution, all of which contributed to extending their influence in western India and throughout Asia.[7]

In the modern area, this area of study has been marked by debates and disagreements among historians and other chroniclers, especially since the nineteenth century. The latter began with the publication of Swedish historian Anders Ljungstedt's study, A Historical sketch of the Portuguese settlements in China: and of the Roman Catholic Church, which ruffled nationalist sentiments by questioning Portugal's claimed sovereignty over Macau.[8] A counterpoint would not appear until C.A. Montalto's 1902 publication of Historic Macau, the first English language study of the Portuguese colony.[9] Varying historical interpretations, at times driven by nationalism and political agendas, later led to the suppression of Montalto's revision of that study in 1929, and the public burning of copies by the government of Macau.[10]

Following World War II, the debate was renewed over the effects of Portuguese colonial policies on indigenous populations and race relations. The most controversial aspect involved the willingness of some scholars to present a sanitized view of Portuguese colonialism that emphasized "benevolent acceptance" of racial groups encountered in India, Africa, and South America, despite historical evidence to the contrary. This perspective was aligned with the nationalist government of Portuguese Prime Minister Antonio Salazar, who wished to soften his country's tarnished public image and defend Portugal's remaining overseas "possessions" in Goa, Angola, and Mozambique.[11]

The new debate reached its height with the involvement of Armando Cortesao, a noted Portuguese historian and the translator of Tome' Pires' "Suma Oriental", and Charles R. Boxer, a prominent British historian, which played out over the pages of magazines and academic journals during the period.[12]

A consequence of this contested portrayal of history, some critics argued, has been a general devaluation of Portuguese historiography, and scant recognition of Portugal's contributions to global development since the colonial period.[13] Since then, the insular nature of research in this field continues to produce narrow views of Portuguese history in the writings of some academics and colonial expatriates.[14] There is recent evidence, however, that this trend may be changing. One of the benefits has been the appearance of research that incorporates the realities of Portuguese colonialization and its racial policies into wider ranging studies.[15] There have also appeared several examinations of Portugal's trade history since C.R. Boxer's seminal studies, and research on indigenous and racially mixed populations in Asia.[16]

In summary, research in this area has left many unresolved issues. These began, in some cases, with an inability or unwillingness to differentiate between European Portuguese and those of mixed racial heritage who succeeded them in virtually all areas of colonial life by the end of the 17th century. As a result, early scholarship was unable to discern the multiple impacts that Portuguese colonization had on non-Europeans, and the degree to which indigenous peoples, and Luso-Asians in particular, contributed to the growth of communities outside Portuguese control. Had these scholars been able to overcome these obstacles, they may have able to recognize evidence that Luso-Asians played important roles in creating economic and political relations between the Chinese and other Westerners in the 17th and 18th centuries when the British, Dutch, and the French were making little headway. They may have also given Luso-Asians credit for adopting early technologies such as printing, which led to the wider distribution of government data and commercial information, thus stimulating the "China Trade" in the 19th century, the precursor to modern global commerce.

In the end, it may have been the inability of some scholars to differentiate the first Portuguese who arrived from Europe from their mixed-race descendants, who we refer to as Luso-Asians, including the Macanese in Macau, that obscured recognition of those achievements until now. Today we see the effects of this neglect by the small amount of research on those groups in the development of modern Asia.[17] Based on a review of empirical studies, analyses, recently discovered materials, and new research, I will attempt to address some of these issues below by proposing common features about Luso-Asian development, beginning with their migrations through India, across Asia toward Macau and Hong Kong, and more recently to other countries around the world.

The Realities of Portuguese Colonization

Despite disagreements among scholars over the intention of colonization, there is little doubt that early Portuguese policies, which effectively institutionalized religious and secular persecution, resulted in four principal migrations and several minor dispersions of Luso-Asians beginning in the early 16th century. The specific reasons and the details about these migrations will be discussed in later chapters. In the broadest terms, these migrations began in the years following the departure of explorer-merchants and missionaries from Portugal in 1419, who later traveled across Africa, Brazil, India, and Asia seeking trade and the conversion of indigenous people.[18] Following the exploration of trading routes to Africa and Brazil through 1500, the first migrations of Portuguese from Lisbon to Goa were launched by the Portuguese monarchy through the Estado da India, which administered the colonization of western India (1511), and the settlements of Indonesia (1509), Malacca (1512), Indonesia (1515), Siam (1535), Macau (1553), and Timor (1556).

As the Portuguese overseas empire reached its peak by the middle of the 17th century, a second and larger migration of Luso-Asian descendants, the result of inter-marriage with local peoples, began arriving in Macau by 1557 due to its proximity to China, and later identified themselves as "Maquistas" or "Macaense". The growing commercial activity of Macau, along with the willingness of local authorities to allow other ethnic groups to settle and work, was a key feature in expanding Portuguese trade in Southeast Asia and securing its survival during later periods of decline.

Almost three hundred years later, after the end of the Opium Wars (1839 – 1860), a third migration began among Macanese workers and their families, who were recruited by the British administration to Hong Kong beginning in 1842. Then following the end of World War II, the fourth and final migration of Macanese dispersed to the United States, Australia, Canada, Brazil, Portugal, and other countries from 1945 to around 1980. There also were secondary migrations that followed trade routes between Goa, Japan, Macau, and Hong Kong to other destinations, including Vietnam, Cambodia, and Timor. The largest of these was to Shanghai, beginning in 1859 where about 4,000 Macanese settled, joining a larger international community that thrived until the Communist Revolution of 1949.

The dates of each settlement vary among the sources, resulting in an overlap in periods. That is, although Macau was settled in the middle of the 16th century, the migration of Luso-Asians from Goa to Macau did not increase significantly until the late 17th century, following the decline of Portuguese trade and the persecution of mestizos and indigenous people after the Inquisition was transferred to Goa in 1560. Each date, however, marks the beginning of a specific period of settlement in a new destination. The fact that this group of Luso-Asians later identified with Macau, rather than with Goa or Portugal, indicates a longer period of cultural development took place in Macau for over 400 years, and persists in the identification of many Luso-Asians to this day.[19]

There also were at least five unique characteristics of Luso-Asian and Macanese culture that unified these communities throughout each migration. Recent studies suggest that the two most common traits are a devotion to Roman Catholicism, a remnant of Portuguese influences, and a creole language or patois, first called "Kristang" in Malacca and later referred to as "Maquista" in Macau.[20] The use of language, in particular, was the result of commercial utility and multiple exchanges with different ethnic trading partners arriving periodically in the port. Another characteristic was a tendency toward large family groups, which we will also discuss, and the associated development of cultural organizations and associations they created. A fourth characteristic was a unique cuisine that was nurtured within familial generations and influenced by multiple cultural contacts.

A final trait, less common among continental Portuguese but indicative of colonial expatriates, was an inclination toward business in each new location out of a necessity to survive as a community. Commerce among Luso-Asians first began with clandestine trade in the South China Sea during the 16th century, then after large settlements appeared focused on small shops and other forms of local commerce. By the 18th century Luso-Asians took on the role of colonial intermediaries, but by the end of the 19th century many Macanese became more entrepreneurial through such innovations as faster sailing and steam ships, and the adoption of print technology, taking advantage of wider distribution and creating products and services that stimulated the larger trade economy in ways that we are only now beginning to understand.[21]

Despite these characteristics, some of which were shared by Luso-Asian communities outside Macau, the identification of these mestizos by outsiders has often been difficult to pin down. For example, beginning in the 17th century, most European traders often referred to the people of Macau as "Portuguese", even though most had never been to Europe. This inaccuracy has contributed to confusion about their origins over the years. Many Luso-Asians from Macau, it should be acknowledged, continue to identify with Portugal because of the city's historic ties to that country since the sixteenth century.[22] But the label placed on them often failed to recognize, and in some cases purposefully obscured, their racial and ethnic origins.

Hidden Heritage

The confusion over ethnic origins may ultimately rest upon the Portuguese clergy's early obsession with a policy known as "pureza de sangue" (purity of blood), a counterpoint to the widespread miscegenation, domestic servitude, and slavery in India, which contributed to growing numbers of mestizos by the end of the 15th century.[23] The disparity in numbers in comparison to Europeans and the need for social stability, however, were incentives for both the Church and Portugal's Estado da India to grudgingly accept varying degrees of racial mixing in later years.[24]

Ultimately, neither racial purity nor the insistence by clerics on marital unions could continue once overseas trade became dependent on the volatile mix of easy wealth and unattached males from Africa, India, South America, and Asia arriving on trading vessels, who joined assorted brigands, criminals, concubines, domestic servants, and slaves in Goa and

Macau. As a result, even while Luso-Asians to the outside world were incorrectly identified as "Portuguese", by the second generation (around the late 16th century) most were actually multi-racial, a blending of Europeans and others from Goa, Japan, Malaysia, Indonesia, Thailand, Timor, and later from Canton (Guangzhou) and other Chinese provincial cities, the result of Portugal's extensive trade relations in Southeast Asia.

To avoid further misunderstanding, since there were relatively few continental Portuguese in Asia after 1700, throughout this study I will use "Macanese" and "Portuguese" interchangeably in reference to the Luso-Asian majority that first populated Macau, and later migrated to Hong Kong, Shanghai and other western countries by the late 20th century. While recent scholarship has discussed Luso-Asians in other regions of Southeast Asia, my primary focus will be on those from Macau who developed a culture in this obscure corner of China for almost five hundred years.

The Origins of Luso-Asian Culture

In order to untangle these historical threads further, the first part of this study will provide a context to Luso-Asian culture that first developed in Goa, the point of origin for all subsequent migrations toward Asia. This requires us to introduce a different perspective that will guide our focus on those who settled in Macau within the context of Portuguese colonialism. In other words, Macau was the beneficiary of diverse patterns of cultural development begun in Goa, the administrative headquarters of the Portuguese overseas empire. During the occupation of western India, a new group of people were born to Portuguese settlers and indigenous women, who scholars first referred to as "descendentes", later as "Portuguese-Asians", and more recently as "Luso-Asians".[25]

Their very existence was a result of political and religious policies, and economic need, the former introduced during the colonization of Goa and the surrounding region.[26] Their Indian ancestors were often domestics, laborers, sailors, soldiers, concubines, or slaves who were forced to adopt Portuguese culture and Roman Catholicism to avoid scrutiny by military authorities and persecutions by the Goan Inquisition. As Portuguese trade on India's west coast initially flourished, and was eventually challenged by the Dutch and the English in the late 16th century, an exodus of those descendants began across India toward Southeast Asia throughout the 17th century, exposing them to multiple influences in language, religion, social outlook, fashion, and even culinary styles.[27] Once expelled from Goa, a significant number were drawn by the opportunities of clandestine trade in the South China Sea, allowing many to become independent traders and intermediaries between China and Japan just as both nations closed their borders to foreigners in the 17th century.[23] Their eventual settlement in Macau made it a center for European and Asian commerce for the next three hundred years.

The Organization of Chapters

In order to provide more clarity, this study is divided into two sections. Part I will include a discussion of the Portuguese empire's rise and decline as we follow the migrations of indigenous peoples and mestizos from India to Southeast Asia. This section is not intended to be a comprehensive analysis of Portuguese colonialism. It is more an attempt at an historical narrative and contextualization of Luso-Asian presence that often has been missing from previous studies. This will involve various chapters on the locations in which they settled, including Goa, Malacca, Indonesia, Siam, Macau, Hong Kong, and Shanghai from around 1503 through the end of the Opium Wars in 1860. Each chapter will emphasize major developments that influenced Luso-Asian communities and suggest their contributions to larger world processes, including as indicated in the title, their role in the development of a global economy introduced under Portuguese and British trading systems from the 15th through the 20th centuries.

Part II will focus on the evolution of the Macanese community in Hong Kong, where large numbers settled in the 19th century, through the documented histories of specific individuals and their families. Each chapter is a case study intended to illustrate the deterioration of trust and a loss of confidence among the Macanese in the Hong Kong government's willingness to protect their interests. As a result, each chapter analyzes their different roles as clerical workers, community advocates, business owners, entrepreneurs, politicians, and wartime refugees as we witness their progression as social actors within a highly structured colonial society that moves toward decline.

In both sections, through historical reviews and intimate glimpses of individuals living through specific events, we will demonstrate the character of cultural development that first emerged in 16th century Macau, through the evolution of a unique identity in Hong Kong and Shanghai that emerged by the end of World War II. We will also witness the transference of that culture in later migrations through local associations in the post-war period. We will then conclude with an assessment of the Macanese in the modern era, and an analysis of different groups within the community who are attempting to maintain a cultural identity across various national borders. Throughout these chapters, my objective will be to introduce the unique history of Luso-Asians and Macanese over the last five centuries, and highlight the relevance of their contributions to future studies of ethnic cultures and colonial societies in Asia.

PART 1

The Rise and Fall of the Portuguese Empire:
The Migrations of Mestizos from India to Southeast Asia

CHAPTER 1
Goa and the Origins of Portugal's Overseas Empire

A Portuguese fleet under the command of chief captain Afonso de Albuquerque first arrived in Indian waters near Cochin in April 1503. The fleet consisted of six ships, three each in flotillas under Afonso and his cousin Francisco de Albuquerque, and were accompanied by small groups of Jesuit missionaries and their retainers. All were under orders from King Dom Manuel I (1469-1521) to build a fortress in Cochin and organize a garrison to protect trade that had begun there three years earlier. [29] They were also told to avoid conflict, to convert local people to Christianity when possible, and to inquire about establishing relations with indigenous groups along the coast. The actual practice suggests that these instructions were more difficult to follow. Upon his appointment as Governor of India in November 1509, Albuquerque overthrew and executed incumbent Moorish rulers, laid siege to their fortresses, and captured their principal seaport of Goa. He then made plans to continue on to Malacca, Siam, and the islands of "Insulindia" (Indonesia) to collect information and bring back samples of merchandise.[30]

By the time the Portuguese succeeded in controlling western India, one of Albuquerque's aides, Tomé Pires, had already identified Malacca and the surrounding region as the principal source of spices and goods that the Venetians and others transported along the Silk Road. Following the Portuguese occupation of Goa in November 1511, Albuquerque was awarded the title of "Captain-General of India" and effectively become the chief architect of Portugal's overseas empire. Pires soon became a reliable source of intelligence from Malacca. In reports that ranged from sober evaluations of resources and local defenses to social commentary, he skillfully catalogued a wide variety of exotic goods, a conspicuous display of wealth, and a high volume of trade conducted by Muslims, Egyptians,

Bengalis, Siamese, Goans, Cambodians, Turks and merchants from many other nations.[31] By employing Pires' detailed assessment of the region, Albuquerque succeeded in elevating Portugal, a small nation of just over one million, into position to bypass the trade monopoly held by Venice, Genoa, and Florence since the 14th century.[32]

Tome' Pires (1468 –1540) was perhaps least likely to become one of Europe's earliest Asian strategists and chroniclers. Although he proved to be a keen observer, Pires began his public life as an apothecary in the Portuguese court of King Joao II and his son, Prince Afonso.[33] Following the death of the young prince in 1491, Pires was attached to the king's physician and continued his education at court, which included an introduction to new methods of commerce. In early 1511 when Pires was forty-three and a widower, the king assigned him to Albuquerque's command in India as an agent or "feitor das drogarisas", a purchaser of Asian and Middle Eastern spices, including all culinary and medicinal varieties. HIs new position included an annual stipend and a store of spices that were sent ahead to Goa for his use. It would be the beginning of a long and sometimes anxious existence, the early years of which Pires documented in a series of letters and reports entitled "The Suma Oriental" (An Account of the East).

Based on his analysis of Malacca, Pires sent communiques to Albuquerque in Goa stating that many nations trading in the South

China Sea were considered vassals of Imperial China, whose relations were protected by a formidable seaborne military. The fleet had forged alliances with sultanates from Asia to the Middle East from 1405 to 1433 through the voyages of Zheng He, a eunuch general under the Ming Yongle emperor Zhu Di.[34] Since then Zhu Di's heirs, under the influence of Confucian clerics, refocused inward, neglected international trade, and remained suspicious of foreigners. China's ambivalence toward foreign contact and commerce effectively left the door open to the Portuguese occupation of Malacca in 1512, which China tolerated from a distance. This situation created an opportunity for the Europeans to set up settlements in regions that make up modern-day Indonesia, Malaysia, Thailand, Burma, and Vietnam.[35]

Pires also advised Albuquerque that the ability of the Portuguese to maintain a presence among these sultanates should not be by conquest, as was the situation in Goa. In Asia, Pires suggested, Portuguese success must focus on incorporation and coercion. The rulers of these nations were in most cases distracted by continual conflicts over territory and power, often with members of their own families. Most rulers were willing to concede control of the surrounding seas to the Europeans in exchange for material support against their rivals. These local conflicts, Pires emphasized, should be exploited to advance the Portuguese agenda through lucrative treaties, which would allow trade, the building of fortifications, and religious conversions in exchange for arms and protection.

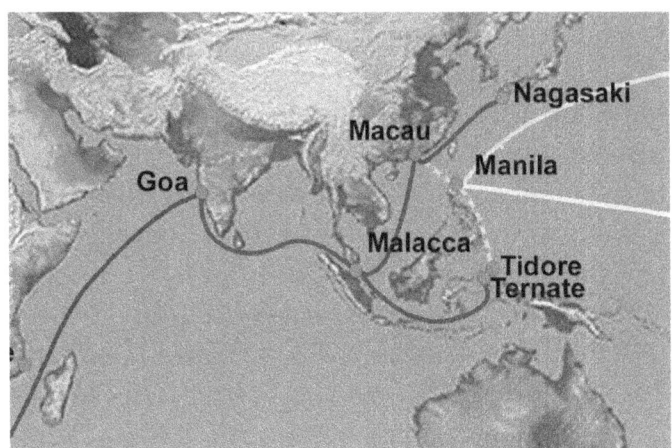

In the intervening years, from 1512 to 1553, before the Middle Kingdom could decide on a policy toward the Portuguese, the vacuum left by the lack of a strong Chinese presence in the South China Sea and disorganization among smaller kingdoms allowed the Portuguese to thrive. Goa and Malacca were quickly incorporated into a series of protected port cities, which extended from the Middle East to Timor.

C.R. Boxer, the noted historian of Portuguese history, observed that:
> Ormuz at one end of the Indian Ocean and Malacca at the other were the two great Asian entrepots for the collection and distribution of luxury goods, including the Indonesian spices that eventually reached Europe via the Levant. [36]

As Goa became the administrative hub of this network, the regions of Portuguese Asia became noted for the immense wealth produced, corruption, religious persecution, slavery, and different forms of pacification.

Colonial Wealth: The Basis of Power
Portuguese power depended on the wealth that could be extracted from its new empire and transferred back to Lisbon and the rest of Europe. To appreciate the scale of this enterprise, we shall attempt to estimate the actual value of Portugal's colonial

prosperity relative to the present in order to understand the stakes involved. Such an illustration may suggest why so many Europeans were willing risk their lives and the futures of their families on the thin promise of foreign riches. This estimate will also help us to appreciate the great social and economic disparities between Europeans and the large indigenous and mestizo underclass in India, conditions this wealth produced.

Any effort to produce a precise tally of trade revenues during 16th and 17th centuries is difficult, however, given fluctuations in the price of silver and gold since then, and five centuries of inflation. On the other hand, a rough estimate of Portuguese revenues transferred to Europe may provide some perspective as to the amount of trade conducted. Given these parameters, we can begin by using historian James Boyajian's estimates of gross values per ship load for illustration, which he placed at 5.1 million silver cruzados each (4.128 million ounces) during a thirteen year period at the height of trading activity (1586-1598).[37] Our calculations also employ Boyajian's estimate of 4.7 ships completing the journey from Goa back to Lisbon annually, and the current price of silver ($15.46 in 2019). If multiplied by the number of ships each year, a preliminary value of goods arriving in Lisbon each year would be roughly $64 million USD.[38] Incorporating other trade destinations into this calculation would increase that estimate exponentially.

Following the introduction of Japanese trade after 1542, for example, large amounts of silver were also transferred annually from Japan to China by Portuguese merchants, then traded for Asian goods to be sold in Europe.[39] Since China had an abundance of gold mines, merchants there were willing to exchange silks and gold for Japanese silver, cotton, tin, copper, and other commodities to sell in local markets. An estimate by economist Kotaba Atsushi of silver exports from Japan for the years 1546 to 1638, converted to current prices, places the additional value of Japanese-Portuguese trade at roughly $9.11 million annually.[40] When added to the previous tally, Japanese silver would increase our estimate of gross revenues to more than $73 million USD each year.

These revenues were offset by the capital invested in ships, men and materials bound for India, China, and Japan, which was often borrowed by Portuguese kings from New Christian (Jewish) investors, whose families were persecuted as heretics in the 15th century by the Spanish and Portuguese Inquisitions. The borrowed funds averaged about 50% of a cargo's value when it reached Europe.[41]

If we accept these estimates, net profits from Portuguese trade would have been approximately half the gross revenues listed above, or about $36.5 million annually (50% of $73 million). Some historians, including C.R. Boxer and C.A. Montalto de Jesus, argued that annual profit margins, especially after 1542 when the Portuguese began trading with both Japan and China, may have exceeded 100%, and in some cases, up to 200% of the initial investment.[42] That would potentially increase the range of European profits, after expenses were paid, from $73 million to $146 million annually.

There was also private cargo that arrived unreported and uncounted on manifests in Lisbon. Many ship captains, officers, agents, and crew members held back small quantities of spices, pepper, gems, or precious metals in personal holds for sale once the ships docked, some of which was permitted under prior agreement, and others that were smuggled for personal use. Bribes to officials for other items, such as cloves and bullion, were also common. In addition, Spanish gold from the Americas and other goods that entered Europe through Seville during the same period was reported to be at least equal to the amount of goods that arrived in Lisbon, effectively doubling the riches that passed through Portugal.[43]

The sum of all these revenues suggests that the wealth reaching Europe from Portuguese and Spanish sources through the 16th century, including permitted and smuggled goods from the Americas, may have been at least $300 million annually. The combined riches from Iberian sources were probably the largest source of wealth in Europe at the time, surpassing even the value of goods arriving via the "Silk Road" controlled by Venice, Genoa, and their Middle Eastern partners, which was reduced, but not eliminated, by the new competition.[44] The accumulation of wealth, local engagement of small and large traders, and the overall stimulation of commerce from both Iberian and Venetian sources during this period was likely a principal catalyst for the transformation of medieval Europe from rural fiefdoms to economies connected to a nascent global economy, leading to the Renaissance and the Enlightenment in Europe. As A.J.S. Russell-Wood observed:

> ... such contacts between Europeans and non-Europeans inexorably heralded a new transcontinental, transoceanic, and transnational age of globalization, which was to be characterized by interdependence, interaction, and exchange. ... The Portuguese were initiators, protagonists, and cultural brokers. [45]

The Effects of Wealth from Portuguese India and Asia

Once a large portion of this capital arrived in Lisbon, all trade from the Portuguese colonies was in principle governed under the royal monopoly. Portuguese kings claimed ownership of all cargos from India and Asia, as well as all the ships leaving their ports and the materials necessary to outfit them. The terms of the monopoly stipulated that only those who represented the king, usually courtiers and landed gentry called "Fidalgos" (sons of somebody), were granted royal contracts or licenses, and could trade in pepper, cloves, and other spices. The list later included other exotic commodities, such as elephants and pearls from Ceylon. The investors were to be repaid out of profits once sales were completed in Lisbon or in Portuguese factories at Antwerp. The king also had the right to sell pepper and other spices to investors at prearranged prices.[46]

This system worked fairly well for the first half of the sixteenth century, as long as Portuguese navigation, technology, and its military controlled western India. The windfall profits were greatly anticipated in early reports of Portuguese agents in the field. In Tome Pires' assessment of Malacca for Albuquerque in 1511, for example, he noted the high volume of trade conducted by merchants from many nations.[47] The variety of goods and precious metals was a revelation to the Portuguese court and most of Europe. Pires calculated that each ship leaving Malacca was valued at about fifteen thousand cruzados, with some up to thirty thousand cruzados. One ship's annual cargo from the Indian city of Cambay was estimated to be worth seventy to eighty thousand cruzados. [48] Due to the priorities of the crown, Pires was especially interested in the large supply of pepper, cloves, mace, nutmeg, and musk, as well as sandalwood, peals, porcelain, silks, and large amounts of gold that passed through the various kingdoms. Each of these commodities could bring even higher profits in Europe.

The vast wealth from the Indies, however, did not lessen the Portuguese monarchy's risk. Even the great sums collected from Goa, Malacca and other ports were not enough to pay the mounting debts of Portuguese kings during this period. Large amounts was taken up by a failed military expedition to North Africa by King Sebastian I in 1578 and the ransom of captives, and in the defense against Dutch attacks on Asian ports following the unification of the Spanish and Portuguese crowns in 1580.[49] More was paid in the form of dowries for women of the royal house, or lost due to increasing competition from native traders who conducted business beyond the reach of Portuguese ships. Another drain was what Boyajian has called "the growing tributary of income ... among a handful of fidalgos (landed gentry) and titled nobility, ostensibly to reward past services." [50] Those privileged few were tasked with collecting revenues in Africa, Brazil, India, and Asia, and sending surpluses back to Lisbon, a system ripe for corruption. In December 1511, for example, Tome' Pires found evidence of such corruption in Malacca while comparing stored quantities of spice against outgoing manifests.[51]

Other factors put the crown at a disadvantage as well. Principal among them was the preference for an immediate return on investments, even at the expense of larger profits later on.[52] This fueled speculation among the investors, who were in positions to buy back pepper cheaply when ships docked in Lisbon and resell the spice in Antwerp and other markets for substantial profits.

But Spanish aggression toward the Netherlands and rebellions in the Low Countries beginning in 1568 forced the temporary closure of Amsterdam and Antwerp, where the financing for most Portuguese trade by New Christians (converted Jews) originated. This tended to dry up funds until the investors could resettle. The death of the last Portuguese royal heir in 1580, resulting in the ascension of Philipp

II of Spain to the Portuguese throne, provided funds for Philipp's military expansion, including funds for the Spanish armada that was defeated by the English in 1588.

As a result, Portuguese kings continued a strong dependence on New Christians for capital, which led to attempts to refinance debts, prompting Boyajian to observe:

> *The Portuguese monarchy – the chief organizer and intended beneficiary of the enterprise – was drifting toward financial insolvency barely half a century after Da Gama embarked Portugal on the road to empire and trade in Asia.[53]*

The Reorganization of Goan Society

Much of the revenues from this trade were the result of confiscated booty after Afonso Albuquerque and his forces succeeded in occupying Malacca in early 1512, and transferred back through Goa, Lisbon, Oporto, and the rest of Europe. Once Goa and Malacca were firmly in the Portuguese orbit, most of Western India and several Asian ports was transformed by trading wealth and the policies of Portugal's colonial administration, the "Estado da India". Along with the influence of the Roman Catholic Church at the time, the governance of this emerging "seaborne empire" was guided by two principal objectives: the trading of Indian spices and other luxury goods for sale in Europe that was governed by the Estado da India, and the religious conversion of indigenous populations encountered by missionaries supported by the Roman Catholic Church, two policies that closely tied the Portuguese Crown and the Pontificate in Rome. The connection between these powerful allies was described by the 17th century chronicler Diogo do Couto, who wrote:

> *The Kings of Portugal always aimed in this conquest of the East at so unifying the two powers: spiritual and temporal, that the one should never be exercised without the other. [54]*

The common perception was that the Portuguese Crown and its authorized merchants came to India in search of earthly riches, while transporting clerics who sought the salvation of pagan souls. In reality, Boxer described Portugal's empire in India as a "military and maritime enterprise cast in an ecclesiastical mould".[55] Despite their vows of poverty, some of the earliest clerics made little effort to conceal the primary reason for their journey east was to enrich themselves and their religious orders through trade.[56]

The initial phase of colonization came at an immense cost to the local region. It began with the overthrow of Muslim elites who ruled Goa's Hindu population for several hundred years. A few years after the Portuguese takeover, local disenchantment grew as Hindu temples were systematically destroyed and replaced by Roman Catholic churches, as local leaders were executed or exiled. Villages were reduced to subsistence farming, and local women were forced to marry low ranking settlers.[57]

In a second wave of repression beginning in 1560, claims of heresy was used by the Portuguese Inquisition in Goa to focus on Hindus and New Christians, Iberian Jews whose their ancestors were persecuted in Europe a few decades before. Most of the latter arriving in Goa were descendants of families who escaped the persecutions in Europe by converting under pressure to Roman Catholicism. Some had become affluent as merchants, bankers, and investors, many settling in Amsterdam, Antwerp, and in a few cases, living in Lisbon.

These "Cristaos-Novos" traditionally gravitated to finance and money lending, sectors of the European economy which had been shunned by landed aristocrats who claimed the status of "Old (True) Christians". Ironically, many New Christian families had provided funding to the Portuguese crown for its first expeditions. Regardless of their suspected loyalties, King Manuel I and his successors grew so dependent on New Christians for borrowed capital that many were granted lucrative trading charters in India.[58]

The royal dependency, however, did not prevent many from being persecuted by the Inquisition. [59] Hannah Wojceihowski has written that more than three hundred New Christians were tried in Goa, many tortured and executed, effectively destroying the community within the first thirty years, and sending the survivors into exile across India and Asia. Hindus and Muslims were also brought before the tribunals and similarly punished.[60] Collective dissent among these groups also became much riskier as censorship, dispossession of property, imprisonment, torture, and execution grew more prominent in the territories where the Church and the Portuguese military remained strong.

As the occupation unfolded, the Estado da Indio in Goa continued to enforce the terms of the King's monopoly under which was determined who could travel to the Indies, and how trading privileges were distributed. As a result, Goan society was largely organized according to those priorities. James Boyajian and C.R. Boxer indicate that the upper ranks were occupied by Portuguese settlers divided among three principal groups: "Fildagos" (translated as "the sons of somebody"), "Clerigos" (priests and other religious clergy), and "Soldados" (the soldiers and sailors of the military).[61]

Many fildagos arriving in Goa were the non-inheriting males of Portuguese gentry, with a large number of "New Christians" sent by their families to look after their trading interests, some escaping persecution in Europe, and other male relatives seeking riches in the Far East. To regulate them all, a priority was granted to "Casados" (married men), who were thought by the crown to provide a stabilizing influence in the colonies.[62]

Below them in rank were "Clerigos", who were sent to fulfill the crown's commitment to the conversion of souls. The lowest European group were "Soldados", soldiers and sailors of the fleet who were often recruited or coerced from the poorest ranks of Portuguese society. Unlike Fidalgos and Clerigos, most in the military were illiterate and often destitute before coming to India. Throughout the sixteenth and seventeenth centuries it has been estimated that only a total of 10,000 Portuguese men and boys of all classes arrived in Goa and western India, including three hundred aristocratic fidalgos and about one thousand New Christians of lesser rank. [63]

Goan Casado – 1596 - Jan Huygen van Linschoten – Courtesy of Columbia University

The ranks of fidalgo casados (married gentry) were likely complicated by distortions of their status, which was fueled by a desire for riches. While a few married fidalgos traveled to the colonies with their wives, many who landed in Goa were without them. When the shortage of European women became acute, King Joao III in 1545 offered dowries for converted mixed-race orphans who could find husbands.[64] Throughout the 16th and 17th centuries the number of European women in Goa and other Portuguese colonies continued to decline. Boxer writes that on average 10 to 15 women traveled aboard ships in the early years, and almost none arrived in Goa after 1550.[65] In their absence, most fidalgos and New Christians took up with local women and servants in Goa, and set up large households of slaves and illegitimate children. The presence of these familial units allowed many men to remain technically in the good graces of the Estado da India and the Church in Goa as they conducted business.

The quality of the Portuguese military was also less than we might imagine. Boxer remarks that there was a tradition in Portuguese society that the crown always favored the clergy first with financial support, then paying bankers, tradesmen, and the military "tarde, mal, e nunca" (late, poorly, or not at all), often in that order.[66] As a result, Portuguese professional soldiers were rare, while those with experience became mercenaries.[67] Men sought for service in the Indies were usually found by clearing Portuguese jails or among the most impoverished living in the countryside far from the sea.

To these numbers were added assorted brigands, former prisoners, vagabonds, and other untrained and illiterate men. Among them were "Lancados", who have been described as renegades and military deserters. Many eventually fled Portuguese India because of the Inquisition to settle in Asia and trade independently.[68] One prominent group of Lancado merchants were New Christians, probably mestizo descendants, who traded frequently between Goa, Manila, Macau, and Japan. Some accounts put their number at a few thousand by the 1580s, and up to five thousand scattered throughout the trading ports in the early 17th century. Many other so-called "undesirables", such as "Degredados" (exiled criminals), defrocked priests, and other fugitives from justice made up a large and shifting group of men who lived on the fringes of society.

The conditions in which Soldados, Lancados, Degredados, and other marginal settlers ultimately found themselves upon arrival in Goa were often as bad as in Europe. While enduring a journey from which many would never return, the common goal was to leave government service as soon as possible, or otherwise remove themselves from the scrutiny of the Estado da India and the Church to participate in some type of trade.

To achieve this, virtually all had to interact with the majority of Goan society, which was now highly diverse due to the expansion of trading partners. Those consisted of Hindus, Muslims, Buddhists, Malaysians, Portuguese mestizos, and a large number of African and Southeast Asian slaves, who made up the total population of about 180,000.[69] In spite of attempts by the Church and the Estado da India to maintain a policy of "pureza de sangue" (purity of blood), the disparity in numbers and the need for trained soldiers were incentives to grudgingly accept varying degrees of racial mixing.[70]

The Central Marketplace of Goa

The social distinctions underlying this condition, especially for the underclass, largely determined the status of Europeans and Non-Europeans in early 16th century Goa. These castes were usually based on perceptions of race and the origins of birth. One of the ironies of the period was that the earliest unions, both legitimate and illegitimate, were encouraged by the Roman Catholic Church and Portugal's Estado da India to maintain stability, provide a military presence, and as a source of cheap labor in Goa. Early precedents had been established by Afonso Albuquerque's alliances with the native population under the force of arms. As conditions evolved following the settlement of Goa, he allowed the preservation of local customs so long as Christian conversions and trade continued and offered incentives for marriages between Portuguese soldiers and indigenous women. [71]

As one 19th century historian wrote:

Albuquerque ... encouraged intermarriages between them, by loading the married pairs with substantial gifts and favours, distributing among them the landed property of the Moslems which had lately been confiscated, and encouraging them to cultivate the mechanical arts for the benefit of the new Portuguese settlement.[72]

Portuguese colonization was hardly benign. De Souza recounts that after Albuquerque conquered Goa the general wrote to King Manuel 1 in 1512:
> *If the Portuguese continue to settle down at the present rate, it looks to me that Your Majesty may have to drive out the natives of this island and give the land to the Portuguese settlers. [73]*

Albuquerque eventually recognized that the shortage of European women would have a long-term effect on his ability to govern. Before his death in 1515, the Portuguese general is reported to have officiated in marriages of his men to captured Muslim women.[74] Many were the widows and daughters of soldiers who died in battle. But his change in attitude may have been based on a realization that the Portuguese military was badly weakened by skirmishes with Muslim forces, the rigors of travel to many ports under its protection, and the prevalence of tropical diseases.[75] To offset the conditions in India, Albuquerque hoped to use inter-racial marriage, a common practice in Brazil and Africa, to his advantage by replenishing the military with local men who shared common values and to induce the formation of a stable and loyal population.

The volatile mixture of long years away from home, slavery, religious persecution, and easy wealth, however, had unintended consequences. The continual flow of men from the Middle East, Africa, Brazil, and Asia with dreams of riches presented a serious social problem in Goa, especially as trade increased. The problem was closely related to the way lower classes were treated. Many sailors and soldiers arrived in Goa undernourished and poor, and remained so until they were paid as needed by the administration.[76] The most desperate men joined criminal gangs that preyed on the local population, stealing food, committing murder and other forms of mayhem that plagued the Portuguese colony throughout the sixteenth and seventeenth centuries.

As a result, one of the first priorities of men upon arrival was to find slave or servant girls with which they could cohabitate, often living off whatever the women could earn. [77] The pervasiveness of "female slave-prostitution", as Boxer called it, paved the way for many casual liaisons between European men and native women. Fidalgos, casados, and some clerics were not immune to temptation. Observers remarked on the "licentiousness" and "sexual license" that was thought to be the leading cause of social unrest.

A letter written by a Jesuit in 1550 described:
> *innumerable married settlers ..., who have four, eight, or ten female slaves and sleep with all of them, as is common knowledge. This is carried to such excess that there was one man in Malacca who had twenty-four women of various races, all of whom were his slaves, and all of whom he enjoyed. ... Most men, as soon as they can afford to buy a female slave, almost invariably use her as a girl-friend (amiga), besides many other dishonesties. [78]*

Households with large numbers of slaves elicited this observation by C.R. Boxer:
> *An ordinary European or Eurasian artisan would have fifteen or twenty female slaves; and one seventeenth-century Mulatto blacksmith at Goa was alleged to own twenty-six women and girls, exclusive of the male slaves in his household. Well-to-do citizens and officials often owned between fifty and a hundred household slaves, and rich ladies sometimes had over 300. These unnecessarily large slave households were maintained to give social status and prestige to the owners, and they were a feature of Portuguese colonial life in Africa and South America as well as in Asia. [79]*

Slavery and casual unions inevitably produced a large number of racially-mixed children who lived in Western India at the time. The appearance of orderly Casado households in which many illegitimate descendants lived belied the turmoil that churned just below the surface. Boxer wrote that:
> *The children of this sexual promiscuity with slave mothers seldom had the chance of an adequate upbringing or education, while*

> those who were born in lawful wedlock were only too likely to be early corrupted by their surroundings. [80]

Their low status due to caste divisions in India and repeated denouncements by the clergy also helped to relegate most racially mixed descendants to the bottom of the social order.

By the middle of the sixteenth century marriages between Portuguese settlers and Brahmin women in Goa were already exceeded by unions with women from Malacca, Ceylon, Mozambique, and other trading ports, increasing the number of "descendentes" born of slaves and domestic servants to 10,000 by 1540.[81] Including Goa and Asia, the population of territories under Portuguese rule by 1695 has been estimated to be 230,000.[82] Boxer indicates that these numbers may have increased due to harsh laws preventing the practice of old religions, inducing many Hindus, Brahmin, and Kotani Indians to adopt Roman Catholicism, European mores, and assume Portuguese names.[83]

A willingness to claim Portuguese ancestry to retain an aura of superiority may have also increased their numbers.[84] Blood lines were blurred by poorly kept birth records and unusual forms of assimilation. Pietro Della Valle, an Italian traveler in 1623, described common rituals such as baptism, marriage, and the celebration of Catholic sacraments through which the children of servants and slaves In Goa were incorporated in Portuguese households.[85] Given the prevalence of slave labor and miscegenation throughout western India, their descendants may have also increased through unions with other mestizos.

Another reason for mestizo claims of Portuguese ancestry were the advantages once they escaped from Goa and began trading beyond the reach of Portuguese authorities. Many descendants had working knowledge of navigation in the South China Sea and family contacts in local ports.[86] Some were familiar with modern weapons, such as canons, and spoke native dialects and languages, which provided information about rouge pirates and the location of Portuguese ships.

As Goa's decline continued, Malacca, Indonesia, and Siam began to rise as alternative ports. Some activity also occurred from 1550-1553 when Luso-Asian traders without royal licenses began exchanging Japanese silver with Wakou pirates for Chinese silk in the Pearl River delta.[87]

CHAPTER 2
Malacca, Indonesia, Siam, and the Decline of Portugal's Empire in Asia

The Muslim sultanate of Malacca (present day Java, Malaysia, and Singapore) was a large merchant center long coveted by the Portuguese, and an early point of entry into China and the rest of Southeast Asia. News of Malacca's strategic location was initially reported in 1509 by captain Diogo Lopes de Sequeira, and confirmed by Tome Pires, who was later appointed Portugal's first ambassador to China.[88]

Both Sequeira and Pires warned that Malacca's Muslim ruler, Sultan Mahmud, a vassal both to Siam and China, had become an indolent despot. As the sultan grew more powerful, he stopped sending tribute to the Siamese monarch, while entrusting the government to one of his uncles, described by the Portuguese chronicler Castenheda as "a great tyrant and an enemy to all".[89] Assisted by a dispute between the sultan and his son and heir, their armies proved to be no match against Portuguese artillery, religious zeal, and commercial ambitions. Utilizing a force of over 1200 men, 17 ships, and cannons, the battle for Malacca lasted from April through August 1510.[90] Once securely in Portuguese hands by November, Albuquerque set his sights on Insulinda and the spice trade of the Moloccas.

Indonesia

The Portuguese presence began with the dispatch of Francisco Serrao in 1512. Following his shipwreck and landing on the Indonesian island of Ambon, Serrao assisted a local ruler against the forces of a rival to his throne. The Portuguese captain was rewarded by being allowed to buy spices, and later built a fortress to protect the acquisition of cloves, pepper, nutmeg, and mace, each coveted by Venetian spice merchants.[91] Several decades later, Francisco Xavier

(1506-1552) and other Jesuits established missions in Eastern Indonesia on the islands of Morotai, Ambon, Macassar, Flores, Tenate, and Solor beginning in 1546. By 1560 there were 10,000 Christian converts. In 1590 there were up to 60,000 Christians in the region, the result of Portugal's policy allowing unions with local women. Many family names, including da Costa, de Freitas, Gonsalves, Mendosa, da Silva, are thought to have originated from these first Portuguese settlers. Although trade and religion were priorities, other influences were evident, including the introduction of a patois blending Portuguese and local dialects, in the architecture of several churches, forms of music, literature, and a hybrid cuisine incorporating Indonesian spices. [92]

The Portuguese influence also appears in early language and cultural remnants incorporated into songs and literature, which evoked images of inter-racial relations that suggest diverse contacts. In the Indonesian song "Kafrinju", for example, a dark skinned Luso-Asian woman from Goa longs to return home with her Indonesian lover after she reveals she is with child.[93] In another song, a Indonesian woman married to a Portuguese falls in love with a Chinese man who must go into battle. Another ancient text reveals the story of a princess who is forced by her parents to choose a groom to marry. Incorporating a modern theme, the young girl rejects a number of suitors in favor of a Portuguese merchant for his assurances of "Renggala", the Indonesia word for showing her a good time. The traditionalist reaction of her parents is illustrated by the closing wedding reception led by a "Bobu", a buffoon or jester, who is thought to express displeasure at their daughter's selection. As Antonio Pinto da Franca observed, the influences on racial differences, cultural interaction, and the clash of traditional and modern ideologies, as shown in these writings, were evident well after the Portuguese left Indonesia for other destinations.[94]

By the end of the seventeenth century, that departure was hastened when Indonesia became a distribution point for opium through the involvement of the Dutch. According to Indian scholar Om Prakash,

> *Before the emergence of China as a major market for Indian opium in the early years of the nineteenth century, practically the entire exports of Bengal opium were directed at the Indonesian archipelago. Between the middle of the seventeenth century and the third quarter of the eighteenth, the principal carrier on this route was the Dutch East India Company.* [95]

The two areas of production outside Portuguese control were Bihar, Malwa, and other parts of Central India. Early estimates in 1688 indicate that up to 46% were distributed to Northern India, while the remaining output were distributed to other markets. The largest market was the Indonesian archipelago, which by 1670 was controlled by the Dutch East India Company. The British East India Company's conquest of Bengal (1757 – 1765) caused the transfer of revenue collection to revert to them and continued until EIC's monopoly of the China Trade ended in 1833.

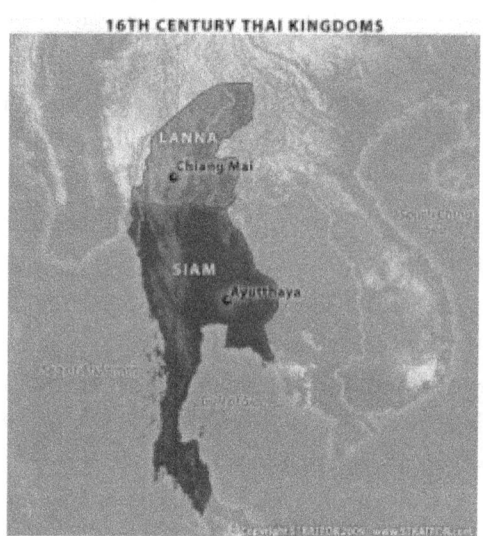

Malaccan, Indonesian, and Siamese inhabitants in the same period

Siam

Albuquerque next sent Simão de Miranda as an envoy to Siamese King Rama Tibodi II in 1511 to seek an alliance and to open trade relations in the region.[96] In a letter to the king, who became an enemy of Sultan Mahmud for his refusal to send tribute, the Portuguese general declared that he would not leave Malacca without defeating the Sultan and all who were helping him. Assuming the Siamese were "Christian – like", Albuquerque added that he would inform the king as soon as he was victorious so that Tibodi's subjects could resettle there.[97] Employing both military prowess and statecraft, Albuquerque's motive was to play on the Siamese king's mistrust of the Muslim tyrant, whose overthrow would benefit both Portugal and Siam, and solidify future relations in the region. His method was to punish the Malaccan Sultan and conquer the town, adding an intention to rid Siam of all Muslim influence.

As Albuquerque was pacifying Malacca, Miranda arrived in Siam with a small fleet of three ships amid great ceremony and bearing rich gifts. [98] The king was so pleased that he provided good lodgings and food, offering to show the entourage many towns and the monarch's herd of elephants. Among his impressions, Miranda reported:

> ... a King who is so powerful that he is able to maintain continuously, at his own cost, ten to twelve thousand war elephants which he rears for this purpose. ... he has at his service more than thirty thousand male and female elephants, for in his kingdom there are large herds being reared, both tame and wild among which the King has one that is white, so highly esteemed in all neighbouring countries that owing to this, he is called "the King of the White Elephant". [99]

Miranda returned to Malacca with a peace treaty and brought Albuquerque a gift of twenty bells and performers that could play tunes on them. The Siamese king also loaded the envoy's ships with rich merchandise and offered personnel and supplies for the Portuguese command in Malacca.[100]

Among Portuguese authorities on the ground, early relations with Siam were focused on ministering to Christians and finding a way to trade in China, two goals influenced by religious clerics. Those objectives were reflected in their correspondence. Writing in 1552 from Sanchan Island in the Pearl River Delta a few months before his death, the Jesuit Francisco Xavier had hoped to enter Canton to begin his mission. But he wrote, "...if God does not wish it, I shall go to ... Siam, and from Siam leave with the embassy which the King of Siam is sending to the King of China."[101]

Siam's relationship with China was also noted by Brother Luís Fróis, writing in 1555 to his fellow priests in Goa. Fróis described the sea voyage between Goa and Japan by indicating that one had to spend the winter in Siam during the monsoons, as did all traders of the time, before finding passage to China.[102] The "carrot" of the Siamese alliance, he observed, was bilateral trade, especially with Portuguese India, which the Siamese coveted and the Portuguese were willing to extend. In 1561 another Jesuit named Jerónimo Fernandes wrote that Malacca is considered by Siam to be "the door to the most glorious missions and enterprises that there are in India". Fernandes emphasized that Malacca is close to all kingdoms, which send their ships loaded with merchandise, including to the kingdom of Siam.[103]

Albuquerque was so convinced of the alliance's success that he reported favorably to Portugal's King Dom Manuel in April 1512.[104] The news traveled relatively quickly. Receiving regular reports from India, the King related the events in June 1513 to Pope Leo X, effectively introducing Siam to Europe. Information regarding Siam and other countries in Southeast Asia was then carried regularly by ship back to the Portuguese court and filtered out to other European monarchs. Regular voyages and trade between Siam and Macau began soon after.

Siam's ruler had realized that the alliance with Portugal could blunt the growing naval power of the Dutch, which would eventually overwhelm his army of elephants. The king invited the Portuguese to establish themselves in his capital city of Ayuthia, and withstood opposition from Muslim and Japanese merchants by replacing them with Portuguese traders. Before Albuquerque died in 1515, the general sent several more gifts to sweeten the deal, including jeweled bracelets and gold snuffboxes to the king's mother. The king also requested missionaries to serve Christian converts and promised to implement trade between Malacca and mainland China.

The alliance led to the building of a port city near the capital, through which a variety of goods could be obtained. In the process, a small group of 130 Portuguese arrived around 1524. The king's request for priests was granted in 1539 with the arrival of two Dominican monks who set up the first ministry in Siam. By the end of the 17th century the Christian population had grown to about 4,000 inhabitants, including refugees from Malacca after 1641 and Macassar after 1660 and several Portuguese-Siamese children, following the Dutch takeover of those ports.[105]

The Decline of the Portuguese Empire in Asia

As the Dutch and English naval presence grew more prominent, each threatened to end the Portuguese monopoly of sea routes and organized separate trading companies: first the British East India Company in 1600, and the Dutch East India Company in 1605. As a result, Portugal entered the 17th century at a disadvantage due to the more scattered and weakened state of its Asian possessions. Boxer observed that persistent attacks on Portugal's settlements were encouraged by the religious antagonisms underlying a temporary truce between the Dutch Calvinists and the Anglicans against the Portuguese Papists. Another weakness was Portugal's unresolved royal succession stemming from the ascension of Phillip II of Spain to the Portuguese monarchy in 1580. This drove a wedge between Portugal's nobility, the local clergy and most commoners not benefiting from colonial wealth, undermining the Asian strategy for the next sixty years.[106]

The intervention of the Dutch, in turn, exposed Portugal's lack of sophisticated weaponry, manpower, and naval experience. According to Boxer, the Dutch had an overwhelming advantage in the number of ships and canons, three times more men trained to conduct battles at sea, and had more experienced sailors, pilots, and commanders. This was an ironic development given Portugal's reputation as a nation of mariners. Following Albuquerque's death, the disorganization of the Portuguese enterprise exposed fidalgo commanders, who lacked the knowledge and competence of their Dutch counterparts.[107] Some Portuguese observers even shamed their own commanders, who were often defeated by lower-born Dutch captains, highlighting the lack of discipline and training displayed by their military.[108]

Another factor may have been the lack of incentives among fildalgos to engage the Dutch due to Portugal's previously unchallenged extraction of wealth from India and Asia. Many European Portuguese in Asia benefited from wide-spread corruption, the exploitation of local peoples, and the general chaos introduced by the Inquisition in Goa. Each instance undermined confidence in the earlier goals of exploration, religious conversions, and commercial expansion, especially the latter, which generally excluded racially mixed Luso-Asians, the backbone of the Portuguese enterprise, from the benefits.[109] As a result, lower-born descendants, who were often persecuted because of race or heretical beliefs in Goa, fled to more secure destinations as early Dutch attacks on Portuguese settlements, beginning with Principe and Sao Tome in 1598, became more frequent.

The influence of corruption was especially evident, as illustrated in Tome' Pires' early report to Albuquerque on Malacca in 1512. Upon an examination of the booty supervised by Albuquerque's "Wardens of War Prizes" following the Portuguese occupation, Pires noted a difference of twenty "arrates" (at 16 oz. each) that was held back in Malacca from each shipment to Goa, apparently lost to theft. This was complicated by Lisbon's use of an old weight system that rated each arrate at 14 oz. Even under different systems, the wardens were taking at least twenty pounds of spices (probably pepper and cloves) from each shipment for themselves, and likely reselling it for substantial profits.[110] When projected across the Portuguese territories, the scale of corruption as noted by other historians of the period suggests that the incident Pires observed in Malacca was widespread by the second decade of the 16th century, and would remain a common practice throughout Portugal's overseas empire for many decades to come. [111]

When the Dutch finally succeeded in expelling the Portuguese from Malacca in 1641, most ship traffic between Goa and Southeast Asian ports was cut off, plunging the entire Portuguese system into jeopardy. The new settlement at Macau established in 1557, which we will discuss in the next chapter, was the only Portuguese settlement that remained as neutral ground for traders because of its strategic location at the entrance of the Pearl River in southern China. Hoping to make up its losses in Malacca, Macau's Senate redirected traders to Manila, a Spanish colony controlled by Phillip II. Relations between Portugal and Spain, however, deteriorated rapidly after 1640, leading to the Portuguese War of Restoration and the crowning of Portugal's Joao IV in 1668. Dutch blockades resulted in the seizure and destruction of numerous Portuguese ships through 1667, including many bound for Manila. As a result, many fidalgo traders in Macau returned to Portugal, leaving Asian ports open and unprotected.

Until then the wealthiest merchants authorized by the Estado do India in Goa had neglected other markets in deference to the abundant profits in Malacca. After conditions changed in the late 17th century, rouge Japanese and Chinese merchants began offering goods in Tonkin (Vietnam), Manila, Cambodia, Laos, and Siam (Thailand). Luso-Asian "country" traders without charters from the Estado da India attempted to fill the void left by fidalgo merchants. Many of the mestizos were familiar with the region due to cultural ties. They also sought shelter from persecutions in Goa, or were Christian refugees expelled from Nagasaki in 1639 and from Malacca after 1641. Some shrewdly made overtures to local authorities to improve relations in attempts to "reinvigorate" trade. Their efforts, according to historian Brian Souza, "established or augmented existing ... Portuguese populations and increased the frequency of trade visits to those states." [112]

The presence of these new traders revitalized commerce in the region. While the data is incomplete, a large number mestizos were former slaves and servants who were familiar with local waterways and realized the opportunities. Others were the descendants of Malaccan women who were abandoned when their European paramours returned to Macau and Portugal.[113] Many congregated southwest of the Indonesian islands in Macassar, a city port in the Celebes. By 1651 there were over 3,000 Christians in the town.[114] As in other Luso-Asian communities, the common language among the migrants was a Portuguese creole closely related to "Maquista", Macau's patois, possibly influenced by Luso-Asians who traded frequently there by the end of the 17th century. Souza noted that these country traders remained close to the Indonesian archipelago where they could purchase native spices, including pepper, mace, and cloves. These were exchanged for rice, silk, cotton cloth, pepper, tin, sandalwood, and silver used to purchase Chinese goods. The frequency of trade was relatively brisk, attesting to the skill of mestizo captains who avoided Dutch ships. At the height of the Dutch blockades from 1644 and 1667, Souza writes, thirty-eight (38) Macau trading vessels reached Macassar, while only one ship was lost on the return trip. [115]

In 1647, however, the Portuguese Crown ordered Francisco Vieira de Figueiredo, a wealthy merchant from Macau, to begin negotiations with the Dutch. Figueiredo had already developed an "extensive mutual cooperation" with the Sultan of Macassar by supplying munitions and artillery while also serving as the ruler's factor, both of which served their mutual benefit.[116] By 1665 the talks had failed, and Figueiredo and his household were forced to retreat to Larantuka on the island of Flores. Following his death in 1667, Figueredo's widow, Dona Caterina de Noronha, who accompanied him to Macassar, returned to Macau and continued her husband's business ventures. In 1680 it is reported that she donated 12,000 taels of silver (about 423 oz.) to the Jesuits, which they invested in maritime trade.[117]

Following the failed talks, the Jesuits in the Celebes returned to Siam, which they considered more receptive than Dutch Indonesia. As Portuguese ships continued to suffer from the Dutch blockade of Malacca, Macau's senate in 1667 also looked to Siam and Prasat Tong's successor, King Narai, for assistance. A large loan was secured consisting of merchandize and 605 catties of silver (about 12,804 oz).[118] When Macau's decline continued, the terms of the loan were renegotiated, and payments were made in annual instalments. In March 1720, upon learning that the final payment was missing, the worried Senators ordered Jesuits living in Siam to present gifts to the King and his family in hopes of salvaging relations.

The Reverend Francisco Telles, acting Captain-Major of Siam, however, reported that the situation was complicated by the "disappearance" of twenty-one silver catties before the final payment arrived in the port of Ayuthia.[119] The revelation may account for the repayment being delayed until July 1723, suggesting that local corruption may have prolonged Macau's crisis for a few more years. To mend the alliance, Macanese officials sent cargos that included several Persian rugs as gifts to the Sultan, which local merchants obtained from their networks.[120] Trade with Siam was eventually restored through the agreement of mutually favorable custom duties. By then the center of the Asian market had already shifted to Macau.

CHAPTER 3
Macau and the Origins of Macanese Culture

Beginning around 1553, after local pirates were driven from the South China coast by Portuguese traders led by Leonel de Souza, mandarins in Canton allowed the Europeans to offer their goods for trade on a small island in the Pearl River Delta. The first treaty to pay port taxes was negotiated by de Souza in 1554.[121] Three years later, without acknowledgement from the Imperial Court, a permanent settlement was approved by local mandarins and built on Macau island. The additional "discovery" of the Japanese islands by Portuguese sailors in 1542, and the successful negotiations for trade by 1580 linking Macau, Canton, and Nagasaki, increased ship traffic to the new territory. This produced immense profits for the Portuguese crown and led to a period of rapid growth for Macau.[122]

During this "Golden Era", from its founding in 1557, to the closure of Japan by the Tokagawa Shogunate in 1639, and ending with the capture of Malacca by the Dutch in 1641, Macau was elevated from a sparsely populated island into a vital trading and mercantile center linking Canton, Nagasaki, Lisbon and Europe for the first time. Partially through Confucian ambivalence and a desire by the Qing, who overthrew the Ming Dynasty in 1644, to keep European merchants at a distance, Macau's emergence, for all intents and purposes, was the harbinger of a new global economy that continues into the present.[123

Chronicles of an Englishman in Asia

Macau's role in this new economy and the extent of its new wealth was unreported in Europe until the publication of an account in 1667 by a British factor (agent) named Peter Mundy. As a seasoned traveler to India and China, Mundy was appointed chief factor of Admiral John Weddell's privateer fleet because of his skill as a negotiator and fluency of Portuguese and Spanish. A future historian would describe his descriptions of Asia as "enchanting", all the more enhanced by "his insatiable curiosity", his "eye for detail", a "... desire for accuracy", and tempered by "strong horse-sense and a balanced judgment".[124] Mundy first exhibited these traits by chronicling voyages to Bengal and Agra, where he was one of the first Europeans to witness the construction of the Taj Mahal. On succeeding voyages, he conducted business in the Portuguese colony of Goa, in Nagasaki, Japan's largest trading port, and along the southern coast of China. Fortunately for researchers, it was Mundy's routine to record his impressions and sketch images of each journey, including his six-month sojourn in Macau from June to December 1637.

The squadron of five vessels reached Macau by way of Goa on orders from Lord William Corteen, a commercial privateer sailing under an English Royal Charter signed in April 1636, who hoped to open trade with China. Beyond the lavish benefits of trade, Mundy's chronicle revealed details about Macau's diverse society at the height of its influence that drew interest throughout Europe.

Dinner at the Palacio

Since their arrival in June, Mundy and the English fleet had been kept waiting offshore by wary Portuguese officials. An encounter on June 28 put Mundy and two other officials ashore with letters of introduction from King Charles I of England and Dom Miguel de Noronha, the Viceroy of Goa, to the Captain-General of Macau, Domingos da Camara de Noronha. On the evening of October 8, 1637, Mundy finally arrived in a small junk on the strand just off the Praia Grande for a dinner at the governor's residence, Macau's Palacio de Goveirno. He accompanied Admiral Weddell, Anglican Minister Arthur Hatch, and Christopher Parr, the Purser of the Dragon, Weddell's flag ship.[125] The meeting was one of many attempts to convince the Portuguese to obtain permission to build British factories (trading offices and storehouses) in Canton, the large port city just up the Pearl River. The dinner was scheduled later at the governor's palace to ease tensions between the European rivals, including introductions to members of Macau's municipal senate and other dignitaries from the Santa Casa de Misericordia (the Holy House of Mercy), which rendered aid to the poor. All were members of Macau's merchant class. The Portuguese military contingent was led by Captain-Major Antonio de Oliveira Aranha, who later invited Mundy to stay in his home for a few days.

The setting at the governor's residence was befitting a rich port at the height of its power and was probably meant to impress upon the visitors that their participation as trading partners was unnecessary. Mundy and others marveled at the richly furnished surroundings, which featured a long dining table outfitted with gold and silver plates with matching cutlery. Exotically decorated chairs and hangings lined the walls. Large Japanese folding screens called "Beeombos" separated portions of the room. Each screen had multiple panels depicting stories and colorful landscapes, which when fully extended measured up to nine feet. Each panel, Mundy later wrote, was "…painted with (a) variety off curious colleurs intermingled with gold, containing beasts, birds, fishes, forests, flowers, fruites…", providing a feeling of tranquility when the assembled group was seated to dine. The Portuguese were quick to mention that the rich furnishings were obtained through Macau's frequent trade with Nagasaki and other Asian port cities.

A savory meal highlighted the evening. Each guest was served portions of meat, which Mundy described as "… broughtt between 2 silver plates…". Several other dishes were offered, the frequency and variety of each attracting special notice. As Mundy observed, "For before a man had Don(e) with the one … there was another service stood ready for him…" Behind each guest was an African servant ready for the smallest request. Beverages were similarly offered in silver goblets "…which were no sooner empty butt there stood those ready that filld them againe with excellent … Portugall wine." In the kitchens, women, probably from Malacca, Thailand, and Japan, stood ready to replenish each course. Light music played in the background, performed by Chinese singers and skilled musicians on harps and guitars from other trade ports, also a benefit of Macau's extensive commercial influence.

Following the dinner, Mundy was entertained in Aranha's home, which the Englishman compared to a well-appointed palace. He was especially taken with the Captain-Major's young daughters, Escolastica and Catharina, whom he described as "pretty mestizninhes (mestizos), and noted: "… except in England, I thincke not in the world bee overmatched For their pretty Feature and complexion, …" The Macanese scholar C.A. Mantalto de Jesus would write almost three centuries later that women such as Aranha's daughters represented a "mixed but legitimate and Christian race" envisioned years before by Afonso Albuquerque.[126]

Mundy took special notice of the young girls' style of dress. In formal settings, each was clothed in small Japanese kimonos "adorned with precious Jewells and Costly apparel." Their hair, pulled up to the crown, was similarly decorated with jewels and other decorations. The Englishman's keen eye observed that most Macanese women dressed in this manner, often covered in public over the head with a shawl-like garment called a "Sherazzee", with a lower kimono around the waist extending to the feet. Out on the avenues and plazas, the wealthier women "… are carried in hand chaires …, all close covered, off which there are very Costly … brought from Japan." Indoors, all classes wore wide sleeved kimonos without the upper shawls, the less costly ones made of cotton and silk, while others were embroidered with gold. Mundy also noticed the subtle differences: "Butt when they goe without (their sedan chairs), the Mistris is hardly knowne from the Maide or slave wenche by outward appearance, … butt that their Sherazzees are finer."

A New Identity

Peter Mundy's chronicle offers a glimpse of an important period in Macau's history. In his short passages we are given intimate details of the cultural influences and class divisions that existed during the port's most illustrious period. At the time of Mundy's visit, Japan was one of Macau's principal trading partners, an example of how religion and commerce worked together under Portugal's system. The Jesuit mission in Nagasaki already had 300,000 Christian converts. In a few years, the Dutch would engineer the expulsion of the Portuguese and the persecution of Christians converts. But the ties to Japan were never completely extinguished. Clandestine trade continued with Japanese merchants who risked their lives for great fortunes. As was the custom for the Portuguese military, Mundy's host Captain-Major Aranha served in Nagasaki from 1629 to 1631 before being assigned to Macau. It was also likely that Aranha, like many Portuguese in Macau, married a Japanese woman, which may account for Mundy's description of his daughters as "pretty mestizninhes", their adoption of kimono-like styles of dress, and other influences that we see in Mundy's account.

Macau's population in 1637 was about 10,000, with about 900 Luso-Asians living in the city.[127] The majority probably included mestizos and indigenous people, made up of Indians, Malays, Timorese, Chinese, Japanese, and Africans, who over time were incorporated into the local culture and involved in commerce related to overseas trade. Despite the broad diversity of groups who settled in Macau, demographer John Byrne writes that Luso-Asians living in trading ports at the time often identified "as one people".[128] While racially mixed from several ethnic groups, they were "homogenous in their ethnic identifications as Portuguese" through their adoption of family names, speaking the European language or a blended creole, and practicing the Roman Catholic faith.[129] Sheyla Zandonai offers a similar assessment of cultural development in Macau. She suggests that the city's multicultural roots of the present evolved from a "distinct and variegated ancestry" through centuries of migrations and trading activity involving these same groups.[130]

The extent of Portuguese expansion from the middle of the 17th century to end of the 19th century was highly dependent on these groups in Macau, which was largely cut off from Goa and Portugal due to Dutch incursions. As Malyn Newitt argues, "… it was the activities of mixed-race Portuguese-Africans and Portuguese-Asians who created a whole new Portuguese identity in remote parts of the world and held together an enterprise that, if it relied on the metropolitan effort alone, would have collapsed at an early stage."[131] Such a collective identity was vaguely acknowledged in Macau several years before Mundy's arrival. On the cornerstone of its largest church, St. Paul's Cathedral, the community was memorialized by Jesuits in a Latin inscription that reads: VIRGINI MAGNE MATRI, CIVITAS MACAENSIS LUBENS, POSUIT AN. 1602. (Great Virgin Mother, the Macanese community dedicates this place in the year 1602.)

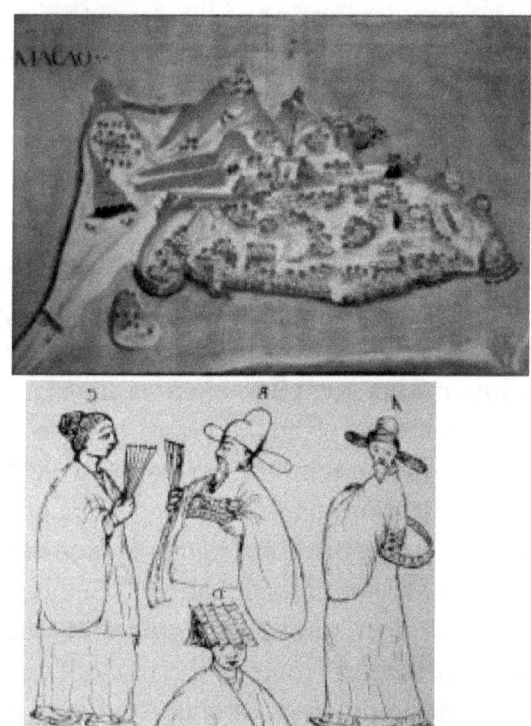

Portuguese Map of Macau and Local People - 17th century

Dutch East India Company - Japanese drawing of Dutch trader

This new identity may have been reinforced by Macau's competition with the Dutch and the English. Dutch raids on Macau's coast had occurred with regularity beginning in 1601.[132] Some English traders even pushed for a combined invasion in 1621, which was rejected by the Dutch.[133] In the summer of 1622, fifteen years before Peter Mundy's arrival, a Dutch force of over a thousand men landed in Macau to meet a small Portuguese militia consisting of local men, priests, and African slaves. After a pitch battle, the Macanese forces, aided by well-directed cannon fire, soundly defeated the invaders. The encounter had the effect unifying the disparate groups defending their new homeland, while remaining free of foreign "heretics", including the protestant Dutch, who were expected to restrict their religious rights.[134] The victory led to the release of the African slaves for their bravery, foreshadowing the prohibition of slavery in Portugal by 139 years.[135]

Following the Dutch withdrawal, Macau accepted Goa's offer to fund the construction of fortifications and a foundry to build canons. The municipal senate, however, remained technically governed by Chinese officials in Canton, and was supervised by mandarins installed in a local fort. Thus, when Weddell's ships arrived in 1637 Macau had already forged a distinct identity and enjoyed a degree of autonomy from Portuguese India, as well as the benign tolerance and supervision of Imperial China, which remained wary of foreign influences. In this environment Captain-General Noronha had little incentive to jeopardize the delicate balance, and every reason to be suspicious of Peter Mundy and his countrymen when they landed on Macau's Praia Grande.

Noronha's reluctance proved prescient. In December 1637, Admiral Weddell grew impatient with the Portuguese when no trade agreement with Canton was reached. His squadron sailed up the Pearl River unannounced and unprepared to force a decision from the Chinese. Along the way Weddell engaged in naval battles with Chinese ships, and soon was forced to retreat. The Portuguese, fearing the loss of the Emperor's support for this affront, refused to resupply the ships in Macau and expelled the British fleet. Weddell's squadron, including his chief factor Peter Mundy, returned to England in disgrace.

Fortunes turned sour for Macau as well. Less than two

years later in August 1639, encouraged by the Dutch, Japanese Shogun Iemitsu Tokagawa succeeded in expelling Jesuit missionaries and Portuguese merchants from Nagasaki and Kyushu, effectively severing Portuguese relations and ending trade.[136] Seeking an end to Jesuit and Portuguese influence, the shogun destroyed churches, expelled Portuguese merchants, persecuted priests, and executed thousands of Christian converts. In another two years, a Dutch fleet captured Malacca in 1641, effectively blocking Goa from trading ports in China and the Indonesian archipelago. As a result of both events, Macau's principal supply of Japanese silver, a major item of exchange for Chinese silk and other goods, was cut off. Many of Macau's wealthiest traders, now without their major source of revenue and virtually without military protection, returned to Goa and Portugal. The Dutch now threatened Portuguese shipping in the Malaccan Straits and controlled the surrounding seas.

<u>The Road Back</u>

To offset these losses, Portuguese merchants in Macau attempted to obtain silver from Manila through Chinese pirates, a violation of a treaty with Spain. As we saw in the previous chapter, that strategy failed and was succeeded by the activities of unlikely players. New Christian merchants, clandestine pirate-traders, and their Luso-Asian descendants, who were no longer restricted by Goan authorities and resentful of their past treatment, sent ships through their networks to British controlled Madras and Calicut (Calcutta), and to Portuguese settlements in Siam (Thailand), Java, the Moluccas (Indonesia), Cochin (Vietnam), Cambodia, and Timor.[137] Their initiative encouraged other Luso-Asians to set up factories and migrate to each location. Once there, traders encountered Japanese merchants also operating illegally, who were willing to exchange silver for other commodities. Many began frequenting Macau in place of Malacca and other ports to buys goods from Canton, using the Portuguese territory once again as an entry point to the Chinese mainland.

Macau, however, was not able to profit from the new trade for several decades. Following the closures of Japan and Malacca, Macau's struggles to replace trade from these ports was hampered by a Mongol invasion and civil wars in China, which led to the overthrown of the Ming dynasty and the ascension of the Qing (Manchus) in 1644. The restoration of the Portuguese monarchy in 1668 also led to divided loyalties in Macau. The result was a temporary slowdown to the flow of goods that flourished only a few years before, leading to food shortages and a temporary halt to commerce.

The effects on Macau were evident only a few years after Peter Mundy's departure. When the English ship *Hind* arrived in 1644, Francis Breton, an English trader on board, was surprised by Macau's "extreme poverty", which Breton attributed to the sudden drop in commerce.[138] Robert Anthony's research indicates that during this period Macau had a reputation as a "seedy" city fit only for vagabonds and outcasts, and was noted for gambling, prostitution, drunken sailors, and frequent street brawls.[139] Almost destitute, and unable to depend on Portugal or Goa for protection from the Dutch, Macau's administrators had little choice than to secure a large loan from Siam in 1667 (Chapter 2), and to consider forming a pact with the British East India Company (EIC).

The Siamese loan and the decision to seek a foreign "partner" came during a period of dynastic change in China and upheaval in Portugal, leaving a void that was to be filled by clandestine and mestizo traders, who could operate more freely. The situation remained stagnant until the second Manchu Emperor Kangxi allowed foreign commerce to resume in 1684. By the end of the 17th century, Macanese ships owners succeeded in developing relations with the British East India Company and added the British ports of Madras and Bengal to their trade routes. Between 1698 and 1715 forty-three Company vessels reciprocated by using Macau as a staging ground between trading seasons in Canton and other Chinese cities. [140] By 1739 the EIC gained permission from Macau's renamed "Leal Senado" (the "Loyal Senate" for support of the restored Portuguese monarchy), to build factories and allow foreign traders to reside in the city. The British presence also enhanced Macau's reputation as a multicultural city by providing "a platform where Asians, Africans, European, and American traders and travelers met..." [141]. Over the next one hundred-fifty years the EIC provided Macau with badly needed commercial stability and military protection against Dutch intrusions, while creating a new strategic alliance.

By the early 19th century, simmering relations between Imperial China and Great Britain came to a head during the expansion of the opium trade, which increasingly flowed through Macau and nearby Lin Tin Island. Despite the efforts of Macanese intermediaries, mounting tensions in 1837 led to the forced closure of European factories by China's Imperial government, the confiscation of over 22,000 pounds of opium in Canton, and armed conflict of leading to the first battles of the "Opium Wars".

There was another development, however, that once again placed the Macanese in a pivotal role as the hostilities ended with the Treaty of Nanjing in 1841. This was their rise as commercial printers during a critical period of economic expansion.

Printing and Information in the Age of Global Commerce

Early forms of lithographic printing were first introduced by Portuguese authorities in Goa and Italian Jesuits in Macau in the late 16th century, who imported rudimentary presses from Europe. [142] Several Jesuits, including the Italian Matteo Ricci, sourjoned in Macau to learn Chinese and printed translated bibles and catechisms while waiting for permission from the Imperial Court to begin their missions on the mainland. Beginning in 1812 Macanese apprentices learned the craft in Canton and Macau under British and American clerics using a press imported by the British East India company. Others were trained by Jesuits at St. Joseph's College in Macau following the donation of a press in 1825.

The British missionary Robert Morrison and the American missionary Elijah Coleman Bridgman were two early adopters of print, each of whom employed Macanese as compositors. Morrison received support from the Select Committee of the British East India Company, including an annual stipend, lodging for his family, and use of the company's press when idle. Bridgman's activities were funded by the largest American merchant in China, David Washington Cincinnatus Olyphant, a dealer in "silks, mattings, and fancy articles" from Asia. The difference between the clerics, who were friends for many years, was that Morrison's funds relied on the EIC's sale of opium. This was in contrast to the adamant refusal of Bridgman's benefactor, David Olyphant, to deal in the drug in any of his business ventures. [143] Working on the same press that the EIC imported for Morrison, both missionaries trained many Macanese, who eventually took over printing operations after several English printers left China in the 1830s. [144]

In the next decade, the EIC press quickly expanded to encompass much of the company's communications with its partners in Southeast Asia, soon becoming "a web of printing, publishing, and journalism". [145] This network tied both Canton and Macau together as gateways to commercial trade in China. [146] Printing proved to be an important tool to expand commerce. Many merchants looked for ways to pass information and knowledge about China and other colonial outposts back to Europe and the Americas. Written correspondence was soon replaced by printed pamphlets, government gazettes, and newspapers produced by Macanese, which were then sent on sailing vessels to their destinations. As trade increased, fast clipper ships and steam powered vessels expanded the circulation of knowledge. Typical printed materials included news of ship arrivals and departures, tallies of export costs, billing, notices of tariffs, and revenue statements, as well as private communications to partners and potential investors.

The conclusion of the Opium Wars (1838 – 1860), which forced China to cede Hong Kong and other "Treaty Ports" to foreign powers, opened the floodgates to information production and mass distribution of knowledge about "The China Trade". By 1860 the use of moveable type was dominated, in the words of one scholar, by a "network of Macanese inter-port printing enterprises". [147] This network accelerated the circulation of information about China throughout the treaty ports via high quality output in multiple languages. Macanese printers had the additional advantage of offering local facilities and competitive pricing to British and American firms that wanted to minimize their investments in Asia. All of these factors provided new tools for foreign and regional commerce in Southeast Asia, propelling the global economy to its next stage.

The Aftermath: Macau at the end of the Opium Wars

As Hong Kong and other "treaty ports" flourished in the new environment under British protection, Macau's deterioration continued through a series of social and political setbacks that took the next one hundred and fifty years to resolve.[148]

Throughout the 19th century the Macau government wrestled with a precarious balance between the distant influence of Lisbon, continued pressures from Imperial China, and divisions among local officials.[149]

The main issues with respect to China was the recognition of Macau's territorial borders, which included several nearby islands, and difficulties in gaining control of the opium traffic from pirates and smugglers. Attempts at interdiction were often recorded in church records and the local press, including one instance that resulted in the death of Caetano Gomes da Silva, a Captain in the Macau Infantry, who lost his life attempting to stop a group of smugglers in November 1873.[150]

The problems apparently began not long after Britain's victory. In 1845, sensing China's weakness following the ceding of lucrative trading ports, the Portuguese government in Lisbon proclaimed Macau's sovereignty by naming it a "free port" and forbidding the payment of duties to local mandarins. The enforcement of this decree was left to a former sea captain, Ferreira do Amaral, who was installed as governor in April 1846. Amaral's imposition of additional duties on native shipping led to several months of unrest among the Chinese population. The governor met local protests with force and military confrontations, including the use of artillery on Tanka junks. leading to his assassination in 1849.[151]

A resolution was not achieved until 1887 with the ratification of the "Sino-Portuguese Treaty of Amity and Commerce" between Portugal and China, which recognized Macau for the first time as a Portuguese territory, but not in the opinion of the Chinese, as a colony. The treaty's major drawback was the failure to specify Macau's maritime limits involving the local islands in dispute. The Chinese also allowed "dual jurisdiction" with Portugal, so long as government policies remained acceptable to China's Imperial government.[152]

Equally significant were inadequate attempts by the Macau government to secure dwindling resources after foreign merchants abandoned the port for more secure territories. One requirement of the treaty was that Macau pay for the regulation of the opium trade by sending duties to the Chinese government. This not only threatened to reduce revenues in one of city's three remaining industries (along with gambling and "coolie" labor), but also impinged upon the Portuguese monarchy's efforts to maintain a colonial presence in Africa funded by opium profits. Under financial pressure, the opium stipulation was ignored by Macanese administrators even after the October 1910 overthrow of King Manuel II and the installation of a Republican government in Lisbon.[153] One of Macau's governors, Anibal Augusto Sanches de Miranda, actively defended the preservation of the government's monopoly on drug sales at an international conference in 1912.[154]

Shortly after, Lisbon's new government pressured Macau's Senate to use opium revenue to "loan" it 270,000 (MOP) to fund operations in Angola.[155] The loan was never repaid, further depleting government reserves, as Macau remained in an economic and social limbo for almost a century.[156] Thus, opium, gambling, and the coolie trade took on added weight, and would remain the principal supports until after Macau's "handover" to China in 1999.[157]

On to Hong Kong

As Macau languished, it became clear to the British Parliament, once enlightened by merchant lobbyists led by James Matheson, that a requirement of maintaining economic dominance in Asia was the possession of protected trading ports and adjoining territories.[158] The Britain occupation of Hong Kong and the acquisition of several "treaty ports" along the Southern coast of China was achieved precisely for this purpose. As we shall see in the next chapter, the aftermath of the Opium Wars not only led to the presence of European and American traders. The end of hostilities provided the next destination of Macanese migration, offering new opportunities and, in some respects, an escape from Macau where conditions remained stagnant. Hong Kong also represented a new challenge for Macanese workers and their families, who would experience a more complicated and structured environment under British rule.

CHAPTER 4
Hong Kong and the Introduction of "Social Distance"

At the conclusion of the Opium Wars in 1860, Hong Kong and Macau remained connected by proximity to Canton and the Chinese mainland as trading ports in the developing China Trade. That connection soon frayed as Hong Kong rose in importance and Macau regressed, leading to restrictions on non-Europeans during the first years of settlement in the new colony. In this chapter, several features of early Hong Kong society will be explored. The most prominent were the widening divisions between British citizens who occupied positions of leadership, Portuguese from Macau, who were hired by trade officials for intermediary posts as clerks, linguists, and assistants, and Chinese from the mainland, who mainly provided labor. In order to understand how this stratified environment influenced social, political, and economic organization in the new British colony, we begin from its origins.

The Founding of Hong Kong

After several unsuccessful attempts to establish relations with Imperial China, the British East India Company ship "Macclesfeld" was first permitted to dock at Canton in 1699, but was not allowed to build factories until 1771.[159] The routine for the next seventy years was to use Macau as a seasonal residence from May through September each year when all Europeans were forced to leave Canton. As the opium trade grew, the Pearl River became increasingly important to foreign merchants. The occupation of Hong Kong as a more suitable site, because of its deep harbors, was advocated as frustrations with the Imperial Court increased. Reflecting English sentiments, a correspondent for the *Canton Register*, who was likely James Matheson, a local trader who funded the newspaper, commented with jingoistic fervor, and some insight:

If the lion's paw is to be put down on any part of the south side

> of China, let it be Hongkong; let the lion declare it to be under his guarantee a free port, and in ten years it will be the most considerable mart east of the Cape. The Portuguese made a mistake: they adopted shallow water and exclusive rules. Hongkong, deep water, and a free port forever! [160]

There was much at stake. Most British "country" traders like Matheson, his partner William Jardine, and Thomas and Lancelot Dent attempted to fill the void left after the East India Company lost its opium monopoly in 1833.[161] They had been headquartered in Macau for over a decade and had acquired large farms in India to grow poppy to produce the drug. Nearly all traders exchanged raw opium for silver at inflated prices to purchase other goods to sell in Europe at a premium. Opium, however, quickly became a source of outrage to the Imperial Court and conflicted interests from the large profits enjoyed by the mandarins overseeing foreign trade.[162] The situation came to a head after the arrival of Lin Zexu, a special commissioner from Peking with wide powers, who ordered the jailing of foreign merchants and the seizure of large drug caches in Canton.[163] Numerous protests and petitions to the British Parliament led to the arrival of a naval fleet. Despite employing Macanese as intermediaries to diffuse tensions, many merchants in Macau feared their factories were vulnerable to attack and regarded Portuguese authorities as unwilling to risk their centuries old relations with the Chinese. Eventually, the conflict pushed traders to look east for a new site.

The leading free traders, including Jardine, Matheson, the Dents, and others lobbied the English Parliament in 1837 to force compensation for opium ceased in Canton, and some form of "Chinese property".[164] As one of the conditions of the Treaty of Nanjing signed in 1841 ending the first "Opium War", Hong Kong island was ceded as an alternative to Macau that Britain alone could control. Five other "treaty ports", Canton, Ningbo, Xiamen, Fuzhou, and Shanghai, were also secured by the foreign powers for trade and residence. By the end of the 1840s, about one hundred traders representing European and American interests were operating in the region.[165] The subsequent defeat of the Qing army in a second war in 1860 led to the occupation of portions of the Kowloon peninsula. A negotiated settlement signed in 1888 called the "Special Articles for the Enlargement of the Hong Kong Boundary" led to a 99 year lease of new territories in the region and over 230 nearby islands.[166]

Fear on the Rocky Island

Some early traders in Macau, unsure of how Hong Kong would be governed, initially ridiculed British attempts to auction off land for settlement.[167] Despite its deep harbors, the island appeared to have little to offer. Even with Macau's drawbacks, it was considered a livelier, more established port with crowded streets and shops, and a quiet enclave away from the Chinese mainland. Hong Kong, on the other hand, had few buildings, and according to a preliminary census in 1841, only 4,350 inhabitants, including government workers, the military, and about 2,000 Chinese boatmen and their families living on the waters of the surrounding area.[168]

The main thoroughfare, Queen's Road, built along the northern shore in 1843, was then only four miles long, around which one observer wrote, "there had grown a straggling ribbon of a town", which contained ship outfitters, twenty-four brothels, and one candy shop.[169] A British naval officer described Victoria, the island's first city built in 1844, as "the fearfullest hole in the world ... inhabited by a den of thieves." [170] Yet another visitor described "a bleakness of life and prisoner like sensation ... arising in great measure from the difficulty experienced in moving more than a mile or two on either side of the town of Victoria, ..." [171]

Conflicts with indigenous Chinese, many fleeing the Taiping Rebellion and in competition with Europeans, only contributed to the turmoil. Hong Kong's fifth governor, Sir John Bowring (1854-1859) was so alarmed by the resulting violence that he instituted a pass system among the Chinese with violations punishable by incarceration, scourges, and "public exposure in the stocks".[172] There was some evidence to support those fears, which were amplified by the poisoning of Hong Kong's bread supply by a local baker in 1842. This incident led to the death of Bowring's wife a few years later.[173]

To add to the tensions, Hong Kong and the surrounding islands were susceptible to pirate raids for several years. The "Hongkong Government Gazette" reported frequent attacks on trading vessels to an anxious readership. During the period from 1856 to 1859 the Gazette reported actions between the British and crews of Chinese and Portuguese brigands over cargos of opium, rifles, tea, and other valuable commodities.[174] Later accounts documented the engagement of the Royal Navy with regular Chinese forces through the end of hostilities in 1860.

The Introduction of "Social Distance" in Hong Kong

To allay widespread concerns about the Chinese and hostile conditions in Hong Kong, the new administration sought to create a more "hospitable" environment for British residents so that the business of trade could be conducted efficiently and largely unimpeded. To achieve this end, an informal system of racial separation and exclusivity began to appear. Although evidence of this condition seems to have existed much earlier, a conceptual description of these forms of "social distance", effectively cloistering the English from local ethnic groups, was not published until 1924 by sociologist Robert Ezra Park in studies of American race relations.[175] Scholars before and after Park refined the concept over the years, suggesting that the practice of distancing groups from each other was not unique to Asia.[176] As others have written, methods of maintaining social distance in British India had been common practice by the late 18th century.[177]

The parallels to social relations in Hong Kong seem unmistakable, suggesting how an ideology of racial division had been maintained for specific purposes. In Park's original phrasing, "social distance" was marked by "... an insistence on social distinctions and differences, ... condescensions, ...for the express purpose of enforcing the reserves and social distances upon which social and political hierarchy rests."[178] These distinctions, for example, were reinforced by institutions and social practices throughout Hong Kong's colonial period. As a result, numerous examples of policies and rules designed to block non-Europeans from reaching the highest levels of government and business led to the virtual segregation of British citizens from the rest of the population, even as the colonial administration advocated a "free trade" policy that was to be impartially administered among all trading partners.[179]

The rationale for maintaining social distance in Hong Kong was complicated and not always absolute. Early forms of segregation in Hong Kong began with housing. Residential restrictions initially directed at the Chinese, and enforced against the Macanese and other ethnic groups as well, were first introduced in 1844 to protect a few hundred British expatriates and soldiers within the city of Victoria. All others were confined to living areas near the docks and warehouses along the northern shore. Small enclaves of houses protected by Indian troops were also commonplace in specific areas of the island. By the 1850s several large mansions for wealthy merchants and stately homes built for government officials began to appear on various levels of the "Peak", the highest hill on the island, as a respite from the tropical heat. Residence on the Peak soon came to epitomize stratification in the colony, with the more elevated locations signifying higher degrees of social status.[180]

The Victoria Peak Hotel and Mansions, 1890s

British institutions that facilitated these attitudes included the large number of exclusive clubs, recreational facilities, and protestant churches located within many of these segregated neighborhoods. Each not only insured isolation from "foreign" contact, but affirmed class positions, allowed the cultivation of business relations among English traders, and encouraged accepted forms of religious worship. Among those organizations were the elite Hong Kong club, the Masonic Lodge, the Hong Kong Cricket Club, the Botanical Gardens, the Hong Kong Jockey club, and St. John's Anglican Cathedral.[181] The maintenance of these venues helped to secure the privileges of the small English minority over the much larger population of Chinese and other underclass groups. It was no coincidence that these policies were enacted just as Hong Kong's population began to swell due to civil wars and migrations from the mainland.[182]

The workplace provided fertile ground for extending these forms of distance. The business of trade was marked by a well-defined division of labor required within the government bureaucracy, banking institutions, and merchant houses that separated British department heads from mid-level Portuguese clerks and Chinese workers. An interesting example is presented in descriptions of "protocols" at the Hong Kong and Shanghai bank in 1886, which included rules restricting contact with Portuguese and Chinese laborers, segregated use of bathroom facilities, and warnings about foreign food and "fraternization" outside the workplace.[183] Frank Welsh also noted the "parochial and restricting snobbery" among Banks executives, who required employees to remain in the colony no less than 10 years and remain celibate with respect to non-British women.[184] Even partnerships between Chinese businessmen and British traders did not prevent segregation in the early years.[185] While there were accounts of British citizens having difficulty maintaining "civil" relations even among themselves due to the "foreignness" of Asia, pressures in the workplace and within social circles often discouraged contact across racial divides.[186] Deeper concerns about racial mixing through personal contact and "contamination" of the English character have been suggested by other scholars.[187] A similar purpose was apparently intended for British institutions in all colonial outposts: to insulate English subjects from the "foreign" environment by limiting contact with ethnic groups.

Economic Supports

Protecting the status of the English population had implications for the local economy and Britain's colonial policies as well. In Hong Kong, it was critical that British managers, Portuguese clerks, and Chinese laborers knew their roles in the workplace, since the economy, which these restrictions supported, was expected to run smoothly as part of England's broader strategy connecting India, China, and Europe. As Tak-Wing Ngo wrote: "The aim of the colony was ... to serve as a foothold for British trade in the Far East, especially in China. ... administering the colony and administering the China Trade were seen as two sides of the same coin." [188] Several other nations were also involved, including France, Germany, and Holland, which followed the colonial division of labor. Deviations from the way Hong Kong was governed, including a change in employing Portuguese "middle-men" as bulwarks and supervisors of Chinese workers, would likely have adverse effects on the economy.

German merchant - staff, 1896

Holland-China Co. staff, 1918

The commercial vehicle that justified these policies during much of the 19th century was the sale and distribution of opium. As more foreign traders operated through Hong Kong in the 1850s, both England's national interests and the China Trade grew increasingly dependent on large exports of opium sold for silver, the main currency that kept foreign commerce flowing, allowing England to maintain a superior position in global markets.[189] By agreement, Hong Kong was the only distribution port for opium in Southeast Asia. Richard Grace writes that throughout the 1860s Hong Kong's largest merchant firms, including Jardine, Matheson and the Dent Brothers, remained heavily invested, earning the bulk of their income by producing opium on their poppy farms in India and from sales for the refined drug to other traders.[190] It was not until an early banking crisis and the diversification of exports in the late 1870s that Britain's economic dependence on the drug began to change.[191] By then the Dents were bankrupt and forced to consolidate their business in Shanghai.

We could speculate that more companies may have failed had political disruptions in Hong Kong occurred earlier or were allowed to go unchecked. If the division of labor had been upended as a result,

British supervisors would no longer be able to control, much less count on the reliability of Portuguese and Chinese labor. Such upheavals could have led to dissension, a breakdown in the workplace, and racial antagonism. Each would likely have impeded commerce. Given Hong Kong's history of political tensions, banking crises, and increased competition from other European powers, an economic recovery would have been difficult.

There was so much was at stake in early Hong Kong that within twenty years the foundation of a permanent system to institutionalize "social distance" in the workplace was set in place. In 1861 it appeared in the form of the Hong Kong General Chamber of Commerce, which joined its political counterpart, the Hong Kong Legislative Council established in 1843. Each organization was the exclusive domain of British-born executives. The Chamber was created "... to watch over and protect the general interests of Commerce", and founded with government approval by Jardine, Matheson & Co., the largest trading house in the colony, which provided leadership for nineteen years. Over the next century, the chairmanship of the Chamber was passed on to a representative of P & O Steamship Navigation for twelve years, to the merchant house Butterfield & Swire for ten years, and to Turner & Co., a commercial house, for another 10 years.[192] Together, these companies and institutions introduced a pattern of control that virtually guaranteed British interests would dominate Hong Kong's society, economy, and civil affairs through the end of the 20th century.

CHAPTER 5
The Macanese Community of Hong Kong

The effects of the new social order in Hong Kong were evident in the lives of most Macanese, who had been generally classified as "Portuguese" because of their origins in Macau and Goa. Many early arrivals were initially surprised at how different life was in Hong Kong, especially for those who worked for British interests in Macau. Among the earliest recorded was Bartolomeu Barretto, the scion of an old merchant family who is mentioned prominently in the correspondence between William Jardine and James Matheson beginning in 1829.[193] Typical of the Portuguese role in the 18th and 19th centuries, Barretto was employed by Jardine Matheson as a "channel of mediation" with Canton to sustain British trade in South China, and was relied upon to intercede with the governor of Macau and Chinese mandarins heading Co-Hongs, the trading guilds assigned by the Imperial government to regulate foreign merchants. [194]

Once Hong Kong was established and commercial relations were dictated by the Treaty of Nanjing ending the first Opium War, there was less need for mediators like Barretto. Most Portuguese from Macau were employed as mid-level clerks, interpreters, or compositors. In the banks and trading houses, Portuguese clerks and bookkeepers worked under English executives, but ranked higher than Chinese compradors, shroffs (tellers), and laborers. There was often little direct contact between the English staff and the Chinese workforce, with most institutions relying on Portuguese "middlemen" to relay work orders down the chain of command. [195] The position of department head was reserved for British expatriates, many of whom stayed in Hong Kong for only a few years. Lower ranking Portuguese clerks reported to a Portuguese Chief Clerk or a Head Accountant, who often was a long-time resident. This was the highest position to which a worker of his race could aspire. Below them were Chinese compradors, who reported to the ranking Portuguese supervisor. The shipping lines, telegraph companies, and sections of the military were similarly organized.

The lines between these positions were almost never breached. Situated between the British and the Chinese, the Portuguese were effectively used as a social and political "buffer" within these organizations, and between the two former adversaries throughout Hong Kong society.[196] Custom, family pressures, and cultural perceptions based on ethnic stereotypes nurtured in Macau prevented Portuguese workers from descending lower in the social order. Colonial policies and company rules created barriers to moving higher. These hierarchies remained virtually unchanged until after World War II.

Macanese Community and Family Life

Outside work, life for most Macanese was similarly isolated from the British, and in many cases, from other ethnic communities. In the first years a small Macanese community was segregated in the Wan Chai district, near the "Chinese quarter" and the naval shipyards, removed from the center of Victoria. Conditions would be considered primitive by present standards. Housing was usually scarce and cramped for large families, with illumination only from oil lamps. Food had to be imported from the mainland through a city gate guarded by Chinese imperial soldiers. Street vendors were unevenly supplied and often sold at inflated prices. Until reforms were adopted in the police force in the 1890s, gangs of thieves and rouge "watchmen" of the constabulary were known to rule the night. There was also little entertainment, except for family gatherings and religious holidays.[197]

As the community grew from around 400 workers and their dependents in 1849, several families began moving near the Jamia Mosque to an area commonly referred to as "Mato Moro".[198] After British officials "annexed" the Kowloon peninsula in 1860 to secure Hong Kong's defenses, small farms and houses were built and a commercial ferry service was introduced in 1896. A large group of Portuguese families, attracted by housing schemes beginning in 1911, many with relatives who worked in government or for banks and trading houses on the island, settled in the Ho Man Tin and Tsim Sha Tsui districts on the Kowloon peninsula.[199]

One of the few shelters from the turmoil of early Hong Kong was the extended family unit. Most Macanese women left the politics of the workplace to their fathers, husbands, uncles, and brothers. Many took on traditional roles as wives, mothers, and critically, as managers of large households. The pattern was a carryover from traditions begun in Macau.[200] To accommodate these households, most family dwellings in Kowloon were built with multiple floors. The layout of most homes followed a similar pattern. On the ground floor were sitting rooms and parlors, with kitchens and servant quarters in the back. On the next level, or the "first" floor, were older relatives' and children's rooms. The "second" and "third" floors consisted of the main bedrooms for the head of the household and his wife, their younger children, and small rooms for Chinese servants who helped care for them. Rooftops and balconies on the upper floors allowed places to dry laundry, play areas for the older children, and vantage points to see other neighboring residents. Extended family were usually included in the household as well.[201] Father Jose "Zinho" Gosano recalled his own family's residence in Kowloon.

> ...besides the 9 of us plus Mother, we had 2 of Mother's brothers living with us. Mother was also looking after another 4 orphans – her brother's children (a boy and 3 girls), and then another family of my mother's (relatives) ... including 2 boys. ..., about 18 or 19 at one stage." [202]

Another son of Macanese immigrants, Horatio Ozorio, also noted that such large families would have been impossible without Chinese "amahs", refugee women from the mainland who worked long hours for low wages that were sent back to relatives on the mainland. He described a typical family unit and amahs:

> ... each family had two amahs, one to cook and the other to do the rest of the chores. Larger families had a third amah to

care for the children. When a family was exceptionally large, say eight or more children, there might be a fourth amah whose main duty was the laundry. In the high humidity tropical setting of the Far East, a heavy load of laundry every day or two was usual." [203]

As Kowloon's Macanese population grew to around 3,000 in the early 20th century, most households congregated in a familiar pattern of ethnic communities around the world. [204] Fr. Gosano's description of his neighborhood was typical:

We lived on Soares Avenue, Ho Man Tin (a Kowloon neighborhood), where there were quite a few Portuguese people who bought the houses around us. ... The house ... was two-storied. It was attached to number 9 Soares Avenue, which was occupied by ... the Sequeiras. Next door to us, Number 13, was occupied by another Portuguese family ... the Barros. In between this house and the next was one ... occupied by a Portuguese family called Guterres. Next door to the Guterres's was where the Yvanovichs (a Ukrainian-Macanese family) lived... . [205]

A Typical Macanese home circa 1910

Over the Bamboo Ceiling

Leonardo d'Almada e Castro

Within these neighborhoods, and due to the lack of external support systems, a few prosperous Macanese began to fund community projects as a way to maintain cultural cohesion. Leonardo d'Almada e Castro, Chief Clerk to Captain Charles Elliot in Macau, the first Superintendent of Trade, was one such example. During his career, d'Almada rose quickly from a junior clerk in Macau in 1836 before the move to Hong Kong in 1842, to "Keeper of the Records" (Head Archivist) in 1844, then to Chief Clerk for the Colonial Secretary in 1846.[206] Less well known is d'Almada's career as a property owner and philanthropist. His position in the Colonial Secretary's office not only placed him in charge of all Portuguese workers, but also allowed him to purchase land near Hong Kong's deep-water harbors. Those parcels were highly prized by foreign traders relocating from Macau, and some that provided cheap rentals for many Macanese when they migrated to Hong Kong.[207] In the 1870s d'Almada also deeded land and a building on Hong

Kong Island to the Italian Canossian sisters for an orphanage and a school. [208]

Januario Antonio Carvalho

Another influential Macanese was Januario A. de Carvalho, an early arrival to Hong Kong in 1842. Carvalho was trained as a clerk and bookkeeper in Macau at St. Joseph's College, where many less affluent boys were taught. Entering government service as an accountant in the Colonial Treasurer's office, he quickly rose to Chief Cashier and remained in that position until his death in 1900. During his career, Carvalho's expert testimony was often used to settle local issues. These included a dispute in 1858 concerning payments and registration of brothels in Hong Kong by Chinese owners.[209] In 1887 he was appointed "Justice of the Peace" to help settle disputes in the Macanese community. Despite being a citizen of Macau, Carvalho's long service in government eventually resulted in a conferral of British citizenship in December 1883.[210]

Carvalho's senior position at the Treasury also allowed him to shepherd young Macanese, including members of his family. His oldest son, Edmund, rose to Chief Cashier after his father's death. Another son, Carlos, was the Chief Clerk of the "local staff" at the Hongkong and Shanghai Bank. Geraldo, Carvalho's third son, was employed as a bookkeeper with Jardine and Matheson in Hong Kong. The Macanese writer Jose Pedro Braga also credited Carvalho's influence, together with his grandfather, Delfino Noronha, in guiding his own career as a journalist and a legislator.[211]

As Braga's principal mentor, Delfino Noronha staked out his own path to success. Rather than work as a clerk or linguist as many had done before him, Noronha, who was trained as a compositor and printer in Macau, founded his own printing plant after migrating to Hong Kong in 1844 at the age of twenty. After two years, Noronha opened his first business, Noronha & Co. By 1859 his company was granted the contract to print the Hongkong Government Gazette,

the colonial government's official record and its principal means of communication. It was from this position that Noronha & Co. grew to become the largest printer in Asia, and Noronha himself became an important link between the government and the Macanese community for almost five decades.

The Production and Distribution of Information

The impact of Noronha's influence has hardly been recognized. He and his protégés virtually dominated the printing and publishing industries in Hong Kong, Shanghai, and other treaty ports from the 1840s through 1941, including the publication of newspapers, pamphlets, tourist brochures, advertisements, product labels, and currency notes for banks in China and Southeast Asia. As a result, Macanese printing through its involvement in news production and journalism, consumer goods and advertising, business services, and tourism, became a pillar of the "China Trade" and the developing global economy. Their printing facilities were the principal means by which information and strategic knowledge about business could be communicated across Asia, and to consumers and corporate principals in Britain, the United States, and Europe. It was through these early methods of "information technology" that business could be conducted between distant locations, in the most efficient manner, and in the least amount of time. (An example of how one large printing company operated during the period is presented in Chapter 9.)

More Than Printing

Noronha's achievements went beyond his success as a printer. His example in business and willingness to help others, including many outside the Portuguese community, ushered in a period of independent enterprise among the Macanese that would continue for the next century.[212] A local directory in 1861, for example, listed just thirteen Macanese owned businesses, including pharmacies, merchant houses, printing presses, a soda water firm, and a shipping company.[213] By the turn of the 20th century, in addition to several hundred printing presses, Macanese businesses included: A. Botelho and F.D. Barretto, a son of the same Barretto family, who in 1895 were flour merchants and shipping agents. There was also Luis Maria Alvares, the youngest son of the Goan and Macau family, who in 1896 was an exporter of ginger, ginseng, and ornamental feathers. Others included A.M. da Cruz and J.M. F. Basto, importers of Australian flour, butter, and dairy products in 1897; and F.J.V Jorge, a rice, food produce, and ginseng merchant in 1901.[214]

Delfino Noronha influence also was reflected in the career of his grandson, Jose Pedro Braga. In 1895 at the age of twenty-four, Braga wrote a widely read pamphlet entitled "The Rights of Aliens in Hongkong", published by Noronha's press and distributed by the English owned China Mail, criticizing government policies and attitudes toward non-British workers. (An analysis of J.P. Braga's early work appears in Chapter 7.) He also managed an English language newspaper, the Hong Kong Daily Telegraph, from 1902 to 1909. Braga was later hired as a correspondent for the Reuters News Service and the Associated Press, and in 1929 was appointed the first Macanese (non-voting) member of Hong Kong's Legislative Council, the colony's government body.

The Ceiling Appears

Despite their achievements, many first-generation Macanese encountered social barriers. Leonardo d'Almada e Castro, for example, was plagued by spurious criticisms of his position in government. As early as 1847 in an anonymous "Letter of an Englishman" printed in the China Mail, objections were raised about d'Almada's appointment as Chief Clerk in the Colonial Office the previous year because a brother and a cousin also worked under him. The suggestion of nepotism was contradicted by the government's own policy placing all Portuguese workers in the Colonial Office under the Chief Clerk. The same writer accused d'Almada, a devout Catholic, of being an "Agent of the Propagandists", falsely claiming that he could neither write nor read English, and must apply to Rome for permission to rent his properties.[215] Several years later, it was revealed that d'Almada was denied an appointment as Colonial Secretary, the second highest office in government, because of local objections to his Portuguese citizenship.[216]

Similar objections were raised of Januario de Carvalho, Chief Cashier of the Treasury Office, who was appointed in 1878 as Acting Colonial Treasurer. His appointment was revoked because Carvalho was labeled an "alien" citizen of Macau.[217] In spite of this setback, Carvalho was granted British citizenship in 1883. Joao Jose Hyndman, a fourth assistant in the Diplomatic Department, was similarly denied advancement because he retained Portuguese citizenship as the son of a mother born in Macau.[218] Alexandre Grand Pre', an officer in the Hong Kong Police Force, culminated a long career with an appointment to Superintendent of Police in 1855. That nomination was also rescinded by the Police Commission because of criticism from senior British officers who objected to Grand Pre's "alien" ancestry (French and Portuguese).[219]

These incidents were not isolated and indicated an institutional bias that favored English-born managers in the highest positions. According to Harold Lethridge, between 1862 and 1941 the upper ranks of the British colonial civil service were chosen from a small group of Oxford and Cambridge trained English "cadet officers".[220] Most served in several colonial ports during their careers and spoke multiple languages. They were often assigned to lead departments in service of commercial trade, a task that could not be entrusted to "foreigners" or "aliens". Three future cadets became Hong Kong governors, five others were high commissioners, and four more were chosen Colonial Secretary. Each of the successors to Grand Pre', Hyndman, Cavalho, and d'Almada came from the cadet ranks. [221]

Among cloistered British citizens, the hiring of foreigners to lead departments would have violated unwritten policies that paid them less than their British counterparts. A review of public officer salaries between 1856 and 1889 revealed that a typical Portuguese worker's annual pay averaged about 60% less than that of a similar mid-level English employee.[222] Legislative Council minutes in 1906 also indicated that during a recent budgetary shortfall caused by higher exchange rates, Portuguese workers were preferred because they could be paid less and were more reliable than English workers than who were similarly trained.[223] Underlying these sentiments was a bitter reality about the British presence. Legislative memoranda noted that English recruits, most with minimal education, tended to stay in Hong Kong only a few years. Some were expelled for petty crimes, while others were ostracized for "consorting" with members of other races. Many other British workers simply returned to England unable to endure the climate, social attitudes, and ethnic tensions in the colony. [224] Portuguese workers, much like the Chinese, were simply cheaper to employ and more likely to remain in Hong Kong for a longer period. Most came from families that arrived in the early 19th century to work for British administrators and companies.

A Legacy of Social Organizations and Networks

There were certain advantages to the Macanese condition, however. An obvious one had to do with work. Throughout the last half of the 19th century and well into the 1930s, Macanese employment remained stable, while neighborhoods grew more settled and the community in general expanded across the harbor into Kowloon. As long as large institutions flourished in Hong Kong's booming economy, the jobs of mid-level clerks, bookkeepers, and linguists were relatively secure, although actual pay grew slowly. As mercantile activity flourished, more members of the middle class sent their children to international schools in Shanghai and Canton, or back to Macau to learn Portuguese. The Chinese, however, many of whom arrived in Hong Kong after fleeing famines and civil wars on the mainland, fared less well. Most had little choice than to become domestic workers or laborers, working inexpensively for Europeans, including the Macanese. The sober reality was that Chinese "shroffs", "amahs", and "coolies" greatly eased the workload in English businesses and in many households, but often supported their families and relatives on the mainland whom they saw infrequently.[225]

Hong Kong's rigid social norms also provided fertile ground for the growth of Macanese organizations outside "legitimate" British society. The insularity of the community, a consequence of colonial policies, English hubris, and racial discrimination, often led to the formation of social clubs, libraries, mutual aid societies, and charitable groups, which were created as alternatives to "British-only" organizations. The purpose of many groups went beyond the social arena, however. As Barnabas Koo observed, many Macanese associations began by providing support and assistance to newly arrived members from Macau or others in need.[226] Emulating the work of Macau's *Santa Casa da Misericordia* (the Holy House of Mercy), a counterpart in Hong Kong named the *Associacao Portuguesa de Socorros Mutuos* (the Portuguese Association of Mutual Aid) began operating in 1868. Several other associations with various other priorities soon followed.

Over next decades these organizations became the foundation of a network of institutions that linked the Hong Kong Macanese community through chapters in Macau, Canton, Shanghai, and other locations across Southeast Asia. [227] There is little doubt that these connections were assisted by commercial expansion throughout the "Treaty Ports" beginning in the 1860s. Providing aid and social links through these networks up to World War II also allowed these organizations to re-assert elements of Macanese culture and identity, a response to homogenizing colonial policies, which extended common bonds to Luso-Asians in other settlements. These cultural elements included the Macanese patois (Maquista) spoken exclusively among members and their families, the observance of Catholicism and religious festivals in local churches built to accommodate them, expressive forms of literature, music, and art displayed in association venues, and the cultivation of a uniquely blended cuisine handed down over the generations. Each were routinely practiced by family members in Goa, Macau and other settlements for over three hundred years, and later by association members in Hong Kong for more than a century. [228]

The most prominent organization was the *Club Lusitano*, founded in central Hong Kong on December 17, 1866 by a group led by Joao Antonio Barretto, the oldest son of the Macau merchant Bartolomeu Barretto, Leonardo d'Almada e Castro, Chief Clerk in the Colonial Secretary, and Delfino Noronha, the publisher of the Hong Kong Government Gazette.[229] First housed in a stately building on Shelley Street near the Macanese "Mato Moro" district, the Lusitano was constructed using donated funds following the dissolution of the earlier *Club Portuguez* in the 1850's. The new club eventually moved to the financial center of Hong Kong on Ice House Street in 1920 after securing a loan from the government of Macau.

Even though its initial purpose was to be an alternative to British men's clubs, the Club Lusitano soon adopted some of the same policies. These included restricting women and Chinese nationals from membership, and in 1885 creating two classes of members, one for "Founders and Owners" who contributed money for construction, and a second category for "General" members who only paid annual dues. The club also offered low cost "refreshments" and "rooms" for bachelors and widowers, while providing venues to entertain friends and family, and sponsoring religious and community events. Membership in 1903 included over 200 men, most of them relatives or business associates working in banks, merchant houses, shipping companies, and government. By the 1920s the *Club Lusitano* had hosted three generations of Macanese workers in Hong Kong, and had affiliated chapters in Shanghai and Canton.

Club Lusitano members were also involved in the creation of other organizations. Lisbello de Jesus Xavier, one of Noronha's protéges, and the founder of the Hong Kong Printing Press in 1888, provided funds for the *Club de Recreio* in 1906 and became its first president. Recreio's mandate was to build recreational facilities and organize sports leagues for Macanese families, initially on Kimberley Road in Kowloon, where a large number relocated away from the crowded conditions of Hong Kong island.

The club was able to expand to a larger facility at King's Park in 1925 through a land grant from the colonial government. Pedro Xavier, who succeeded his father as president of the Press in 1909, and as a member of both the *Lusitano* and the *Club Recreio*, had already moved a factory to Kowloon in 1924, and employed several Macanese who lived on the peninsula. Located on Bowring Street near the corner of Nathan Road and Jordan Road, the factory joined several other Macanese businesses, newspapers, social clubs, churches, and parish schools that served the community for several decades. Like the *Lusitano*, the *Club Recreio* had affiliated chapters in Shanghai and Bangkok.

Several other organizations made similar impacts. *The Portuguese Library*, founded in 1857 and described as the "heart of the community for decades", was joined in 1889 by the *Club Lusitano Library*. The combined 4,000 volumes were later merged in 1920 into the *Royal Lusitano Library of Hong Kong* and remained a community resource through the 1960s. Mutual aid societies were also active. These included the aforementioned *Associoao Soccorros Mutuos*, which provided burials for indigent Macanese, and the *Little Flower Club* founded in the 1910, which raised money for Church charities. *The Portuguese Association of Mutual Aid* in Hong Kong, founded in 1915, offered a variety of social services in several cities, including Macau, Canton, and Shanghai. During World War I the *Liga Portuguesa*, through patrons such as Pedro Xavier, raised money for the families of Portuguese soldiers killed in Flanders. Between the world wars in 1929, a successor to the Liga called the *Portuguese League of Hong Kong* even tried to align its membership with the nationalistic policies of Portugal's Salazar regime, and distributed propaganda at the request of the regime's State Intelligence Service.

Despite their varying agendas, these organizations filled a void for active involvement in Hong Kong society and provided a reaffirmation of cultural practices that had been largely denied the Macanese since they left Macau. Many associations offered members opportunities to assist others, as well as social venues to maintain old acquaintances, to discuss business ventures, and to pass on Macanese culture to new generations. Each helped sustain the larger community as more Macanese migrated to Hong Kong from other cities in Southeast Asia.

A Fitting Epitaph

The progenitors of these social networks were the first generation leaders of the Macanese community in Hong Kong. Both Club Lusitano founders Leonardo d'Almada e Castro and Delfino Noronha, for example, were among the first landowners in Kowloon, where a majority of the Macanese community began settling at the end of the 19th century. As mentioned previously, d'Almada offered affordable housing to many immigrants and supported local charities and religious orders. Delfino Noronha became a noted horticulturist, experimenting with various tropical plants and fruits on his Kowloon farms, and sold produce to families and local restaurants. In the 1870s Noronha became a partner with another Macanese immigrant, Marcus Calisto do Rozário, on ten acres in Kowloon set aside for farms and housing. This venture was followed by more extensive land development schemes in 1911, 1920, and 1931.[230] During the 1880s Noronha also operated a rudimentary ship service between Hong Kong and Kowloon, the precursor of the British owned "Star Ferry", providing a convenient way for Macanese workers to commute to the central island. [231]

A lasting impression was made on many of their descendants, including Delfino Noronha's grandson, Jose' Pedro Braga. Almost from birth, the young Braga was exposed to a wide range of political and cultural ideas offered by Noronha's activities, and from the dialogue with many guests who dined periodically at the elder's table. Many years after his grandfather's death in 1900, Braga reflected on Noronha's influence as his own career as a journalist and politician was coming to an end, providing a fitting epitaph for many pioneers in Hong Kong.

> *By dint of hard work and thrift, and in spite of the ravages of the climate and other handicaps of life in Hongkong's early days, Mr. Delfino Noronha brought up a large family of children and grandchildren and built up a prosperous business. ... He was small and slight, and was always immaculately dress, and he was my ideal of a perfect gentleman.* [232]

CHAPTER 6
The Macanese Community of Shanghai

The port city of Shanghai became another important settlement for the Macanese, and an alternative for migrants from Macau. Long before it was conceded by China as a "Treaty Port" at the end of the first Opium War, Shanghai had been settled by the Tang Dynasty in 746 and served as a commercial center beginning in the 12th century under the Song emperors. Under the Ch'ing (Qing) Dynasty (1644-1911) Shanghai was described as a "A City Built by Guilds." Over two dozen associations and guilds were active in the 18th and 19th centuries. These merchant organizations helped expand the original city by constructing guild halls, rental housing, and temples, as well as buildings for manufacturing and commerce. The guilds also provided civic services through their benevolent projects.

Thus, Shanghai was unique in the Chinese Empire. Major cities of the empire tended to be administrative or political centers. By contrast, Shanghai was a commercial city engaged in both domestic and international trade. By 1830 the volume of shipping going through the port was reported to be equal to London.[233] Strategically located on a main tributary of the Yangtze River, and in proximity by ship to Hong Kong, Taiwan, Korea, and Japan, Shanghai soon played a key role in expanding European trade in Asia.[234]

In November 1843 under the Treaty of Nanjing, also known as the "Unequal Treaty System" following the first Opium War, the British, French, and American governments exercised extraterritorial powers leading to the creation of "concessions" in Shanghai that housed commercial factories and residences for foreign traders. Shortly after the treaty was signed, the

British and American administrations merged to form an "International Settlement" to be governed by a joint municipal council. This was followed by the creation of a separate French council in 1849. Each nation initially appointed foreign merchants as Vice Consuls until professional diplomats took over in the late 19th century. [235]

The Macanese Community

Due to Lisbon's diminished influence, racially mixed Portuguese from Hong Kong and Macau, with no national concession to support them, settled slowly in Shanghai's other foreign settlements based on their occupational roles. Among the first six Macanese listed by the North China Daily News and Herald in 1850, four were mercantile assistants in large companies from Hong Kong and the United States that set up offices in the British-American concession of Shanghai. Two others were employed as compositors by the Herald, headquartered in the French quarter. [236] The population of the community did not change significantly until after the 1887 "Treaty of Friendship and Commerce" between Portugal and China, which attempted to solidify Macau's permanence in China by taking advantage of the latter's weakened state. [237] A local census in 1895 listed 1,936 Portuguese workers and family members, increasing to as many as 4,000 through the end of the 1940s. [238] As a relatively small group among almost 111,000 foreigners in Shanghai, the Portuguese were well represented in commerce and social life.

Although the evidence of their origins before Shanghai is incomplete, a large number seem to have come initially from Macau and then through Hong Kong throughout the late 19th and early 20th centuries. The paths were not always one-way. Many were among the back and forth migration of individuals looking for work, joining relatives, or retiring later in life. Some examples include Antonio J.H. de Carvalho and Cypriano Euzebio do Rozario, who came as compositors from Hong Kong 1850 to work for the North-China Heald in Shanghai. Carvalho later returned to Hong Kong, while Rozario remained in Shanghai. Henrique Carlos Lubeck, a ships navigator born in Macau, came to work in Hong Kong as a compositor for the "Echo de Povo" (Voice of the People) in the late 1870's. In 1880 he moved with his wife to Shanghai to work at the Hong Kong and Shanghai Bank.[239]

The majority lived in the French concession in an area known as "Siccawei" (Xujiahui), where the Jesuit missionary Matteo Ricci began his mission around 1560. The area is named after a Chinese Christian convert and scholar named Xu Guangqi, who donated large plots of land for the building of a church and an astronomical observatory which still exist today. Unlike Hong Kong's restrictions on non-English workers, there were fewer barriers confronting the Macanese in Shanghai until the 1930's. Two distinguishing features were most evident: a wide dispersal of Portuguese workers across different sectors of the economy, and a large number of social organizations, which suggests extensive personal networks. As we shall see, the latter tended to allow many connections to exist between the Macanese communities in Shanghai, Hong Kong, and Macau. Let us look at these characteristics in more detail.

Working in Shanghai

Some of the earliest Macanese arrivals listed in the North-China Heald in 1850 worked as "mercantile assistants", that is, as clerks or bookkeepers, for large foreign trading companies. T.P. Cordeiro, for example, worked as a mercantile assistant at Wolcott, Bates & Co., a New York based firm that imported teas, silks, satins, hand-made shawls, oil, and pepper from Canton and Shanghai to Massachusetts, Liverpool, and Amsterdam. Another was J.S. Baptista, who worked for Dent, Beale & Co. in Shanghai, which was the main competitor in Hong Kong to trading giant Jardine Matheson & Co. Baptista began working before Dent consolidated business interests in Shanghai in 1867 after defaulting during a banking crisis. Another worker, P.J. da Silva Loureiro, Jr, was employed by the American firm Russell & Company, which included a grand uncle of Franklin Delano

Roosevelt as an investor. Another was António dos Santos, also a mercantile assistant, who worked at two English trading companies, first at Holiday and Wise, Co. in 1850, and then later at Gilman, Bowman & Co. As mentioned previously, two other Macanese were employed by Shanghai's first English newspaper, the North-China Herald. António J.H. de Carvalho, who later founded a newspaper of his own, was listed as the "Overseer", while Cypriano E. do Rozario, was the paper's sole compositor.

Among the largest employers of the Macanese after 1850 were printing companies owned by Macanese from Hong Kong or Macau. One of the earliest was Carvalho & Co, founded in 1857, which was owned by the same Antonio J.H. de Carvalho, the younger brother of Januario de Carvalho, Chief Cashier of the Hong Kong Treasury. The company was reorganized in 1875 due to poor sales, then sold in 1878 to Noronha & Co., the largest printer in Hong Kong. Up to its closure in 1893, the firm employed at least fourteen Macanese printers and compositors. There were also seven other printing companies, which were owned and operated by Macanese between 1867 and 1940 in Shanghai. Each of those employed an equal number as Carvalho & Co., and several hundred Chinese and other foreign staff. It is estimated that about half of the owners were from Macau, and the others from Hong Kong.

Compared to Hong Kong, however, the number of Macanese enterprises outside the printing industry seems to have been far less, largely in partnerships that began operating later in the period. Wang Zhisheng's research indicates that there were only six recorded Portuguese enterprises in Shanghai from 1900 through 1949, although he does not name them.[240] Those included an exporter, two importers, an independent industrialist, and two dealers. The six Portuguese enterprises, Wang wrote, employed twenty-six Chinese staff members, four Chinese workers, and eight other foreign staff members. According to Ho Tin Wong's research, printers in Shanghai and their families comprised the majority of the Macanese community.[241]

Cultural Networks

The most important sector of the Macanese community in Shanghai was not business, however, but associations. Most local organizations and clubs combined to form networks that supported churches, community schools, and businesses, while creating bonds among expatriate families that lived in the treaty port for over a century. Two important functions were providing a sense of identity and military protection. In many cases, members either belonged to similar organizations in Hong Kong or had relatives who were members.[242]

The oldest of these organization was the *Club Portuguez*, founded in 1882 by a committee made up of Joao Carlos Danenberg (Danish - Macanese); H. Pereira; Francisco Simão dos Santos Oliveira; and Antonio Joaquim Yvanovich (Ukrainian - Macanese). Each member was born in Macau and migrated from Hong Kong or moved directly from Macau to Shanghai in the 1860s. Nearly all had relatives belonging to Hong Kong social clubs. The same could be said for the *Club de Recreio* founded in 1893 and affiliated through relatives with Hong Kong's *Club de Recreio* in 1903. Another sporting club was the *Clube Lusitano de Shanghai* founded in 1910, which was connected to relatives in Hong Kong's *Club Lusitano* founded in 1882. Like its counterpart, the Shanghai *Lusitano* club was considered a more exclusive "men's club" for Portuguese gentlemen who were denied membership to other European clubs. There were also benevolent organizations in Shanghai similar to Macau's *Santa Casa de Misericordia* (Holy House of Mercy) founded in 1569. These included the *Associacao Macaense de Socorro Mutuo de Shanghai* (1910), a women's auxiliary named the *Associação des Senhoras Portuguesas* (1920), and the *Portuguese Benevolent Association* (1945).

The premier organization was the Portuguese Volunteer Company, a militia of the Shanghai Volunteer Corps (SVC). The larger multi-national Volunteer Corps was made up of units totaling less than 2,500 members, drawing from the British, American, French, Italian, Spanish, Japanese, and Korean residents of Shanghai. The SVC was first organized in 1853 by British and American units in response to the "Small Swords Society's" uprising during the Taiping Rebellion, and fought its first battle in 1854 against Chinese Qing troops. The Shanghai Volunteers were then reorganized in 1861 until disbanded in 1942 by the invading Japanese army. [243] As part of the larger Corps, the Portuguese Company was slow to gain acceptance until early 1906. Once reliant on other militias for protection, the lack of an organized company remained an embarrassment for Portuguese businessmen until volunteers were formally recognized by the international municipal councils and trained by the British army.

The importance of the "Portuguese Volunteers", as they were called, to the larger Macanese community was significant for several reasons. The company was ostensibly created to protect the community from periodic riots and other actions threatening Shanghai's borders. Throughout the short history of the "Portuguese Volunteers", however, the presence of uniformed members at ritual gatherings, rather than infrequent calls to arms, became the principal rationale for the organization's existence. Composed primarily of prominent men who were long-time residents, the membership of the "Volunteers" was well established in government and business. Many members had parents and/or grandparents who migrated from Macau and Hong Kong in the 1840s and 50s. Those factors provided credibility and gravitas within a community where many Macanese settled with great frequency as the trade economy in China expanded or contracted. Some members of the volunteer militia were advocates of Portuguese nationalism, and had long term interests in maintaining positions in banks and trading companies, as well as the social standing of their families. Many families had lived in Shanghai for three or four generations by the dawn of the 20th century. Shanghai essentially provided them with an opportunity to climb the social ladder and maintain themselves unbounded by old world restrictions. Most had interests in securing a place in society that, in some instances, had been denied in Macau and Hong Kong.

Even as Shanghai grew into a busy port city and financial center for European trade, the growing demand for middle level workers necessary to keep international commerce moving made it clear that, at least for the Macanese in the late 19th century, the majority of the community remained in Hong Kong. As more archival material, documentation, and analysis have become available, the details of colonial conditions for second generation Macanese, those born in Hong Kong after settlement in 1842, can now be discussed in greater detail.

PART II

Macanese relations continued to evolve as the political and economic climate changed over the next century. By the late 1890s, evidence of discontent began to appear among the "second generation", the first Portuguese from Macau who were born in Hong Kong. In the following chapters, several case studies will be offered to illustrate how varying forms of dissatisfaction were manifested through an analysis of Macanese participation in several key events. These events included a public debate over worker rights in 1895; the participation of ethnic communities in an annual horse racing derby in 1918; the rise and fall of a Macanese printing house that hit its peak in the late 1920s; a sensational trial involving a mixed-race (Macanese and English) couple in 1931; the selective evacuation of British subjects as war with Japan approached in 1940; and the story of Macanese refugees and cultural renewal during World War II.

Throughout each chapter, the goal will be to analyze the changing conditions in which the Macanese community lived. Each case study also documents the efforts of Hong Kong born Macanese to resist intrusions on civil rights and demonstrate a reassertion of cultural identity that had been suppressed. Finally, the evolution of community attitudes and sentiments over time are offered to explain how the Macanese and their unique culture adapted to new, and at times unexpected, conditions as the 20th century progressed.

CHAPTER 7
J.P. Braga and "Alien" Workers in Hong Kong

Among the Macanese, it was clear that the system of working within colonial institutions and businesses in Hong Kong involved more than performing the duties of clerks, linguists, bookkeepers, and merchant assistants. There was also evidence of disenchantment among the first generation, including Leonardo d'Almada, Januario Carvalho, Alexandre Grand Pre', and Joao Jose Hyndman, who each rose from the lower ranks, only to be denied positions of authority due to race or national origin. In fact, beginning in the 1890s there seems to have been a steady erosion of confidence in the willingness of Hong Kong's colonial administration to treat the Macanese as true British subjects, which was suspected among the first generation and fully realized by the second generation.

As we begin to explore the histories of workers and their families from approximately 1895 up to the end of 1941, there are indications of mounting pressures on groups and individuals that not only redefined their work roles, relationships, and psychological attitudes, but also perceptions on their future in Hong Kong.

In a previous chapter, we saw that Hong Kong's division of labor depended on many first generation workers carrying out tasks under the direction of English department heads and executives, and at times in supervisory positions over Chinese compradors, shroffs, and laborers. As a result, the Macanese traditionally functioned as a buffer between the two communities, providing an extra level of "distance" to British elites from the lower levels of colonial society. While these conditions were tolerated and accepted by the majority of workers, English-born employees often feared being displaced by

Macanese who rose to high positions of authority. As we saw in the cases of Macanese moving into positions as Chief Clerks and other supervisors, English subjects began pressuring colonial administrators to intervene. In most cases, critics not only questioned Macanese abilities and loyalties, but their right to work in government, and by implication, their rights as British subjects.

These attitudes were reinforced by segregated policies protecting British residential areas, clubs, churches, and recreational facilities that excluded other groups. Clearly, not all English-born residents condoned policies of exclusivity, nor harbored discriminatory attitudes. The prevailing ideology of maintaining social distance from other groups, however, effectively created an environment for racial intolerance that remained part of colonial society throughout much of the 20th century. While it is difficult to pinpoint when the ideology of British superiority was first questioned, a documented response from the Macanese community first appeared in 1895 with the advocacy of "alien rights" by Jose' Pedro Braga, a young journalist who led public debates both inside and outside Hong Kong.

J.P. Braga, as he was known professionally, was a community advocate and writer who later became a prominent businessman and historian among the second generation of Macanese. Born in 1871 in central Hong Kong into a family of early settlers, Braga rose to become the managing editor of the Hongkong Daily Telegraph from 1902 to 1909, often as a critic of government policies, and served as a correspondent for both the Associated Press and Reuter's news service from 1906 to 1939. In 1910, following the example of his grandfather, Delfino Noronha, managed his own printing business, JP Braga & Co. In politics, due in large part to his advocacy, Braga was appointed to a number of positions, including as a Justice of the Peace in 1919, a member of the Sanitary Board in 1927, and in 1929 as the first Portuguese non-voting member of the Legislative Council, Hong Kong's ruling body. His public life culminated in awards from both the Portuguese (1929) and British (1935) governments.[244]

Braga's personal life had an important bearing on his career. He was the estranged son of Vicente Emilio Braga, who was an unsuccessful real estate investor and the owner of a failed soda water company. [245] Following those ventures, the elder Braga found work as a clerk at the British Oriental Bank in the accounting department. In 1867 he moved to the newly created Hong Kong Royal Mint under the direction of Thomas William Kinder. After the mint went bankrupt in 1870, Kinder was hired away by the Japanese government to establish a new mint in Osaka. Upon Kinder's recommendation, Braga was recruited as the mint's chief accountant in 1871. He later served in the Ministry of Finance as head instructor of bookkeeping in Japan's Mejii government. Through the 1880s, Vicente Braga helped train a generation of Japanese bookkeepers, and is credited with instituting western accounting practices that allowed Meiji era businesses to compete in the new global marketplace.

In order to accept the position in Japan, however, Vicente left his wife and seven children a few days after his youngest son Jose was born, to live alone in Osaka. There is no record of him ever returning to Hong Kong. Braga retired to Shanghai in 1897 to live with his oldest daughter and her family, and died there in 1911. [246] His acceptance of the new position, after much debate and turmoil, understandably created a rift in his close knit family. Braga was married to the eldest daughter of Delfino Noronha, the prominent printer and philanthropist, and had been living in his household for several years. In his father's absence, Jose' Braga and his siblings was raised by Noronha and his wife, who cut off all ties to their son-in-law Vicente.

The tensions created by Vicente Braga's absence marked the beginning of Noronha's early influence on his grandson Jose. Following his son-in-law's departure, Delfino Noronha was said to consider all the Braga children like his own and prevented Vicente from contacting the family. Stuart Braga writes that Delfino Noronha's influence was so great that both Noronha and his wife were godparents as well as grandparents, providing each of the eight siblings (one had died before their father's departure) with the middle name "de Noronha", and describes the family group as "a patriarchate as much as a household." [247]

Young Jose' was apparently one of Delfino Noronha's favorites, and was encouraged to excel at his studies under French Lasallian Brothers at St. Joseph's College in Hong Kong. He was later sent by the family to Calcutta to train as a barrister, eventually winning an award at Albert Memorial College in 1889. A smallpox epidemic in Hong Kong that year, however, took three of his brothers, resulting in his mother's pleas to return home to work in Delfino Noronha's business.

As Jose's earliest mentor and grandfather, Delfino Noronha, was very much a self-made man. Arriving in Hong Kong in 1844, he founded a printing company at the age of twenty. By 1859 Noronha was producing the Hong Kong Government Gazette, the official record of the administration's affairs, and was soon the largest employer of Portuguese in the colony. His belief in Hong Kong's success was such that in 1883 he petitioned for British citizenship and was one of the first Macanese to be granted the privilege. Noronha's influence over his grandson also was shared by a circle of like-minded elders, which included Leonardo d'Almada e Castro, Chief Clerk of the Colonial Superintendent of Trade, and Januario de Carvalho, the Chief Cashier of the Colonial Treasurer and Jose's uncle. Together, they guided Jose' Pedro Braga's intellectual growth and social outlook.

Among Braga's earliest projects was the publication of a pamphlet, "The Rights of Aliens in Hongkong", which addressed racially charged criticism against Macanese government workers in the English press, as it highlighted the contributions of all non-British workers to the economic and political life of the colony. The positive reaction from local and international readers was probably a surprise to the twenty-four year old Braga. The many themes touched upon, however, especially an acceptance of subordinate but autonomous status, and a clear pronouncement of cultural identity, each bore indications of Noronha's influence. A closer examination of Braga's early work will illustrate some of the conditions facing the Macanese community at the time and a model that Braga proposed to address them.

First Steps on the World Stage

In the fall of 1895, the "China Mail", Hong Kong's largest daily, published the Postmaster General's annual report, which noted that a Portuguese postal clerk had been dismissed for stealing 50 registered letters, many containing currency and script. [248] The incident had been preceded by thefts a few months earlier involving two other Portuguese clerks in the same office, who were convicted of their crimes. In the latest case, the Postmaster announced that no prosecution was conducted because the clerk's father had paid restitution. Ten days later a controversy grew over the right of all Portuguese to work in government, with several accusations against the community printed in local dailies. Over the next nine days a debate quickly evolved into questioning the rights of all "Non-British" workers in Hong Kong. It was later revealed that there were only five Portuguese workers among the forty employees at the Post Office on staff during the incident.

In response, Jose' Braga, then working in his grandfather's printing business, published a lengthy essay questioning the criticisms. [249] The essay was written in collaboration with five newspapers: three English language papers: the Hongkong Telegraph, China Mail, the Daily Press, and two Portuguese language dailies in Macau: O Extremo Oriente and Echo Macaense. Through the support of the Telegraph's editor, Chesney Duncan, who was somewhat sympathetic to the criticism, Braga was able to print and publish the 125 page supplement for distribution to about 5,000 English speakers in Hong Kong. [250] The wide circulation among the colony's most influential dailies, in two languages, suggests the importance each placed on the issue of "British only" employment in government, and the larger issue of racial discrimination in the colony.

Braga began the essay by conceding that the daily press was an invaluable record of social issues in Hong Kong, but argued that minority opinions could easily be lost, particularly on questions of class and racial prejudice, unless an even handed discussion could be aired in public. His reliance on a "free press", even within a colonial setting, was the principal reason he chose a newspaper supplement to address the issue. To those who might object to his arguments, Braga wrote that the question of whether the children of non-British parents have a right to work in government, or anywhere else in the colony, contradicted long held English principles of "fair dealing and fair play". This alone, he argued, should have exposed the controversy as "offensive", and as an "unwarrantable intrusion" on human rights. While Braga was not advocating the substitution of Portuguese workers for "true-born Britons", he asserted that when "reason is blinded by prejudice" it was his duty to come to the defense of alien workers, even when their position in society was weaker. Writing in language that blends Rousseau with a unique perspective on British rule, Braga boldly stated:

> *The good old days when might was right have happily passed away, never, it is to be hoped, to return, and justice is, especially throughout the length and breadth of the British Empire, dispensed with due regard to the common rights of all mankind, and with the important fact ever in view that 'the labourer is worthy of his hire' be he alien, native, or true-born Briton.* [251]

Beyond the moral argument, Braga also pointed out that the rights of children of foreign born subjects had been decided by the Secretary of State for the Colonies in 1862. Using language that suggests no reservations as to their status, Henry Pelham-Clinton, the 5th Duke of Newcastle, had written: "There is little doubt that the children of foreigners born in the British dominions are entitled to the character, rights, and privileges of British subjects," [252] Since then, all governors of Hong Kong had accepted the opinion.

Despite the long standing policy, both Braga's critics and supporters wrote anonymous letters to argue their positions, some suggesting that English-born workers should be hired first, while others questioned the loyalty of the Portuguese in times of crisis. Those seeking to deny Portuguese worker rights used such names as "Justitia", "Another Victim", and "Purge the Portuguese".[253] The fear of recrimination probably played a part in the attempts to hide their identities. The choice of names was probably not lost on Braga and his supporters. From our vantage point more than a century later, each provides clues to the tenor of the controversy.

A letter written by "Another Victim" questioned why "foreign" Portuguese clerks were hired to work in government or other positions of authority. These views seemed to represent working class Britons who came to Hong Kong seeking better paying employment within colonial institutions. A response by "Nepenthe" likely represented a Portuguese who argued that their sacrifices and contributions to Hong Kong's success gave them the right to equal treatment. The use of "Nepenthe", referring to a potion given to Helen to quell her sorrow over the death of Paris, may indicate a belief that tolerance of racial prejudice may have been the price for economic stability and good jobs. It also suggests that there were regrets associated with early Macanese settlement, when many families suffered from discrimination and unequal treatment. Ironically, it was an English correspondent for the Singapore Free Press who suggested the crux of the Macanese condition.

> *We (British) take advantage of their poverty, of their need of employment, of the limited area within which they can alone hope to obtain work. ... We pit them one against the other in the race for work, and we give a preference to him who asks least.* [254]

Braga acknowledged those sacrifices and systemic barriers, but also mentioned the advantages enjoyed by many coming to Hong Kong, "as well as the benefits derived by their employers ...". Braga then notes that most Britons came for economic reasons, the majority staying no longer than a few years seeking to make their fortunes. The Portuguese, by comparison, arrived at the request of the British government, who employed many in Macau from the 1820's. Braga argued that his generation, most of whom were born in Hong Kong, could claim a stronger tie to the colony. But tempering his remarks in recognition of a more powerful adversary, Braga, the shrewd colonial, adds:

> *Far be it from me to under-rate the importance of the higher stratum of our population. Its superior intellect, better culture and enormous influence wielded by virtue of exalted position and wealth, command, and must ever continue to retain, our profound respect and sincerest admiration.* [255]

Nevertheless, Brag concludes, justice and fair play should be conceded in the spirit of Hong Kong's "grand Free Trade policy", the same principles on which the British Empire and the Colonial Administration had been so successfully based.

Braga's visibility as a community leader was no doubt enhanced by his new celebrity on behalf of those who, up to then, had little voice in Hong Kong's affairs. Another supporter was Robert Ho Tung, a prominent Chinese businessman and leader of his community, who applauded Braga's stance. Ho Tung had raised concerns about curfew laws that applied only to the Chinese about the same time that the essay was published, leading to a life-long connection.[256] Braga's grasp of cultural history also suggested that the "Portuguese", whom he pointed identified as "Macaense" from Macau rather than Portugal, had a rich and important history that had not been acknowledged in Hong Kong society, or in some cases, by the Macanese themselves.

Braga's arguments raised another theme that would resonate in his later writings. He mentioned that many Macanese who were born in Hong Kong occupied a certain "place" and rank in relation to the British and the Chinese. In this regard, J.P. Braga can be seen as a man of his times. By emphasizing a common sentiment that the Macanese had always been supportive of, but remained subordinate to British rule, he represented a new generation that accepted their class position. The difference now was that his generation would be actively invested in Hong Kong's future as self-contained and increasingly motivated members of society as businessmen and property owners. This also may have been a result of their earlier isolation, either by imposed policy or by choice through the creation of Macanese associations. In Braga's view, the Macanese and all Hong Kong residents, regardless of origins, should have the same rights as all British subjects, and expect livable wages, equal opportunities, and other privileges because of their contributions to the colony's success.

In this light, how we might understand "The Rights of Aliens in Hong Kong" reveals the significance of J.P. Braga's efforts. Primarily, Braga's essay suggests that he was aware of walking a fine line between several competing themes in the debate and, in his case, an emerging point of view. These include addressing the extreme position of a "British only" workforce, which was unrealistic given the needs of Hong Kong's growing economy. Indeed, as the British editor of the Siam Free Press pointed out: "We need not dwell upon the fact that Hongkong owes much of its present wealth and prosperity to aliens. ... the question is, can Hongkong do without the aliens." [257]

There was another view that public criticism of government was viewed as a sign of disloyalty, or at the very least, ingratitude, both ideas shared by some British and first-generation Macanese. Many in the latter group also accepted without question that the "Portuguese", an identification they preferred, and the great majority of Chinese in Hong Kong should always occupy a subordinate position. Braga, on the other hand, was proposing an alternative view that calls his British critics to task based on the government's own well-publicized ideology: the principles of free enterprise, open trade, and unfettered competition, which the rhetoric of exclusion and racial discrimination seemed to contradict.

Braga thus seems to be writing as both a revisionist critic and a cultural Macanese that the logical extension to traditional British ideals, such as "justice and fair play", is equal treatment in the workplace, and by extension, throughout society. In doing so, Braga must acknowledge the conditions of his colonial surroundings, accepting the reality that the Portuguese, despite their contributions to Hong Kong, are regarded as second class citizens, a "middle class" between the British and the Chinese. But Braga considers himself a British citizen by birth, and expected to be treated as one, then pointed to the discrepancies in workers' rights and the racial attitudes of some British colonials to make his case. While Braga only briefly mentions his own ethnicity, he skillfully identifies colonial opposition to his community's right to work as blind "prejudice". In this assertion, his arguments suggest a new cultural identity, not of Macau or Portugal, but one that is unique to the next generation of Macanese in Hong Kong.[258]

And so, at the age of 24, Jose' Pedro Braga took his place in history. In writing the essay, Braga demonstrated that racial attitudes and prejudice could be questioned, and perhaps reconciled within the colonial context of Hong Kong, even while the fundamental right to work is asserted based on policies that had not been fully realized. Whether or not Braga's arguments would have any impact remained to be seen; he had no way of knowing how future generations would perceive his efforts. But by claiming rights as workers, even if they were the rights of "aliens", Braga spoke for a new generation Macanese and other ethnic workers who sought greater control over their own destinies. The underlying reality was that most English in Hong Kong held tightly on to the privileges they expected vis a vis the Chinese and other groups in the colony. Despite Braga's widely read opinions to the contrary, many simply presumed notions of "privilege" and "tradition" that seemed to justify their positions of authority. Given the importance placed on "free" and "open" economic activity by the British administration, however, other Macanese adjusted to these attitudes in unusual and telling ways.

Among the trappings of success enjoyed by Jose Braga and

other Macanese during this period was a middle-class lifestyle. Despite the acknowledged ideology of British "high culture", the segregation of organizations and facilities, and the general cloister of ethnic communities, Hong Kong still basked in the glow of a vibrant economy. This included, in some cases, the ability of some Macanese to participate almost as equals in social events. As we shall see, in the early years of the new century, there were a few occasions in colonial Hong Kong that allowed different ethnic groups to mix and class distinctions temporarily to blur. As Henry Lethbridge reminded us, one was the annual St. Andrew's Day Ball in late November. [259] Another was Derby Day in February at the Happy Valley Racecourse. This event and the tragic consequences in 1918 will be the subject of the next chapter.

CHAPTER 8
The Happy Valley Racecourse Fire of 1918

February 1918 in Hong Kong was unusually dry and heavy with anticipation. The Great War was in its final months, and the effect on trade in Asia, the control of which was now shifting to the Americans and Japanese, was a cause for concern. [260] The Japanese government, in particular, had been growing increasingly militant and self-assured, following victories over China in 1893 and Russia in 1905. Among superstitious Chinese and Europeans in Hong Kong, two small earthquakes on February 13 and 14, 1918, and an outbreak of spinal meningitis leading to 968 deaths, were ominous signs for the future. Just a few weeks earlier a storm had damaged the dock and beach area around North Point. Since then no rain was recorded on the island, and as a result the weather remained unseasonably warm. [261]

The dry weather, however, suggested to other residents the coming of spring, and with it the opening of the horse racing season at Happy Valley, an annual event in Hong Kong since the 1840s. Located on low-lying swamp land less than a mile south of Hong Kong Harbour, the racecourse sits in a valley ringed by tree-lined hills. One of the earliest impressions of the surroundings was recorded by the Marquis de Moges, a French adventurer and diplomat who stopped in Hong Kong in 1857. In a journal he wrote:

> ... we came down the hill, making a circuit to see the Happy Valley, where the English have staked off a drive and a race-course through a superb meadow. The turf is rolled down regularly, as in the English parks. The name Happy Valley, given to this place, comes from the cemeteries which surround it. [262]

Matsheds

The racing season was a much anticipated event in Hong Kong. To those involved in the colony's social life, the afternoon race on Derby Day at Happy Valley, in particular, was the equivalent of the Queen's Race at Britain's Royal Ascot. The derby also signaled the appearance of matsheds, multi-storied Chinese buildings made of bamboo and palm leaves that were built to accommodate the growing number of racing enthusiasts, particularly among the Macanese and Chinese who often brought their families to watch the spectacle. Due to the popularity of the viewing stands, the right to construct the temporary sheds was licensed through an annual auction to groups of businessmen and government employees of many nationalities, some who stood to make substantial profits from betting and refreshment sales carried on in each structure. [263]

The first sheds were erected in 1878 to accommodate the large crowds. Due to the growing demand, a government auction was initiated in 1891. Thereafter, applications increased to the extent that the government hired professional auctioneers and created a set of conditions to guide the process. In 1918 the rules included an auction conducted in English and Chinese, the assurance of a police presence, and a prohibition against gambling. [264] Adapting to local customs, the process of permitting and building the matsheds had become a time-honored tradition. Tenants paid about $700 Hong Kong dollars for each license and $180 to build an individual structure, together almost twice the average annual wage for government workers. [265] Most were two or three stories high, measuring about fifty feet tall, and were licensed to hold up to 300 people. The design was based on theatrical structures used in Chinese religious ceremonies. Many were erected by local contractors in less than three weeks. [266]

Most matsheds followed a simple design. On the middle floor, the main level of the structure, was built a large wooden counter for betting and a window facing the racecourse, with the only door at the back of the structure leading to the street and the tram stop. Below the main floor was a basement level accessible only by an inner ladder, where food counters serving tea cakes, pastries, and hot tea kept warm on charcoal braziers called 'chatties' provided by the vendor. The top floor of the structure, also accessible from the main level by ladder, was another popular location for bettors who wanted an expansive view through larger windows after wagering on each race. The entire edifice was supported by thick bamboo pilings, all resting on wooden planks laid below the shed and lashed to other matsheds that were built beside it. All were connected to the adjoining temporary structures, one to the other, with the first attached to an adjoining brick wall of the Hong Kong Jockey Club. Each ultimately depended on connections from the first matshed tied to the brick facade, the only permanent structure allowed to be built on the course. [267]

Due to the dry conditions in 1918, Public Works officials later stated that the ground had been too hard for supports to be driven into the turf, which was protected under an agreement with the Jockey Club. As a result, the main uprights were not inserted into the soil, instead resting only on the wooden planks under each structure. There also were no regulations concerning the length or thickness of the poles, the height of the sheds, or the lashings supporting the sheds, despite concerns expressed in previous years. [268]

In line with liberal attitudes toward regulation, government enforcement of the licensing conditions was traditionally light. Supervision of matshed construction fell to Hong Kong's Public Works Department, and ultimately to the inspector of the race course, identified in press accounts only as "Mr. M. Sara". Testifying during the inquest, Sara noted: "... matsheds as a rule received very little inspection... No tests of strength were made officially." Sara also stated that while he '... carefully inspected all the matsheds, and had never previously reported irregularities ...', all the structures rested on half-inch wooden boards to protect the race course's turf, none reaching the ground. [269]

Police and fire officials seemed to acknowledge that perfunctory inspections of each structure were made in anticipation of 10,000 spectators, including women and children, many of whom would occupy the sheds during the races. The process usually involved informal tours of the matsheds by young police cadets or Chinese watchmen a few days before the races began, and approval was apparently rarely denied. [270] The scant oversight was also reflected in the police presence. Records indicate that fifty (50) regular officers were assigned to the races that year, and eight reserve officers were positioned outside the racecourse, presumably for crowd control. [271] There is no record of police or fire personnel assigned to the matsheds during the races.

The prohibition against gambling was also apparently ignored. When asked if he was aware that the sheds had been used for gambling, the Superintendent of Police, a Mr. M. Messer, acknowledged: "I supposed that cash sweeps were held there." He then added: "We have never interfered with pari-mutuel (betting) and cash sweeps either in the grandstand or matsheds. The Governor did not instruct me ... to interfere... The same police orders were issued in previous years." [272] The benign attitude toward gambling by the authorities was probably influenced by several factors, including the traditional popularity of wagering among many groups in Hong Kong, government revenue from the auction, and the commissions earned by those who licensed the sheds. Government records indicate that the nineteen matsheds licensed in 1918 yielded over $13,400, the equivalent today of about $3.3 million US dollars.[273] Given that wages in Hong Kong for mid-level Macanese government workers were about $500 HKD annually, the figure is impressive, and much less than the profits from gambling. While no actual accounting from 1918 survives, net profits are estimated to be as high as double the licensing fees paid by each matshed tenant. [274]

The winning bidders of the auctions reflected old and new money interests, and ambitious newcomers. [275] Based on government rolls, the first three matsheds were licensed to the Hong Kong Jockey Club, representing the merchant and landed class of the colony, and attached to the club's brick facade. Sheds 4, 5, and 6 were two-story structures licensed and built by John Olson II, the son of a Swedish landowner and tavern manager, and two Englishmen, J.J. Blake and Charles Warren, the sons of prominent landowners and merchants. Numbers 7, 8, and 9 sheds, all rising to three stories, were licensed to three Portuguese families and their partners, the first owned by the family of Pedro Xavier, who owned the Hongkong Printing Press, and others who worked as clerks and bookkeepers at local banks and merchant houses. Matsheds 10 to 14 and 16 to 19, also three stories high, were rented by large groups of Chinese government employees, shroffs, tailors, cooks, and laborers, some selling as many as 88 shares. The last shed, No. 15, was two stories tall and licensed to the Japanese Benevolent Society. [276]

The licenses, the building of the matsheds, the wagering, and the perfunctory oversight, like the races themselves, were part of a long-held tradition. The rich purses at Happy Valley drew horse owners from all over Asia, including in previous years the governor of Hong Kong, Sir Henry May, who was an avid racing fan. Purses were paid for by a percentage of matshed rental fees and gaming revenue, both policies approved by the government.

Grouped Matsheds in 1918

Derby Day 1918

Late on the morning of Tuesday February 26th, Carlos d'Assumpcao took the Star Ferry from his home in Kowloon to meet his good friend Aureliano Jorge for lunch at Wiseman's restaurant in Central Hong Kong. Aureliano was a solicitor from Macau who was born into a prominent merchant family, and the father of fourteen children with another due in April. By some accounts, he was a man of wide interests and tastes, including land speculation, rare stamps, and Chinese porcelain. [277] His friend Carlos, a prominent Mandarin linguist, was a diplomat who previously served as the Portuguese Consul in Canton. Like Aureliano, Carlos headed a large family as the father of eleven children. [278]

Carlos d'Assumpcao *Aureliano Jorge*

Carlos and Aureliano shared a love of horse racing and gambling with many in the Macanese community. It was not unusual for entire families to attend the races together and place bets on their favorite thoroughbreds. The children, at least those who were too young to gamble, often mimicked their elders. Carlos' youngest son, Bernardino, who was twelve and attended the races that day, described later how he and his friends learned to act as "bookies", stating in an interview:

> *We would run around selling these 'tickets' to whoever wanted to place a small bet of ten or twenty cents each, depending on the importance of the races. Naturally, we always retained for ourselves a ten percent commission, earning one or two dollars in this way: which to us was a fortune then!* [279]

On this day, Carlos was struck by Aureliano's persistence about joining him for the Derby. But Carlos declined because of a previous engagement at the Club de Recreio later that afternoon. So he accompanied Aureliano as far as the tram stop, bade him good luck and took the ferry back to Kowloon. [280]

Another Macanese in attendance was Francisco de Paula Xavier, one of the owners of his family's shed at No. 7, and a compositor at the Hongkong Printing Press. After the morning races ended that Tuesday, he joined several relatives and friends for lunch. They included his stepbrothers Jose Maria Xavier and Ludovino 'Bino' Xavier, and nephews Paulo and Vasco Xavier, who were eighteen and twenty years old, and sixteen-year-old niece Daria. The younger relatives were the siblings of Pedro Xavier, the owner of the Press. They were joined by at least eighteen other members of the Macanese community from Hong Kong and Kowloon. [281]

Despite restrictions on the number of people allowed in the sheds, prior to the racing season Francisco Xavier claimed to have distributed about 500 tickets to English, Portuguese, and Chinese friends for Derby Day. [282] He planned to admit only those with tickets, offering food, alcohol, and betting, while deducting a 15% commission on the latter. He later claimed that some people were admitted without a ticket, and he did not know exactly how many people were in his shed during the afternoon race.

Francisco had instructed his contractor to build a three-story shed to accommodate the large group, with a basement floor used for food and drinks sold by Chinese vendors. He noted that the police did not object to having a refreshment room in the matshed, which used an oil lamp for light and a charcoal chatty for heating tea. The main floor was designated for pari-mutuel and cash sweeps betting. Francisco's brother, Ludovino Xavier, was in charge of managing the family's gambling operations and for securing its cash. The top floor, built to only half the size of the lower floor, was reserved for ladies in attendance. [283] Francisco built one entrance on the first floor, but none on the top or bottom floors, adding in later testimony that the doorway to the main floor was about six feet wide. [284]

Several other Macanese were involved in operating matsheds that day as well. A Mr. G. Remedios, a clerk in the Mercantile Bank, had been a partner in shed No.8 for fifteen years. He shared proceeds from the main floor betting with Jose Rosario. Another partner in No. 8 was A.G. Remedios, an assistant at the Hong Kong Electric Light Company, who also worked on the main floor. S.M. de Cruz, another clerk at a local bank, ran the betting in matshed No. 9. He was assisted by J.D. Barros, an interpreter at the American Consulate, and another of the partners, an Englishman named Mr. Richie. Another was Joseph Gonsalves, a clerk, who sold betting tickets in No. 9 that day. [285]

A Multi-Ethnic Experience

On the same morning, John Olson was at the race course to inspect sheds No. 4, 5, and 6, the matsheds he owned with his business partners, J.J. Blake and Charles Warren, who was also Olson's brother-in-law. Olson had hired the Chinese firm, Taz Hop, to construct the three structures in early February, but the crew of 70 workmen had only completed the work two days before the season opened. [286]

Four years earlier, Olson had complained in vain to the Clerk of the Course that the Xavier owned matshed No. 7, which stood three stories high, was too weak and had given way, compromising his own structures. [287] In 1918 Olson instructed his workers to build only two-story matsheds and to follow government instructions that the supporting struts were not to be driven into the ground. Instead the Taz Hop crew, as required by the auction rules, rested the support poles on wooden planks above ground and lashed Olson's shed to the adjoining matsheds that were being built at the same time.

Olson did, however, order his contractors to build 'double uprights', bamboo braces to reinforce the betting and refreshments counter on the bottom floor, expecting, as he stated later, 'more of a crush at the counter' that year. [288] In No. 6, Olson also allowed the use of charcoal 'chatties' for cooking by a Chinese vendor, M.Y. San, but instructed San to have three large barrels of water on the bottom floor, and eight full fire buckets on the upper floor. [289] Olson and Blake stated later that they had a verbal agreement with members of the Hong Kong Jockey Club, owners of the race course, to allow Chinese ladies and their 'amahs' to purchase cash sweeps and pari-mutuel tickets in their matsheds for the races that year. This had been the practice since the Jockey Club erected its own matshed in the 1890s. Blake stated that he thought that gambling was permitted in his stand since it was allowed for many years in Happy Valley's Grand Stand, where only members of the Jockey Club and other colonial dignitaries were allowed to wager. [290]

Many Chinese residents of Hong Kong also had shares in the matsheds, some apparently seeking to benefit from their employment with the same government agencies responsible for oversight. Chan Siu Tong, a clerk in the Public Works Department and a sergeant in the police reserves, and Fong Cheun, another Public Works clerk, each paid HK$10 for their shares, among the 25 shares for matshed No. 10. Another employee and partner, who was not identified in the press, stated that ten of the partners worked in Public Works, and he sub-let the betting floor to four others who also worked in the department. [291]

So Chee, another Public Works employee, was a partner in No. 10 who supervised cooking in the shed. He later testified that there were two charcoal chatties for tea and others for the two cooks who were employed to prepare food. Other workers were also involved. Lo Cheuk San, a shroff in the Hongkong and Shanghai Banking Corporation, claimed that there were 88 shares in matshed No. 11. Lo Hok Chan, another shroff in the mercantile group Bradley & Co. Ltd., stated he had owned a share in shed No. 13 for five years with 34 others. Others like Chan Kwai Yu, a compradore at J.D. Hutchinson & Co., was a partner in No. 14 with seven others. Lo Yuk Nam, a restaurant accountant, was a partner in No. 16 with five others. [292]

Thus, the expectation of a large payout on Derby Day seemed to be shared by many. Middle and working class men from different ethnic communities, some who pooled their funds to pay for licensing and construction, stood to make substantial profits from gambling and food concessions. [293]

The Matsheds Collapse

As the betting period ended after lunch, the horses approached the line for the premier race of the afternoon amid the excitement of the crowd gathered in the stands. The last thing anyone expected was the chaos and terror that was about to unfold. A reporter for the Hong Kong Daily Press gave this eyewitness account:

> *At a few minutes to three o'clock, just after the third bell had rung for the first race ... , the whole row of Chinese booth(s) and matsheds ... collapsed, and awful confusion ensued.... The stands fell gradually ... falling ... outwards ... and made the sound like a rasping of a saw. It looked as if the tops of all the stands had been connected by a wire ... and that ... had been pulled over gradually. The stands and booths took about 10 seconds to collapse.* [294]

Young Bernardino d'Assumpcao described the stands falling one by one in a row toward the racetrack like 'long grass being blown down by a strong gust of wind.' In that moment, he and his friends realized the danger, and quickly climbed down one of the stands and raced across the track to safety. [295]

His father's friend, Aureliano Jorge, probably arrived just as the afternoon race was about to begin. Bernardino estimated that he disembarked at the Happy Valley tram stop with the rest of the crowd and rushed to meet a group of friends to make his only bets that day. There is speculation from other relatives that Aureliano may have been among those who rushed to the front of a matshed when the race began and may have been caught in the crush of humanity. [296]

Francisco Xavier was on the first floor of matshed No. 7 when he heard what sounded like running and shouting, and thought it was strange to hear such a commotion before the start of a race. Then the shed began to push forward. He fell on top of his two sisters as the crowd from the top floor of the shed poured in. There were shouts for help as he frantically looked for his wife and children who were also present. Once the family members were located, some punched holes through the matting with their hands and feet to help the children out. Xavier counted eighteen members of his family who escaped from the fallen structure. [297]

A newspaper account reported that Mr. G. Remedios also heard people running when shed No. 8 began to fall. He shouted at them to stay calm, but suddenly felt himself going down with the rest of the shed and was pinned under the debris. He remembered hearing cries for help and people jumping over him in an attempt to escape. Reaching into his pocket, Remedios found his small knife and was able to cut a hole in the matting to free his head. Forcing the hole bigger, he freed himself and dragged his wife through the same opening. [298]

At approximately the same moment, John Olson and J.J. Blake were standing near the refreshment counter in matshed No. 6 about to ring a bell signaling the end to betting. News accounts state that Olson and Blake heard a cracking sound in the direction of No. 7 and saw a portion of the wall fall into their stand as women and children burst through it. Olson was momentarily stunned by the collapsing wall and the crush of people. But he was able to free himself by pushing through the debris, as he directed others to safety. [299]

Blake ducked under his own reinforced counter just as the walls of the matshed fell around him, saving himself from being crushed. As he was exiting the front of the stand, he heard the cry of a small Portuguese boy and pulled him out from under the matting but was injured by a bamboo piling and had to be rescued by a policeman. [300] Police constable J. Deskin, who also was in Olson's stand 'assisting in the pari-mutuel', testified later that the partition between Olson's No. 6 and Xavier's No. 7 stands swayed back and forth just as the panic started. Then Deskin witnessed a stampede of people going for the exit as the collapse was occurring. The constable was thrown forward in the crush, but was able to escape before the fire began. [301]

As the Matsheds begin to fall, people take notice.

The Matsheds begin to burn and quickly collapse from the weight of too many spectators.

The Fire

The delay between the collapse and the fire was noted by a Hong Kong Daily Press reporter. He wrote that it looked as if those who had fallen from the stands would be safe, since some were breaking holes in the matshed roofs to escape. But suddenly white smoke and flames appeared on the side of the stands and began to spread. He wrote:

> *The flames were seen to rise from one of the sheds, and they quickly spread to the whole ... While the flames were raging, the wind refreshed, and the heat became terrific. ... There was a terrible crush, everyone struggled to save himself. ... The outbreak caused a terrible panic ... and hundreds were thrown to the ground who would have otherwise have had no difficulty ... escaping ... . Once (the flames spread) it was a case ... finished. The clouds of smoke ... must have suffocated many. ... Children were swept hither ... , and I fear that several of them must have*

been trampled to death ... [302]

Lieutenant Colonel John Ward of the Hong Kong Metropolitan Police gave this account:

Within 20 seconds of the collapse (I) saw smoke issuing from the wreckage ... about half way down the rear of the collapsed roof between sheds No. 8 and 9. At first it appeared as if it came from burning oil, then a bright red flame shot out through the roof. The smoke was very dense and black and gave the impression of being connected to burning grease or oil. ... It took 23 minutes before the whole of the matsheds were involved in flames ... There was a light breeze blowing from south-east to north-west ... The fire burnt itself out in about 45 minutes. [303]

Other witnesses reported that Daria Xavier was sitting with family members in stand No. 7. [304] The young girl had been at one of the tables on the lower floor, perhaps taking refreshment and reading the results of other races on a large blackboard. Then the matshed tumbled. A few seconds later the chatties ignited and quickly engulfed the structure. During the commotion, people panicked and ran to the only door up to the main floor. Daria was apparently trapped under a bamboo table. [305] Daria's older brother Paulo and others tried to free her, but Paulo was badly burned on his arms in the attempt. Years later, Paulo related how Daria told him it was no use and to flee for his life. Paulo stayed until the last possible moment, suffering burns on his arms until a police sergeant pulled him to safety. [306] A young police cadet, identified only as 'L.L. Lopes', is credited with the rescue of other members of the Xavier family trapped in the shed. [307]

Once Bernardino d'Assumpcao and his young friends were out of danger, he noticed smoke rising from the collapsed stands, followed immediately by fires from every side. In less than a minute he stated, 'thousands' who had been trapped under fallen bamboo and palm leaves had no time to escape. Years later, the memories were still fresh in his mind. He wrote that those who had escaped to the infield were ...

> ...stunned by the awesome sight ... : a very, very huge fire and smoke rising up to more than two hundred ... feet, accompanied by ... loud screams from everywhere. Young as we were then it was most certainly a sight and experience ... none of us could ever forget![308]

He added that the screams of the victims were accompanied by muffled 'popping' sounds, like the dull explosion of fire crackers under sand. One of the older men explained to the boys that it was the sound of skulls bursting under the intense heat.

Ludovino Xavier was said to have been visiting friends in No. 9 and escaped the fire by fleeing to the safety of the infield. But he apparently realized that he left the family's cash box behind in No 7. [309] Rushing back into the flames, Ludovino was caught in the confusion and joined many others who perished. He was later found under piles of debris with about 200 other victims.

The fate of Aureliano Jorge suggests a more generous ending. There is speculation that he placed bets with friends in matshed No. 7, then went to the top floor to observe the next race. Press reports noted that the initial collapse came after people rushed to the front of the sheds when the horses approached the line, then feeling the sway of the structures, overreacted and rushed back toward the shed's only exit door. [310] Like others, Aureliano was able to escape from the top floor of the shed. But according to witnesses, he returned to the burning structure to assist one of his group, a Japanese businessman who was trapped under the debris. Despite several attempts by his friends, Aureliano and his companion were felled by a burning piling as they struggled to escape. [311] After the fire, Carlos d'Assumpcao was able to identify Aureliano's remains only because a prized gold watch was found underneath him. [312]

Hong Kong Officials assess the damage and loss of life

The Aftermath

An inquiry by the Hong Kong government officially listed the dead at 670, including many Chinese women and children who watched the race from the sheds. Several remains were never identified and left uncounted, with hundreds more injured. The exact number of fatalities and their ethnicity have never been fully tallied. [313] Based on records provided by other sources, there were at least seventeen Macanese killed in the fire and several more were probably injured.[314]

A few weeks later the Macanese community met at the Club Lusitano in Hong Kong to express sympathy for the families and relatives of the victims. Many conveyed their thanks with tokens of sympathy from military, government, and religious leaders. These included an offer of free board and tuition to the sons of Ludovino Xavier at the Seminary of Macao. [315] Requiem masses were conducted for Macanese victims in Hong Kong, Macau, and other Chinese cities. A correspondent at the ceremony in Canton wrote that almost every member of the Portuguese community attended, adding:

> ... the service was more than a conventional expression of sympathy. It was indeed an outward manifestation of genuine sorrow, not only for the relatives and friends ... but also for the hundreds of human beings who have been victims of an appalling catastrophe. [316]

Testimony at a Coroner's inquiry dragged on for weeks. The causes of the tragedy were recounted in numerous press accounts. Metropolitan Policeman John Ward, who had worked as a London building inspector specializing in building collapses, expressed this opinion:

> *Part of the problem was the number of people admitted to the stands ...many more than would have been permitted had current regulations been followed. There was also an absence of cross-bracing in the front and rear of the sheds, which was a major cause for the collapse because there was no resistance to the sheds falling forward.* [317]

Ward noted that since there were 300 bodies alone found in matsheds No. 8 and 9, most had probably fallen down the staircase connecting the floors or within the staircase itself. Ward and others also pointed to the inadequate water pressure available at the race course, which did not allow the fire department to extinguish the fire quickly.

Assistant Superintendent of Police T.H. King, who had previously served as Deputy Superintendent of the Fire Brigade, recalled that in 1914 he visited Happy Valley to test the water system. He found that the water pressure was down 40% from what was needed to put out a fire in the stands. King wrote to the Director of Public Works informing him of the results of the test and recommending at least 100 lbs. of pressure. The director responded that 60 lbs. was normal for that facility, and in any case could not be increased due to the size of the water main. As a result, no other precautions were taken. [318]

Professor Middleton Smith, of the Engineering Department at Hong Kong University, suggested that dry weather conditions before and during the races may have caused the bamboo in the sheds to shrink and crack. Prolonged exposure in contractors' yards for several months before the racing season began may have also weakened the building material. Smith recommended close inspection of the sheds before the races, and that none should have been built over two stories. [319]

Hong Kong Coroner J.R. Wood, frustrated by many weeks of testimony, and perhaps feeling pressure from the press, finally stated that he was unable to assign blame.[320] Wood added, however, that there was no doubt that the evidence showed the matsheds were used as 'common gaming houses' at the race course, contrary to current gaming ordinances and the rules of the auction. He also stated that even though the government auctioneer read out the conditions against gambling in Chinese and English, the prohibition was never intended to be enforced. [321] Summing up, Wood concluded that: '... this calamity ... could most probably have been prevented by the exercise of foresight ... expected before the event ...' [322]

This led Governor Sir Francis Henry May, who was a regular at Happy Valley, to take official responsibility for the fire. [323] Calling it 'a most regrettable affair', May admitted that more precautions should have been taken. He concluded: 'I blame myself as regards the non-provision of fire precautions, because I was head of the Police here for nine years and I never anticipated a fire in these matsheds.' [324] Then, to his credit, the Governor permanently banned matsheds from the racecourse, stating: 'There will never be any more matsheds there (at Happy Valley.) I think I may state that.' [325] The construction of permanent grandstands was begun soon after.

Meanwhile, many victims of the Happy Valley fire remained unidentified. A reporter described the following scene:

> *The charred remains of the victims were laid out in rows in a matshed enclosure on the scene of the disaster, and relatives and friends of the missing ones were admitted to see whether by a shred of clothing, an article of jewelry, or a shoe ... identification could be arrived at. ... Very few bodies ... were recognizable. Many people came to identify the dead. Police were assigned to keep the crowds in order until late into the night. Detachments of military forces were stationed at intervals to keep order ... Police Reserves and other units were assisting in the*

work. [326]

The memories of that day have long faded, together with a monument erected in 1922 behind the old racecourse. [327] Today racing continues at Happy Valley, where the excitement of Derby Day attracts thousands each year. But with the passage of time, perhaps the ghosts of the tragedy, representing the many ethnic groups that were present in 1918, may now rest knowing that their story has finally been told.

An assessment of the Happy Valley incident also reveals an underlying current, suggesting an important moment of reckoning among the Macanese in Hong Kong. While rising only to the level of an "omen", a harbinger of things to come, the fire's aftermath led to a series of events between the world wars that signaled an inexorable decline in confidence among the Macanese, the English underclass, and the Chinese majority in the willingness of the Hong Kong government to protect their interests. The lack of oversight and laissez faire attitudes toward ethnic minorities, in particular, could now be linked to the contradictions that Jose Braga identified earlier in the government's promotion of "fair dealing and fair play". That rhetoric could no longer be reconciled with reality after decades of discriminatory practices and social neglect that ultimately led to the deaths of hundreds of women and children in 1918. As we shall see in the following chapters, relations among lower ranked groups to colonial society in the inter-war years touched on economic, social, political issues.

CHAPTER 9
Macanese Printing: The Hongkong Printing Press

A few decades before the Happy Valley fire, a different Macanese response to the ideology of English privilege in Hong Kong had begun to emerge. While less overt than J.P. Braga's challenges to work relations at the turn of century, a limited form of autonomy developed through the founding of new businesses among the Macanese to take advantage of the colony's open economic policies, almost as a test to British commerce. The change took several decades to take hold. In 1861, as mentioned earlier, a local directory listed just thirteen businesses owned by Macanese. [328] By the turn of the 20th century, Macanese businesses included several printing companies and international trading firms.[329] This entrepreneurial approach contradicted the stereotype held by some English residents that most Portuguese were content to remain as underlings. During Braga's debate, one editorial suggested that the best way to benefit from "fair play" and free trade was to go into "handicrafts" and other forms of business. [330] A common argument was that launching a successful firm might demonstrate that the Hong Kong model could work for anyone who worked hard enough within the system.

J.P. Braga contended in 1895 that early arrivals from Macau had little choice than to find work in government as low paid clerks and bookkeepers. He also pointed out that with more education, the development of local associations, and an increase in the number of businesses, more Portuguese could become successful. [331]

Braga's family was a prime example. His grandfather, Delfino Noronha, was the largest printer in Southeast Asia.

Several of the printing businesses owned by Noronha's protégés had grown and prospered since 1849, outnumbering any other ethnic group, despite the small number of Macanese in Hong Kong. Several set up firms in Canton, Shanghai, and other "Treaty Ports", expanding their products well beyond printing government notices. Whether the growth in Macanese businesses actually "proved" anything was another matter. To understand how a typical business developed, let us consider a case study of one Noronha protégé and his family who attempted to move the printing industry in new directions.

Information and Commerce in the Treaty Ports

In the decades leading to and following the Opium Wars, merchants, colonial departments, and missionaries relied heavily on information contained in printed reports and government notices distributed through several "Treaty Ports" conceded by China. As print scholar Hoi To Wong writes: "Access to knowledge about China was essential to create an information network for merchants and missionaries..." [332] The emergence of printing was important to the growth of these networks. Through the creation of pamphlets, books, newspapers, and weekly periodicals, printing was the means by which information and knowledge could be distributed to international sites by clipper and steam ships. The Pearl River Delta became the nexus of the first network, beginning with the arrival of the British East India Company's press in Canton in 1812 and a second press at St. Joseph's College Seminary in Macau in 1825. This critical juncture, it could be argued, was the next step in what Geoffrey Gunn refers to as "The Eurasian Exchange" in ideas, languages, and philosophies that transformed Europe and Asia from the 16th through the 18th centuries, leading to cultural "crossovers" that ultimately produced Macanese printing shops across Southeast Asia.[333]

By the middle of the 19th century, high concentrations of Macanese printers could be found in Shanghai, Canton, Hong

Kong, and other ports along the southern coast of China. Many partnered with British and American publishers, who out-sourced their printing and composition. In the 1860s, the growth of commerce in Hong Kong and Shanghai became the main stimulus for large numbers of Macanese to be trained in lithography. Through the end of the 19th century, Macanese printers like Delfino Noronha in Hong Kong and A.H. de Carvalho in Shanghai led the industry, taking over businesses started by Britons and other Europeans, and inspiring a boom in journalism, business news, and pamphleteering.

As businesses became more competitive, companies and their affiliated outposts in other ports relied on information that enabled the acquisition of raw materials, reported the availability of manpower, estimated costs, and offered different methods of distribution. Information and knowledge soon became critical resources in their own right by offering insights on supplies, competition, and market demand that could determine expansion, and often, the success or failure of new ventures. Further developments related to journalism, the publication of books and popular novels, rudimentary data collection, advertising, product packaging, postage stamps, and banking services, many created by Macanese entrepreneurs who used printing as a basis, contributed to a system of communications and product development.

The variety of goods passing through the treaty ports reflected these changes. In the decades following 1840, traditional goods like spices, tea, silk, opium, and porcelain were gradually supplemented by cotton, textiles, metals, machinery, sea products, dry foods, oils, vegetables, medicinal products, stone, and fuel. Virtually all information related to these products published in newspapers, government notices, and advertising, as well product labels, lottery tickets, and bank currencies were set to type by former residents of Macau. Economists Wolfgang Keller, Ben Li, and Carol Shiue estimated that between 1868 and 1947 commercial activity in China grew rapidly at 6.4% per year.[334] Hong Kong, the center of Britain's holdings in East Asia and the headquarters of many presses, accounted for one quarter of all China's imports and exports.

The Entrepreneur

Like many of Delfino Noronha's apprentices, Lisbello de Jesus Xavier was born in Macau in 1862 in the parish of Sao Lourenco near the Lilau district, where Portuguese immigrants first settled in the late 16th century. Church records indicate that this branch of the Xavier family had lived in Macau since about 1780, while family lore suggests their forbearers likely migrated from Goa.[335] Due to the insularity of the Macanese community, later members of the family married other Luso-Asians, whose families migrated from India in the same period, further deepening cultural ties.

Lisbello Xavier was educated at the St. Joseph's College, founded in 1784 close to his home parish in Macau. During a period of declining opportunities, the curriculum of the school involved training in languages and the mechanical arts, which included lithographic printing. Learning this skill was possible after the school acquired a press from the "Gazeta de Macau", a government newspaper which ceased publishing in 1825. According to recent scholarship, both Lisbello Xavier and Delfino Noronha were probably trained on the College's press, and apprenticed as print compositors with firms in Macau, albeit several years apart. [336] By the time Xavier arrived in Hong Kong in 1880, Noronha & Co. was already established as one of the most successful printers in the colony.

Family chronicles note that Lisbello Xavier worked as a compositor for Delfino Noronha from 1880 through 1888. In 1888, informed that his protégé wanted to open his own press,

Noronha subcontracted Xavier and his new venture, "The Hongkong Printing Press", to publish government notices and the Hong Kong Government Gazette on its own. To finance the operation, Lisbello sold a prized clarinet to purchase his first linotype machine. The clarinet was eventually bought back by the family in 1919.

Lisbello Xavier incorporated his company on June 1, 1888. Because of the intense labor involved and the high cost of printing, usually only government printers like Noronha could afford to operate. Xavier was fortunate to take over printing of the colony's notices just when business activity in Hong Kong was growing. Like Noronha before him, the Hongkong press's high profile became the basis of the company's expansion. Besides government printing, the new company produced tourist guides for other port cities where immigrant Macanese settled, including Canton, Shanghai, and Macau. The additional revenue from sixteen (16) editions of the guides beginning in 1893, and expansion into the new field of product labeling, allowed the company to flourish. To keep up with the demand, the business moved in 1905 to a new factory site at No. 3 Wydham Street in central Hong Kong.

The success of the press and Lisbello Xavier's rise in social status was confirmed by an invitation to join the Club Lusitano in 1903, which emulated "British only" associations, where social and business relations among Macanese were often forged.[337] Three years later, Lisbello provided funding and was elected the first president of the Club de Recreio in Kowloon. Recreio's purpose was to encourage informal gatherings through athletic competition, and by building cricket and soccer fields for Macanese who moved to the region after the English annexation of Kowloon in 1860. The club was a timely addition for the families of bank clerks and merchant assistants seeking a haven away from the crowded, and often unwelcoming, environment of central Hong Kong. Other Macanese investors had already made the transition, including Delfino Noronha, who owned a large farm on the Kowloon peninsula.

Lisbello Xavier spent the next decade expanding the business, while buying property in the New Territories north of Kowloon, bringing his sons and other relatives into the firm. Unconfirmed reports suggest his death in May 1909 may have been the result of an altercation outside his business. [338] At his passing, Lisbello's eldest son, Pedro d'Alcantara Xavier, became the company's next president just six months before his twenty-third birthday.

A New Generation Emerges

Pedro D'Alcântara Xavier

In the year that followed, after settling his father's estate and the affairs of the firm, Pedro Xavier began devising a strategy that would lead in a new direction. The most significant change involved replacing the old method of lithographic production with "offset printing", a new technology introduced in 1901 that allowed color reproductions and security measures to be incorporated into the process. [339] This strategy led to several new product lines, which included illustrated newspapers, magazines, brochures, stationery, and books, as well as labels for numerous consumer goods moving through Hong Kong and other "Treaty Ports".

Another lucrative source of revenue was the printing of currency notes issued by local banks. In the absence of a central banking system, and a dearth of efficient financial institutions after the fall of the Qing Dynasty, many Chinese banks from 1900 through 1940 guaranteed transactions by issuing their own script and currencies backed by silver or gold bullion. Debin Ma describes the practice in those years:

The greatest transformation in China's monetary and financial system occurred with respect to paper money and banking de-

> posits, ... The growth of paper money occurred in the so-called era of "free banking" where private foreign and Chinese banks, as well as Chinese governmental or provincial banks, freely issued bank notes circulating as media of exchange. [340]

Another economist estimated that the share of bank notes and deposits in the total money supply increased from just over a third in 1910 to over two thirds by 1926, with a corresponding decline in the share of silver and copper coins. Throughout the period up to the beginning of the second world war, current notes were supplanting hard specie as accepted forms of payment. [341]

In isolation, the change in production methods offers few clues to the significance of Pedro Xavier's activities as a second generation printer and a social actor in early 20th century Hong Kong. To explore these roles in more detail, we will focus on Xavier's leadership in business and his involvement in local affairs as his firm grew. Each activity provides a different perspective from which to observe him navigate the rough environment of early Hong Kong and the continued development of the Macanese community during those years.

A Short Introduction

As the eldest of Lisbello de Jesus Xavier's eleven children, Pedro was born in Hong Kong on October 19, 1886, a few years after his father began working in Delfino Norohna's printing company. Pedro was educated with other Portuguese students at St. Joseph's College in central Hong Kong by French Lasallian priests (also known as the "Christian Brothers"), the same order that taught his father in Macau. It was likely that Pedro took both primary and secondary courses at St. Joseph's, since the latter were not offered separately until it's successor, La Salle College, was founded in 1917. By then Kowloon had grown to become home to many Macanese families, including the Xavier residence on Barrow Terrace (now Grandville Road).

At age sixteen, Pedro left St. Joseph's to work as a bookkeeper for a German merchant, Carlowitz & Co. [342] In June 1904 through April 1906 Pedro worked for his father's printing business, then joined the Kowloon-Canton Railway Co. as an assistant bookkeeper and was quickly promoted to "Head Correspondence Clerk". For unknown reasons, Pedro returned to the Press for good in September 1906, working as a compositor until his father's death less than three years later. While remaining in the printing business after his father's death, Pedro Xavier's revised strategy took advantage of Asia's economic boom by serving China's "free banking" sector. But like all Macanese, he also was drawn to developments in Macau.

New Connections in the Treaty Ports

Despite Macau's perceived "inferiority", and acknowledging its cultural embrace, many immigrants like Pedro Xavier continued their connection to the Portuguese colony, often blurring the line between culture and business. [343] In 1910, for example, shortly after becoming president of the Hongkong Printing Press, Pedro was elected a director of the Royal Aerated Water Manufactory Co., a soda beverage company in Hong Kong. It was no coincidence that the company was managed by his first cousin, Francisco de Paula Danenberg, a relative by marriage whose family was from Macau. [344] It was likely that the press's partnership with Royal Aerated Water utilized familial connections to conduct business in the Portuguese territory, including the printing of soda labels.

Pedro also remained a member of the Club de Recreio, founded by his father in 1906, and served on a leadership committee. The club had become a central part of the Macanese community in Kowloon since the region was ceded by China in 1860. By 1916 Pedro also was a member of two organizations associated with republican causes in Macau and Lisbon: the Liga Portuguese and the Royal Geographic Society of Lisbon. Both were active in programs providing soup kitchens, education, and raising funds for war veterans and their families. Pedro was reported to have donated $10,000 HKD to support wounded soldiers who survived the Battle of Flanders in which 7,000 Portuguese were killed. [345]

Within this milieu, Pedro Xavier was able to identify other opportunities, partially a result of his familial connections and his ability to anticipate new markets. According to family records, there are indications that he prepared in advance. On August 5, 1913 Pedro sold the Hongkong Press offices at #3 Wyndham Street to the British owned South China Morning Post for $55,000, gaining a profit of $15,000 on the sale. The next day the firm purchased #31 Wyndham Street, a three story building with 21 rooms and a large basement, for $69,000. The Press also began renting out space to other businesses for $800 monthly. [346]

The larger building was to accommodate modern printing presses intended to mass produce currency notes and other security items for banks located in the region near Swatow (Shantou), a treaty port 300 kilometers north of Hong Kong in Guangdong province. Initially a landing spot for American missionaries, Swatow was known for hand embroidered table linens, silk lingerie, and handkerchiefs crafted by Chinese women using local silk and cotton obtained from India. By 1941, the industry was estimated to employ 300,000 workers producing goods for European markets. [347]

As both a manufacturing and transportation hub for central China, Swatow offered a fertile environment for businessmen like Pedro Xavier. In the years from 1913 through 1940, the Hongkong Printing Press contracted with at least fifteen (15) private banks to produce currency notes of various denominations. Eight banks were headquartered in Swatow. Five others were in Guangdong, Kwangtung, Fijian, and Fukien. [348] In an especially active period from 1916 to 1921, Pedro Xavier traveled to Swatow six times to secure bank contracts. Interestingly, during the same period he acquired a contract to print currency notes for Macau's Banco Nacional Ultramarino, while also printing labels for the municipal government. Several years later it was revealed in a letter to the British Consul in Macau that the Press actually had been producing duty tax stamps for opium, liquor, and toilet articles since 1918.[349] Despite local restrictions, family records indicate that these connections continued to be frequent and new markets remained lucrative through 1940.

A Revised Strategy

The business of printing currency, checks, and script was apparently profitable enough to begin a second re-evaluation of HKPP's business model. In October 1922 Pedro Xavier indicated this change of course by giving up the production of the Hong Kong Government Gazette and official notices altogether, selling the concessions to two English investors for $30,000. [350] By April 1924 the old headquarters of the Press in central Hong Kong was also sold and relocated to Kowloon with the purchase of #3 Bowring Street for $52,000. Family accounts indicate that the sale allowed Xavier to concentrate on less labor intensive, and more profitable, banking services by using modern presses to produce color security notes. [351] The density and rising cost of real estate on Hong Kong island may have been an additional factor.

While the end of government printing could be interpreted as a departure from his father's legacy, it seems that both cultural and commercial interests were involved. The Press' new location reflected Lisbello Xavier's belief, as evident from the founding of the Club de Recreio, that Kowloon would remain the center of the Macanese community for the foreseeable future. Pedro's factory, near the corner of Nathan Road and Jordan Road, also joined several other Macanese businesses which supported multi-generation families, as well as social clubs, churches, and parish schools for several decades. [352]

New Partners

The next phase of the reorganization began in November 1928 when Pedro Xavier's mother, Estaphina, granted him power of attorney over all assets and property of the firm. This action effectively made Pedro sole owner, allowing him to begin an ambitious strategy to expand the company's business across Southeast Asia. [353] Soon after Estaphina Xavier's death in January 1929, the remaining assets were sold and transferred to a newly named company called the *Hongkong Printing Press Limited*, which was to be co-managed by Pedro Xavier and Cheng Tien Tau, a director of the Nanyang Brothers Tobacco Company Limited, the largest producer of cigarettes in China. The alliance was apparently intended to generate more revenue through product labeling and packaging.

Other directors and companies were also part of the new plan. They included Sam Pak Ming, Comprador of the Yokohama Specie Bank, the largest bank in Japan; Leung Yan Po, Comprador of the Hongkong Electric Company Limited, the largest utility provider in the colony; and Jose Maria de Noronha, a grandson of Delfino Noronha and Head Cashier for a large French-Belgium bank, Credit Foncier d'Extreme Orient. [354] Each director was expected to direct a portion of their company's printing orders to the Press and was granted shares on the expectation of future sales. [355]

The choice of companies suggests both the promise they held for Pedro Xavier's business and the potential drawbacks of using middle-men without direct access to capital, which may not have been clear at the time. Above all, this particular group through their connection to various business interests in several countries was intended to impress both clients and future investors.

The association with the Hongkong Electric Company, for example, suggested the approval of Sir Paul Chater, the head of the utility, and a wealthy land developer. Chater was a self-

made Indian immigrant of Armenian descent who was in partnership with the Sassoons, an equally powerful Jewish family from India and Iraq. The Company was also the principal supplier of electricity to all the major banks, including the Hongkong and Shanghai Bank which employed many Macanese workers.

Another formidable connection was with Jose' Noronha, a grandson of Delfino Noronha, Lisbello Xavier's old mentor, the largest printer in Hong Kong. The Noronha family's influence among the British and wealthy Chinese reached the highest levels of government and commerce, including friendships with governors and the first Chinese and Macanese members of the Legislative Council. As an investor in local businesses and the owner of large property holdings in Kowloon, where the majority of the Macanese community lived in the 1920s, the Noronha connection provided credibility to the Press's new partnership and encouraged other clients to remain with the firm through the transition.

HKPP opium tax stamps and cigarette packaging

Two more directors suggested more dubious ties. Cheng Tien Tau, co-manager of the new Press representing the Nanyang Brothers Tobacco Company, was a case in point. The company's principal product was a well-known brand called "Double Happiness Cigarettes", of which Pedro Xavier expected to print at least 25% of the packaging. In a curious scheme revealed during the incorporation process, in addition to Cheng's position as co-manager, Chan Lim Pak, Managing Director of the tobacco company, and the company itself were each granted seats on the Board of Directors, as well as company shares. [356] This partnership effectively gave Nanyang Brothers more than equal standing with the Xavier interests, which according to family records, now owned only 15% of the business. [357]

Why such an arrangement was approved by Pedro Xavier, without family consent, which was not required, given the tobacco company's reputation, remains a mystery. The promise of new business and ready capital were perhaps two incentives. On closer scrutiny, Nanyang Brothers Tobacco shares were controlled by Lou Lim-lok, a wealthy investor whose family had obtained the first gambling and opium franchises in Macau in the late 19th century. Both franchises were eventually lost: the latter with the cessation of opium sales by Macau in 1919 (Under the Hague Convention of 1912). The family's gambling concession expired in 1937 and was acquired by a young Stanley Ho and some partners during Macau's isolation following the end of World War II. Lim-lok's father, Lou Kau, was a notorious gambler, investor, and philanthropist, whose downfall and subsequent suicide while escaping his creditors was well-known on the Chinese mainland. [358] Another potential problem were his son's connections to legitimate and illegitimate Chinese businesses in Macau and Hong Kong, as well as rumored links to the Triads. [359] We can only conclude, despite the reputation of these new investors and without a record of tangible guarantees, that such associations were accepted by members of the board on the anticipation of future growth.

The final director, Sam Pak Ming, representing the Yokohama Specie Bank (YSB), with branches in Hong Kong, Tokyo, Bombay, Beijing, Tianjin, and Yantai, raised another concern.[360] The YSB specialized in foreign banking and was a major funder of the Japanese military build-up at the turn of the 20th century. In addition, through Macau's Banco Nacional Ultramarino and the Kwantung Provincial Bank in Hong Kong, the Japanese bank was now associated, through the Press partnership, with the Chinese Nationalist Party of Sun Yat Sen and Chang Ki Shek. The potential conflict of interest of the Yokohama Bank, now technically in partnership with both Chinese nationalists and Japan's militant government, which were antagonists and moving closer to war, could not have been overlooked. This alliance also was accepted into the Press' new board, apparently based on the Yokohama bank's cash reserves and projections of future sales.

Such an eclectic mix of commercial and political interests could exist in the world of 1920's Asia, but would be sorely tested in the coming decades. Like all the companies on the Press' board of directors, each became the pillars of a fragile alliance, remaining dependent on potentially adversarial governments to keep borders open and maintain light restrictions, so long as their respective national interests remained compatible.

The Reorganization of the Press

The first indications of distress appeared even before British Hong Kong's relations with China and Japan deteriorated. By 1923 the Yokohama Specie Bank, which had offices in Hong Kong and Shanghai, was suffering liquidity issues among clients affected by Japan's Kantô Earthquake, and by a series of financial crises beginning in 1927 leading up to the world economic depression of 1929.[361] Support from the Japanese government of YSB saved it from insolvency, allowing the bank to fund the

Imperial Japanese military leading up to WWII. But tensions during the Sino-Japanese War of 1931 resulted in the confiscation of the bank's assets in China, and the exit of the bank from the colony and the Hongkong Press' board of directors.

In 1931 another shareholder, the Nanyang Brothers Tobacco Company, was also encountering difficulties.[362] New competitors, including British and French interests, as well as aggressive Chinese-owned cigarette factories, seriously depressed its business. In 1934 Chan Lim Pak, general manager of Nanyang Brothers and a shareholder of the Press, also was charged by the company's head, Lou Lim Kou, with embezzling funds. Chan fled Hong Kong and was soon declared a fugitive from justice. As hostilities worsened, the financial condition of the tobacco company was considered precarious. After the Japanese occupied Manchuria and the coastal areas of China near Hong Kong, Nanyang plants were placed under Japanese military control. The plants remained idle even after Japan's surrender in 1945 due to a lack of funds.

Pedro Xavier's initial response was to reshuffle his company's board of directors once more, replacing Nanyang Brothers Tobacco and the Yokohama Bank in 1936 with a British mercantile company, Gibb Livingston & Co. That strategy also failed. Like other companies in the partnership, Gibb Livingston was not able to live up to the 25% sales quota. It was at this point that Xavier considered eliminating the present board of directors completely and begin again, as he had done in 1928. Although the Press's regular printing business, which included the Kwangtung Provincial Bank in Canton, and work for the Macau and Hong Kong governments, remained healthy, Pedro slowly realized that associations with most of the new partners were not paying dividends. The projected sales of "at least 25% of cigarette packets" from Nanyang Brothers Tobacco Company and the bank note orders from the Yokohama Specie Bank simply did not materialize. Xavier also found that the shares he gave up in exchange did not improve the Company under the new management scheme. As a result, the firm's revenue began to suffer. By late 1936 Pedro concluded that the future of this "new" Hongkong Printing Press, which he had hoped to expand throughout Southeast Asia, could only be salvaged by another reorganization.

In a final move before World War II, Pedro transferred all remaining assets and re-incorporated the business once again as the "Hong Kong Lithographic Company Limited" on November 14, 1936.[363] All Shares of the new company were placed under the control of Pedro and the Xavier family, and all future business that he generated would be without any further encumbrances. The once "strategic" plan, however, was now reduced to a hope for an end to hostilities and to remain solvent. The declining fortunes of the Press continued up to the Japanese invasion, and were not reversed until 1946.

CHAPTER 10
The Trial and Marginalization of Jesuina Xavier

In spite of periodic declines, Hong Kong's steady development from the late 19th century through the 1930s had the effect of creating a social and political "bubble" among residents of the colony, one in which public acknowledgment of China's deterioration between the world wars could be pushed to the side. Even as the presence of Japanese troops occupying Manchuria loomed large, and the bombing of Shanghai and the attack on Nanking in 1937 heightened fears, many Europeans in Hong Kong seemed to ignore the reality that a threat existed.[364] The historian Frank Welsh observed that affluent men and women seemed especially distracted by social position and rank.[365] As these illusions persisted, racial antagonism and mistrust in government continued among working class Britons, Eurasians, Macanese, and Chinese, largely hidden from public view. Describing the European underclass, Henry Lethridge wrote:

> ... working class Europeans existed on the periphery of both European and Chinese communities, although their presence was essential for the smooth running of the colonial economy and society. They lived, in other words, in a terrain vague between the communities. ... He did not belong to Chinese society and, it can be surmised, never wished to. ... each despised the other, the underdog European particularly so. Although the latter usually lived in Chinese quarters of the town, spoke pidgin English or a little Cantonese, and often lived with a Chinese woman, this did not make him necessarily feel less British. He was, it can be inferred, as jingoistic as his counterpart in Liverpool or London, buoyed up at times by a sense of racial and national superiority. He did not belong to Chinese society and, it can be surmised, never wished to.[366]

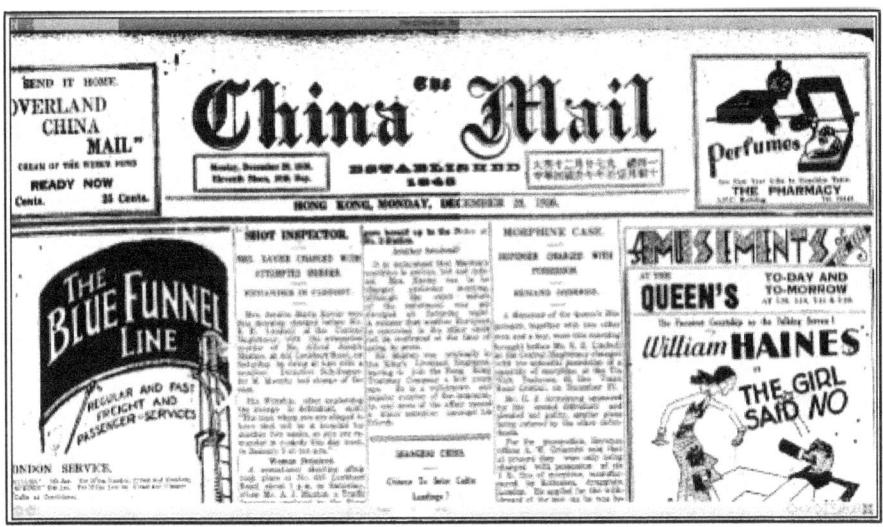

Tabloid Journalism

In the popular press, as reports on the Japanese threat and the prosecution of Chinese crime continued, cases involving the "habitually slighted" Macanese sometimes captured the collective imagination, especially in incidents involving race, sex, and violence.[367] Perhaps it was because such cases provided a diversion from the turmoil in China, or that these occurrences were so unexpected. The prevailing assumption in Hong Kong was that most "Portuguese", as they were known, were law abiding subjects, family oriented, and hard-working members of a community who rarely deviated from the norms established by the Catholic Church and Macau's old world traditions. Each avenue emphasized time honored modes of social behavior, especially for women. When members deviated from those norms, the implications (not to mention the humiliation) rated banner headlines. Such was the case in the shooting of Alfred Joseph Manton, an English tram inspector, by Jesuina Maria Xavier, the owner of a Wan Chi boarding house, in December 1930.[368]

The Arrest

According to police reports, Jesuina and Alfred had lived together for six years in a second story flat in her establishment on Lockhart Road in Wan Chai, a poor district of Hong Kong occupied by Chinese and the European underclass. Alfred had apparently spoken to Jesuina over a period of months about a "parting of the ways" and had mentioned it again on December 27th. Described by her lover as in "a highly-strung condition", Jesuina took the Star Ferry that morning to Kowloon to visit her younger sister, Ceilia Maria Xavier, to seek advice. During the talk, Ceilia excused herself to take a bath, but Jesuina secretly took her sister's house keys and unlocked a wardrobe where a revolver was kept, then went back to the apartment she shared with Manton in Wan Chai.

Wan Chai Boarding House - 1930s

When Alfred returned for lunch, he noticed that Jesuina was in the kitchen with the amah (a Chinese servant) cooking. Jesuina then sat down at the table and told Alfred that she had made arrangements to stay with her brothers and sisters, then refused to accept a $50 monthly allowance that Manton had offered previously. Then she returned to the kitchen for a plate of fish, placed it on the table, and walked to a bedroom behind where Alfred was seated. Just as he reached with his fork and knife to eat, Alfred heard two shots go off behind him, and after a short pause another shot was fired. Realizing he had been hit multiple times, Manton testified:

> *I jumped up and turned around and saw the accused crouching away from me toward the bedroom with a revolver in her left hand. The muzzle was pointed upward. I rushed at her and took the revolver from her and then found I was bleeding from the right arm, and called the amah. She came and I told her to fetch a policeman.*[369]

Jesuina was held at the No. 2 Police Station in Hong Kong and charged with attempted murder. When asked about her motive by the arresting officer, Jesuina was at first silent and expressionless, but later stated she "… would never harm him". Alfred first claimed that he did not know of a reason for her behavior but noted Jesuina's habit of "neglecting the house by going out gambling". [370] He later testified that this was one reason for deciding to end their relationship. But before Manton left for the police station, he added an interesting aside. Jesuina had begged him to: "Shoot me before you go."

So, the police were left with several questions. Was Jesuina Xavier, the jilted lover of an English trolleyman, responsible for attempting to kill him out of revenge? Did she harm Manton in a fit of rage, or was it an accident due to her "mental instability"? What was her actual motive? We may also ask: Why did this particular incident attract so much press coverage? What implications did Jesuina Xavier's behavior suggest about the Macanese underclass during this period? Before answering, let us learn more about the principals.

The Cast of Characters

Her full name was Jesuina Maria Lourdes (do Rosario) Xavier, born in Hong Kong on October 17, 1886. When she was twenty-three, Jesuina married Jose Maria Xavier on May 29, 1909, ten years her senior and a distant cousin of the family that owned the Hongkong Printing Press. Jose worked as a Clerk for the Banque de l'Indo-Chine, a well-known French firm from at least 1898. But Jesuina apparently left him without a divorce around 1924 but continued using his surname while operating a boarding house in Wan Chai. She met and began living with Alfred Manton in 1925 until the shooting in December 1930. Jesuina was 44 years old at the time of her arrest. There is no record of any children from either union.

We know less about her accuser and lover, Alfred Joseph Manton. Scant information from press reports indicate that Manton was a British Train Inspector for the Hong Kong Tramways from at least 1924. Prior to Hong Kong, Manton served during World War I in France as an enlisted man in the King's Liverpool Regiment. Further research indicates that Manton died in Hong Kong in 1933, but it is not known whether his death was connected to wounds suffered in the shooting. No other information about Manton could be found. British Europeans like Alfred Manton, however, belonged to a working class segment that was excluded from "acceptable" society, and rife with racial and status divisions. This exclusion may suggest why Manton and Jesuina Xavier became involved in the first place. As Lethbridge wrote:

> The European lower orders were excluded from the social world of merchant and official and forced either into isolation within the circle of their own occupational and status group or into a segment of the underdog Portuguese or Eurasian communities.". (A working class British male) ... was more at ease with Portuguese and Eurasians; but his social contacts with them were often touchy, prickly, and patronising; for even the déclassé European knew he was a member of a dominant race. [371]

Two other witnesses, on the other hand, were established members of the Macanese middle class. [372] They were Jesuina's younger sister, Ceilia Maria Felicitas do Rosario, and her husband, Renaldo Gustavo Xavier. Ceilia was apparently a housewife and mother. Renaldo was the Manager of the Hong Kong Printing Press and the sixth child and second son of its founder, Lisbello de Jesus Xavier and Estefinia Francisca dos Santos. Ceilia and Reinaldo had nine children at the time of the trial: a tenth child would be born in December 1931. Both witnesses were thirty-seven years old.

One of Jesuina's defense counsels, who could be considered among the Macanese elite, was a young barrister named Leonardo d'Almada e Castro Jr., the son of a prominent family. His grand uncle, Leonardo Sr., was one of the first Macanese to arrive with the British Superintendent of Trade in 1842 and rose to be a prominent civil servant, a property owner, and philanthropist. Leonardo Jr. is interesting because of who he became <u>after</u> the trial. In 1937 he succeeded Jose' Pedro Braga as the second Portuguese "non-voting" member of Hong Kong's Legislative Council. As we shall see in the next chapter, when the threat of a Japanese invasion grew imminent in 1940, Leonardo d'Almada Jr. won wide respect for criticizing the Legislative Council for devising an evacuation plan only for British citizens.

<u>A Cultural Pariah</u>

The popularity of this case had as much to do with culture as it was for the notoriety of the crime. Based on what we know about the Portuguese community in Hong Kong during this period, the pressures and social stigmas would seem to be much greater on a Macanese woman than on her British lover. The public narrative offered in the press was that Jesuina Xavier was thirty-eight years old when she left her older husband, a respected member of the Portuguese community, to live with a "foreigner" out of wedlock for almost six years. She then was arrested for committing a violent crime and may have suffered a mental breakdown. Each would have been considered violations of religious and social conventions. Even suspicions of her possible involvement in a crime or an association with mental illness would have meant Jesuina being ostracized from regular social circles.

Due to the prevailing ideology of maintaining "social distance" from lower classes, there also were unwritten rules that dissuaded mixing between the British, Portuguese, and Chinese communities. Personal "fraternization", even within the scope of marriage, was frowned upon. When this occurred outside of marriage, a woman from any community was often shunned, labeled as "fallen" from grace, and in Jesuina's case, potentially tried as a criminal, similar to the prosecution of a prostitute. This was especially true if the liaison involved a member of a racially "superior" class, as was Alfred Manton, a British citizen, and a partner from a subordinate class, as was Jesuina Xavier, a Macanese. In doing so, Jesuina crossed a divide that probably brought ridicule and shame from both the Portuguese and British communities. Those factors may have been the principal reasons why the story ran for several issues in Hong Kong's major dailies.

St. Teresa's Church - 1932

The Catholic Church in Hong Kong was no less forgiving. In the case of Jesuina's first marriage, divorce was not an option, and a secular annulment would have been forbidden under the threat of excommunication. That may have been one reason she technically remained married and use her surname, as well as the cache' that a prominent family name would have brought. After separating from her husband and living out of wedlock with an Englishman, however, Jesuina was in violation of breaking her marriage vows under Church law, which also would have resulted in excommunication.

Either violation would have prevented her from receiving the holy sacraments, including attendance at Mass and the right to confession, receiving communion, attending weddings and baptisms, and the final rights at death. She also would have been excluded from celebrations on religious feast days, which were important events for the Macanese community. Finally, expulsion from the Church would prevent her burial in Catholic cemeteries set aside for the faithful. Thus, Jesuina's rejection from her community and religious separation by excommunication had multiple repercussions on her cultural and family life, essentially removing her from accepted society in this world and the next.

The weight of these social millstones by association, even before the trial began, would have been burdensome on extended relatives. Related by marriage through her sister to a well-to-do family, Jesuina Xavier no doubt was thought to bring shame to her in-law's household, and adversely affected their standing in social and business networks. Given the insularity of the Portuguese community, we can only imagine the knowing glances that Renaldo and Ceilia Xavier endured when attending church each Sunday. We may also picture Renaldo's encounters at the Club Lusitano, the most prominent Portuguese organization in Hong Kong, in which Xavier males were members since 1902, and his painful attempts to avoid references to his outlawed sister-in-law. We might also visualize the embarrassment of Ceilia's children at school as the trial was followed in the press by parish priests and nuns, and the whispers of mothers and amahs (servants) behind Ceilia's back as they gossiped about her beloved sister. All of this ridicule and innuendo was to be endured in silence, as reflected in Jesuina's demeanor during her interrogation. What must have been going through her mind throughout this ordeal? How much could she be expected to endure?

Hong Kong's High Court circa 1930

The Trial

As Alfred Manton recovered from his wounds, Jesuina Xavier remained in prison until her trial began on February 2, 1931. When the trial resumed, Hong Kong's Public Prosecutor, H. Somerset Fitzroy, surprised the defense by reducing the charge from the "attempted murder" to "malicious intent to maim, disfigure or disable". The new charge, however, could still result in harsh conditions and a lengthy prison sentence.[373]

The trial led to some important revelations that determined how the defense would proceed. Defense co-counsel P.W. Hodgson first called to the stand Sub-Inspector Michael Murphy, the first policeman to arrive at the Wan Chai flat following the shooting. During his questioning, Murphy noted that Jesuina was distraught and was reluctant to speak. But reading from his notes he recalled the following quote from the defendant: "I don't think I have anything to say." she stated, "My conscience is quite clear of any guilty act, especially against Manton. I would never have harmed him." Murphy then was asked if he had found any other evidence in Jesuina's Xavier's flat following the shooting. Incredibly, Murphy stated that he had not looked before returning to the police station. He had only collected some spent gun shells on the floor near where Manton was shot. No other part of the room seemed to be out of order and was not searched, Murphy replied.

Hodson then called Jesuina's sister, Ceilia Xavier, to testify. Ceilia spoke to her sister on December 27th when Jesuina visited her house in Kowloon, but then excused herself to take a bath. When she returned, Jesuina was gone. Three hours later a note was delivered by a servant from Jesuina telling her that she had taken the gun from the locked wardrobe and intended to commit suicide. The letter was then produced and submitted as evidence. Ceilia also stated that a second letter from Jesuina addressed to Manton had been found in a bedroom drawer by Ceilia's husband after the incident, which the police had not discovered. The letter contained an apology to Manton and stated that Jesuina wanted to end her life because he was ending the relationship. Hodgson produced the letter for the court, but it was dismissed because its origins could not be confirmed. The appearance of the second letter suggested that police investigators had failed to recover evidence that was pertinent to Jesuina's state of mind in the commission of a crime. It was now inadmissible.

Assault or Accident?

The most important revelations, however, came from a review of the shooting. Alfred Manton had testified earlier that he knew of no reason why Jesuina would harm him, but also noted that she was distraught and upset over his plans to leave her, and repeated Jesuina's request to "Shoot me" as she lay on the floor of the dining room. Now it was clear that the defense team must put Jesuina's statement into context in order to prove her innocence to the charge of intentional wounding. The strategy involved shedding light on the nature of Manton's injuries.

Leo D'Almada, Jesuina's co-defense counsel, called Dr. I. Newton, a specialist from the Government Civil Hospital. Newton testified that the accuser received three wounds: two to his upper back near the shoulder blades and one that pierced and exited the fleshy part of the right arm. None were considered serious because the bullets were old and deteriorated. Newton also noted that the shots were fired from about three feet away with "considerable variation of aim", which suggested that Jesuina pointed the gun wildly and did not appear to be concentrating on any one part of Manton's body.

D'Almada then recalled Alfred Manton to the stand. He asked Manton what he would say about a person who had never fired a revolver such as the gun in question. Manton stated: "... in the case of a person who has never handled (a revolver) before, anything could happen. ... Anyone who had not received instructions ... is liable to cause an accident." D'Almada then asked Manton again about the gun immediately after the shooting. Manton said that the revolver was in Jesuina's left hand and the muzzle was pointed upward with Jesuina's back to him, three feet away. He also testified that Jesuina Xavier was right handed.

An Alternative View

Given this testimony, Jesuina's defense counsels began to construct an alternative explanation of the incident. The probable cause was Alfred Manton's decision to end a six year relationship. There seemed to be no evidence, as suggested in his early statements, that Jesuina kept an "untidy household" or had a gambling habit. Instead, Jesuina may have had a mental breakdown, perhaps feeling ostracized once she realized that her British lover was leaving, and she saw only one solution: Suicide.

Her actions supported this theory. Writing two suicide notes, Jesuina traveled to her sister's house in Kowloon to retrieve a gun. Jesuina left the first note with the servant with instructions to deliver it to Ceilia and Renaldo Xavier later that afternoon. Jesuina then returned to her flat in Hong Kong and placed the second note in a place where Alfred would find it, in a drawer of their bedroom. Then she went to kitchen to help her servant prepare lunch.

Upon Alfred Manton's arrival, Jesuina went into the bedroom to retrieve the gun from the same drawer where the second suicide note was kept. She then returned to the kitchen and placed a plate of fish in front of Manton. Just as he picked up a fork and knife to eat, three shots rang out behind him. Manton turned to see Jesuina "facing away" from him toward the bedroom, with the gun in her left hand and the muzzle pointing upward. He then took the gun from her hand and threw her to the floor.

Because Jesuina fired "facing away" from Manton toward the bedroom, a shot to his back and right arm would only have been possible if Jesuina had been pointing the gun in her left hand facing backwards, without seeing her alleged target. The fact that there was, in Dr. Newton's words, "considerable variation" in her aim, suggests that the shots were wild, and consistent with someone who was highly distraught.

The most plausible explanation, P.W. Hodgson concluded to the jury, was that Jesuina waved the revolver erratically, firing a gun she had never used, hitting Manton three times as she missed her actual target, *her own head*. The magistrate then asked Hodgson to clarify his theory for the record. His answer, paraphrased by a reporter, summed up Jesuina Xavier's defense: "...The shooting was an accident. Mrs. Xavier did not want to fire at Mr. Manton. ... she wanted to shoot herself in front of him." [374]

The Verdict

The evidence seemed to point to an acquittal, but there is no record of the final verdict. News accounts following the trial have been lost, presumably in the turmoil that was about to engulf Hong Kong and the rest of Asia during World War II. But from what can be determined from the accounts we have,

Jesuina Xavier was not convicted of the charges, and probably disappeared from the pages of history after spending time in a psychiatric ward. Given recent studies of mental health treatment in Hong Kong, that may be considered a punishment in itself.[375] However disappointing it is not knowing her ultimate fate, the limited information available suggests that Jesuina Xavier and other women and men in Hong Kong's Macanese community often endured harsh scrutiny according to prevailing standards of conduct, often set by racial and class boundaries, religious doctrine, family history, and rigid cultures, all of which were magnified in cases like this by the local press.

Hong Kong's Mental Asylum

Such pressures served as an undercurrent during periods of economic growth and political vitality, as we saw in the previous chapter. But expectations based on societal norms and perceptions of the working class in Hong Kong created added weight for people like Jesuina Xavier and Alfred Manton, who lived on the margins of society, especially when anxieties increased due to the disintegration of China and the rise of Imperial Japan. As we shall see in the next chapter, those anxieties seemed to reach a climax in the summer of 1940 during a period of heightened fear.

CHAPTER 11
The Sum of All Fears: The Evacuation of British Subjects from Hong Kong

As mentioned, one of the co-counsels in Jesuina Xavier's trial was the young barrister Leonardo d'Almada e Castro, Jr., a rising advocate of ethnic rights who succeeded Jose Pedro Braga on the Legislative Council in 1937. As a member of the Council in June 1940, d'Almada was a critic of London's response to fears of a Japanese invasion of Hong Kong that resulted in an evacuation of government and military dependents to Australia. As the details of the new policy emerged, the impact on Hong Kong's middle and working classes, its most vulnerable residents, became more clear. After witnessing several weeks of confusion caused by the deportation order, d'Almada and other legislators stood before the Hong Kong Legislative Council on July 25, 1940 to ask the Governor and the Colonial Secretary why the compulsory evacuation was so haphazardly enforced, and why it only included "… British women and children of pure European descent".[376]

To understand the level of anxiety during that period, we must place the evacuation order in historical context. Like all residents of Hong Kong, d'Almada had read news reports describing the Japanese invasion of Manchuria in 1931, the bombing Shanghai in 1932, and the sacking of Nanking in 1937. He then watched in alarm as Japanese troops massed along the border with Guangdong. A few days after France fell to Nazi Germany on June 25, 1940, the British War Cabinet, in response to numerous requests from the Commanding General of Hong Kong's military forces, ordered the colonial government to evacuate approximately 3,500 British women, children, and some elderly men to Manila, and then to Australia. The deportation of forty-one percent of the British population by the local police on a few days' notice, and without financial support or information about their return, created an uproar that reverberated across class and racial lines in a colony that was already showing signs of disintegration.[377]

The targeted groups were to be, as one scholar describes them, "All British women and children under eighteen 'of European race' who were unnecessary for the defence or essential services to the maintenance of the colony..." .[378] Most were the dependents of enlisted military personnel or low level government workers who were to be protected by the colonial government due to their status as British "sojourners", identified by London and Hong Kong officials as "non-domiciled" or short term residents. Those who were not British, including Chinese, Eurasians, and Macanese, even families with males working at higher levels in the military or government, were mostly excluded. There were some exceptions, including twelve Chinese women who were married to military personnel. But most were returned to Hong Kong from Australia before the war.[379] The government's explanation was that those groups not evacuated were originally "domiciled" in other countries and should be repatriated there when necessary.

The shock expressed by British families to the abruptness of the evacuation order was immediate, but given deteriorating relations inside Hong Kong, not entirely unexpected by other ethnic groups. According to recent scholarship, many British evacuees began writing letters complaining to local newspapers and petitioned officials in London, Hong Kong, and Australia.[380] Many inquired about the government's motives and the lack of settlement arrangements once they arrived. Others questioned why the families of high ranking members of government were able to avoid the deportations, or seemed to be settled comfortably outside Hong Kong.[381]

Some challenged the compulsory order in court, and gained the support of high ranking business executives, including the heads of the Chamber of Commerce and the Hongkong and Shanghai Bank. Their legal threats temporarily suspended the order but was followed by new regulations that forbid the return of any evacuee then in Manila or Australia under penalty of arrest.[382] The decision by the government to rescind the order in late 1940 created both resentment and confusion. The unequal granting of exemptions to "official families" was roundly criticized. The abrupt cancellation of the mandatory deportation also implied that the government now saw no imminent threat of invasion.[383]

The evacuation order was seen from a different perspective among the Macanese, Eurasian, and Chinese populations of Hong Kong. Although some were initially allowed to board ships, most Chinese and Eurasian evacuees were turned away at the docks by police officials who noticed their racial features. Others, as reported by Council members d'Almada and Lo Man Kam, a Chinese representative, were "identified" by self-appointed British women in Manila as "ineligible" and were returned to Hong Kong.[384] But many non-British subjects were already making alternative plans for evacuation in the event of war. Some wealthy Chinese families took the advice of their representatives and departed for Macau, Singapore, and Canton to escape the turmoil.[385] Many Macanese families from Shanghai and Hong Kong had already begun the journey, according to witnesses and news articles noting increased ship passages to Macau beginning in 1937.[386]

The reasons for their willingness to leave Hong Kong may be understandable in light of the crisis, and their historic positions in society. As presented in Chapter 4, the reins of colonial power and authority were held tightly by the administration, while those not born in the British Isles were usually considered racially inferior, subordinate, and kept at a distance.[387] This history of discrimination suggested to the Chinese, the Macanese and other Eurasians that the 1940 evacuation was more serious than past slights and condescensions. Rather, this latest act tended to confirm their collective pessimism, and was the culmination of decades long frustrations with the Hong Kong government's unwillingness to protect their interests, and those of most non-British subjects. In this regard, vaunted safeguards under "Free Trade" policies and the ideals of "fair dealing" were gradually exposed as social myths hardly realized in the stratified environment of Hong Kong for nearly a century, and apparently intended only for commercial and government elites. Many on the margins of society, including some born in the British Isles in the lower ranks of government and the military, historically were left vulnerable in times of crisis. [388]

This decline in trust was evident in the criticisms of Jose' Pedro Braga, a second generation Macanese born in Hong Kong, in his defense of the "Rights of Alien Workers" written in 1895.[389] Another example was the government's neglect of fire and building codes, as well as police protection, which exposed thousands of Macanese, Chinese, and other ethnic groups in 1918 to danger during the Happy Valley Racecourse fire.[390] Even in an "open" economy benefiting from Hong Kong's free trade policies, ethnic owned businesses like the Hongkong Printing Press in 1928 had to rely on well-placed compradors and clerks, who were essentially "intermediaries", for access to large scale capital, which was not always assured.[391] These secondary relations were vulnerable to corruption, geo-political events, and often resulted in a loss of control. By the decade of "malaise", Hong Kong in the 1930s, public trust in government was further eroded by cultural isolation, marginalization, and the weight of religious and familial pressures, as we saw during the trial of Jesuina Xavier, a Macanese woman accused of assaulting her British lover in 1931.[392]

The botched evacuation of British women and children in 1940, and the public exclusion of other ethnic groups, could therefore be interpreted as a final step in a long history of discontent in Hong Kong based on generational experience with class and racial discrimination. This resulted in the declining confidence of many foreign communities in the colonial government since the 19th century. Among English subjects this realization may have occurred as late as 1940, a bitter surprise that colonial officials made decisions based on institutional biases as an invasion loomed on the horizon. In an editorial, the

China Mail alluded to the loss of faith by stating: "It is doubtful, ... there has ever been a time in the modern history of the colony when sympathy between public and government has been so strained." [393] Many ethnic subjects, whose families were heavily invested in businesses, property, and the social fabric of the colony for generations, including many who obtained British citizenship, grudgingly realized that a "British subject" was more than a legal designation. It could only be "held by those born in the British Isles..." of "pure European descent".[394]

Leonardo d' Almada, a second generation British citizen, concluded by July 1940 that this final slight, publicly exposing racial and class preferences just as the need for trust was greatest, would have long term effects on the Macanese and others as the war approached. When a vote to approve additional funds for the evacuation came before the Legislative Council, he offered this warning:

In this matter of discrimination, ... Government, ... has forfeited to a very great extent the respect and confidence of the community. That, of course, is Government's business. But that is not all. Government has also placed an appreciable strain on the loyalty of a large section of the community, and I am not going to be an accessory after the fact ... [395]

The final solution, making all debates and protests moot, came with the Japanese invasion of Hong Kong on December 8, 1941. The fates of all British subjects would now be left to the whims of foreign aggressors. In a cruel twist, the identification of Allied sympathizers by the infamous Japanese military police, the Kempeitai, including many "pure born" British in Hong Kong, led to summary executions, imprisonment in concentration camps, and transfers to the Japanese mainland as slave labor. Those not classified in those groups, including many Macanese considered "Third Nationals" and neutral non-combatants, were allowed to evacuate to Macau for the duration of the war. The fate and resilience of the Macanese in this new setting, which had a direct impact on their future in Asia, is the subject of the next chapter.

CHAPTER 12
The Macanese at War: Survival and Identity during World War II

One of the least known narratives of World War II can be found in the experiences of the Macanese. The story of their return to Macau during the war as refugees after a century in Hong Kong and other trading ports documents the plight of a racially-mixed people forced to survive and maintain their families in exile.[396] Their accounts provide a ground level view of the Japanese invasion and life in Macau, a neutral site described by witnesses as Asia's version of "Casablanca".[397]

The Macanese presence in Asia during the critical years of 1942 to 1945 was significant in other ways as well. As colonial Eurasians, war-time relations with the British, Chinese, and Japanese will illustrate the tangled but important roles the Macanese played during the conflict. How the Macanese managed their new environment in Macau also offered them new identities that were unique to the conditions they faced. Their efforts to keep families intact, the foundation of their culture, also appears during an important juncture in their history, during which pre-war hierarchies and social divisions began to break down, culminating in new opportunities and immigration to other countries in the post-war period. This chapter thus offers a different perspective on war-time Hong Kong and Macau by providing a detailed view of the conditions under which the Macanese went to war and how they survived as a community during the conflict.

The Defense of Hong Kong

Hong Kong in the 1930s had begun to suffer the effects of the world economic depression, civil unrest in Asia, and Japan's military takeover of Manchuria. As we saw in the previous chapters, internal tensions among different ethnic communities had also been building. As the Sino-Japanese war of 1937 moved closer to Hong Kong, trade weakened as the result of Britain's diminishing influence in Asia. Meanwhile, the colony's population swelled with an influx of refugees from the mainland and other trading ports, including Shanghai, Canton, Tientsin, and Ningbo.[398] As long term residents, the Macanese generally remained loyal to Britain and joined in the preparations for war. The fate of Macau, their ancestral home for three hundred years and isolated like Hong Kong, also weighed heavily on their minds.

Given the pressures on Britain at the time, the defense of Hong Kong and Macau, the latter Portugal's responsibility since its defense was not in British hands, was largely considered unimportant to the Allied war effort. By 1935 the British government still viewed Hong Kong as a minor outpost on the fringes of the civilized world. Writing in his post-war memoirs, Winston Churchill believed that if war came the defense of the colony would be an "unnecessary distraction" in light of the threat at home posed by Nazi Germany.[399] This attitude was apparently shared by the Colonial Office and the British Parliament, which allowed Hong Kong's defenses to remain outdated and its military garrisons undermanned. Meantime, the Portuguese in Macau looked to its own defenses by building fortifications and bringing in reinforcements from Mozambique.[400] (Geoffrey C. Gunn, Encountering Macau, a Portuguese city-state on the periphery of China, 1557-1999, Westview Press, 1996, Chapter 7.) Portugal also asserted Macau's neutral status and renegotiated its relationship with Japan, which were not options for Britain.

Yet Hong Kong represented a symbolic and material obstacle to the Japanese empire as it continued its war with China

 through 1937. To blunt counter-insurgency and win over hearts and minds, Japanese propaganda relentlessly focused on English racial arrogance and colonial imperialism, convincing some to collaborate in both Hong Kong and Macau even as propagandists ignored atrocities committed by their own troops on the mainland.[401] A more immediate concern was the reality that Hong Kong had become a haven for Allied spies, and a gathering point for supplies, fuel, and munitions for the embattled Chinese Nationalist army.[402] (The South China Morning Post, Editorial, January 15, 1946.) With the Japanese capture of Canton (Guangzhou) in October 1938, these developments made Hong Kong and its surrounding territories likely targets in late 1941.

When the Japanese invasion of Hong Kong finally began on the morning of December 8, among those on the first line of defense were members of "Portuguese" regiments in the Hong Kong Volunteer Defense Corps (HKVDC). They numbered about 500 Macanese men, some recruited from the local police force. Most recruits were concentrated in two infantry companies, the No. 5 Machine Gun Company and the No. 6 Anti-Aircraft Company, and in other support units.[403]

The great majority served in the HKVDC only on weekends, and virtually none had seen combat before. The Macanese contingent was joined by the Royal Scots Regiment, as well as Chinese and Eurasian regiments, each organized along racial lines. Those troops were part of a regular British force of 14,000, which included 2,000 inexperienced Canadian troops who arrived in Hong Kong only weeks before. Many of the Macanese, in spite of their historic treatment as second class citizens, had volunteered out of loyalty to the British government, never expecting to face 60,000 battle tested Japanese troops who fought in China over the last decade.[404]

Anticipating an invasion from the north, several thousand soldiers were deployed in the New Territories north of Hong Kong along the "Gin Drinkers Line", a defensive placement of pillboxes and bunkers that stretched across the Kowloon peninsula. Officially, the defenders of varied in age from 17 to 45, many taking leaves from jobs as tram operators, teachers, bank clerks and bookkeepers. Many Macanese recruits relied on outdated equipment and suffered from a lack of training. One writer described the conditions and the attitude among those in the field:

> *No. 6 Company, ... had old Lee Enfields (bolt action rifles used in World War I), Smith & Wesson revolvers and one Lewis gun (a heavy machine-gun like weapon), which had to be held on the shoulder of the firer and steadied by (another), whose left hand beneath the drum was burned raw and black at the edges...They fought and withdrew, fought and withdrew and ... the Japanese broke through the Gin Drinkers Line, that phony lane of pillboxes built to defend the north which the troops all knew was useless without reinforcement but ... was a great place to have a tipple,...* [405]

The youngest volunteer was a fifteen year old student named Eduardo (Eddie) Hyndman. He was not among those stationed in Kowloon at the time of the invasion, but enlisted following the first attack after telling recruiters he was seventeen. A mature youth, Hyndman was the only son of Eduardo and Laura Hyndman, whose families were Dutch and Portuguese originally from Macau. Alarmed by her son's plans, Hyndman's mother convinced Lt. George Palmer, who was married to her cousin, to transfer him to Palmer's Engineer's Unit to keep the boy near the family on Hong Kong island. An account of Hyndman's service follows:

> On the 20th (of) December, George, his Chinese driver, in the front seats, and Eddie, safely in the back seat of their staff car, made their way under fire from Japanese planes to the Peak. When they arrived at Magazine Gap Road they received heavy strafing from one of the planes, followed by a bomb which hit the back of the staff car. George and the driver were blown free...and landed on the road, unhurt. ... but poor Eddie ... received severe injuries and was rushed to the War Memorial Hospital.[406]

Eduardo Filomeno Hyndman died of his wounds eleven days later. At fifteen, he was the youngest defender of Hong Kong to perish.

Macanese Civilians in Kowloon

Many civilians were surprised by the swiftness of the attack. On the morning of the invasion, ten year old Basilio (Basil) Xavier dressed and prepared to leave as usual for La Salle College for Boys with his younger brother Eugenio (Gene), then met his cousins, Daniel and Tony da Rocha, on the street in front of their house.[407] The school was three miles from Basil and Gene's home in Ho Man Tin, a Kowloon district. As the boys were leaving, their father Vasco listened to radio reports on KZPI, the voice of the Philippines, that the Japanese had attacked Pearl Harbor. He cautioned the youngsters that if there was trouble to go to an uncle's home in Kowloon Tong, which was closer to their school. The boys considered the request to be odd given the attack was more than 4,000 miles away but relied on their father's assurances that they would be safe. On the way to school, they walked a few paces behind a Russian woman they knew who had fled the Bolshevik revolution. Suddenly, fighter planes appeared in the sky to their right. Basil's memories of those moments are poignant:

Look! Spitfires! Someone said. But they were not British Spitfires. They were Japanese Zeroes. And soon the sound of bombs bursting in the distance greeted our ears. We were not really aware of what was happening. But the White Russian lady in front of us cried out in terror, and the despair and fear in her voice galvanized us into action. The memory of that cry forever haunts me. Instinctively, I knew that it was the anguish of horror remembered. We turned and ran. Ran for all our worth towards home. My rattan school bag was heavy with my books, but we ran as fast as we could, and did not stop ... [408]

When Basil and Gene arrived home, their father decided it was no longer safe to remain in Kowloon. Stripping beds of their sheets, the family filled them with clothes and other valuables, including a statue of Our Lady, tied the bundles together and gathered them on the floor. Then Basil's family of six walked a few doors down the street to his uncle Pedro Marques' home, collected his family of four, and all of them made their way to the home of the Portuguese consulate near the docks that had been opened for refugees. [409]

They soon learned that the house and surrounding compound was overflowing with evacuees. Some of the families, including Basil and his relatives, were housed in the adjoining home of a French family. The older boys and other able bodied men in the group were organized into a security force to protect the grounds and the surrounding houses from roving Chinese gangs and looters. Setting up a defensive perimeter, boys patrolled in shifts while Japanese regulars fought the remnants of British troops falling back into defensive positions toward the harbor.

In the midst of the chaos, Vasco Xavier, as the designated "Air Raid Chief Warden" of the Hong Kong and Shanghai Bank, felt obligated to report for duty on Hong Kong Island. Japanese troops were still mopping up in Kowloon and bombarding Hong Kong in anticipation of the final assault that would begin on December 18. Despite pleas from his family, Vasco left with other bank employees on the last ferry across the harbor as bombs began falling on Hong Kong's northeastern shore. Meanwhile, Basil's family and relatives endured meals of rice and celery, and learned to live under the Japanese occupation. The two families shared a single room. Five children slept crosswise on a large bed. Elga Xavier, Basil's older sister, was given a cot, while the adults slept on mattresses laid on the floor. Sandbags outside the building protected them from stray bombs while frequent gun battles outside added more stress on the families.[410] Several days later, after Vasco's difficult return to Kowloon, the two families and several hundred refugees boarded one of the last ferries for Hong Kong island behind the advance of Japanese troops. There they remained for several months.

The Invasion of Hong Kong Island

On the morning of December 8, Reggie Pires and his friend, Terrence Pomeroy, attended Mass for the Feast of the Immaculate Conception at Our Lady of the Rosary Church in central Hong Kong, then proceeded to school late, knowing they would be excused by his teachers, the Christian Brothers.[411] Waiting at the tram stop, the boys heard the familiar whistle, then saw the tram halt abruptly several blocks away and the passengers disembark. Just then, Tommy Castillo, a seventeen year old neighbor, stuck his head out a window just above their heads and shouted: "Go on home. There's no school today. We're at war with Japan." Tommy wore the uniform of the HKVDC and had just returned from a week of duty along the "Gin Drinkers Line". He was visiting the home of his girlfriend, Rosy Murphy, who lived above the tram stop.

Arriving home, Reggie watched the bombing of Kai Tak Airport from his family's apartment on a hill above the Happy Valley Racecourse and saw the first British anti-aircraft shells falling helplessly short of their targets. He could see the planes close enough to recognize the rising sun on the wings, and feel the concussion of the bombs as they fell to earth destroying buildings and neighborhoods he knew well. Listening to Philippine radio, Reggie and his father, Humberto, heard the first reports that the invasion had begun in the New Territories and was moving toward Kowloon.

Realizing now that war was imminent, Humberto sent his servants out to buy dry goods, returning later with a case of Argentine potted beef. Still believing the conflict would be short lived, he shaved and went to work at the Cable and Wireless Ltd. in Hong Kong's central business district. But Humberto soon learned that the tram service was permanently suspended, and was forced to walk the rest of the way to his office. A few hours later he returned home with his boss and assistant in tow. Both lived in Kowloon Tong and were cut off from their families. The men were given rooms and food by the Pires family and waited for the invasion to begin.

From his balcony, Reggie continued to watch troop movements on the Kowloon peninsula and the exchange of artillery between the British and Japanese armies. One day he saw a sobering sight. In the distance atop the Peninsula Hotel, he noticed a large flag with the familiar red ball flying from one of the masts. Immediately he knew the significance. Calling his father and the other adults, Reggie pointed toward the harbor and told them what he saw. In disbelief, Humberto used a pair of binoculars to confirm that the Japanese army was indeed in control of Kowloon. They all knew it was now only a matter of time before the final assault on Hong Kong would begin.

The Pires family learned from news reports that the Gin Drinker's Line was breached in two days. The evacuation from Kowloon to Hong Kong began on December 11 under a heavy aerial and artillery bombardment. Reggie recalled reading that ferries containing civilians were fired upon by Japanese troops as the ships crossed the one mile distance across the harbor to the island. One of Humberto Pires' fellow workers at Cable and

Wireless Ltd., Vicente de Souza, later recalled witnessing gun fire from Chinese collaborators who had picked up weapons left by retreating British soldiers. A woman standing next to Vincente on the Star Ferry was shot and killed before reaching Hong Kong Island.[412]

The family and others prepared as best as they could. The group pooled all the provisions they could gather, stored them in refrigerators on the upper floors of their building, and slept in the stairwells for protection during the bombardments. As the power was cut off after the Japanese captured the electrical station at North Point, frozen food thawed so quickly that it had to be eaten in a few large meals. When the surrender came on Christmas Day 1941, everyone living in the apartment was abruptly ordered to evacuate in twenty-four (24) hours. The Japanese had designated their building as its command headquarters. Nearby, Happy Valley Racecourse was to be used as a staging ground for trucks and machinery. More troops were bivouacked in other buildings around the island.

Like others, the Pires group gathered food and valuables in bed sheets and walked downtown toward the Club Lusitano where the Portuguese consulate had set up a temporary shelter. On the way, an employee of the Belgium Bank offered them a large office to stay in before the refugee ships arrived. Overcrowding at the Lusitano made the proposal appealing, since the first vessels would not depart for several weeks. Reggie's family of four and eight other refugees lived in the one room office for almost two months until leaving for Macau.[413]

Those who survived the attack on Hong Kong lingered on for several weeks, unsure of their fate. Despite the dangers, some Macanese families continued to live in damaged homes and offices, barricading themselves against marauding gangs of looters, thieves, collaborators, and drunken soldiers, many who sought food and other valuables, while threatening women with rape.[414] Others who wished to evacuate waited on the Kowloon docks for several days for ships to ferry them across the harbor, some separated from their loved ones at the last minute because of citizenship papers.[415] The Acting Consul for Portugal, Francisco P. Soares, offered his home in Kowloon to serve the large Macanese community there, and heroically interceded with the Japanese authorities to provide food, temporary shelter, and travel documents to many refugees who were stranded.[416] Many more were held in camps set aside for Eurasian, British and American prisoners, while others preferred to remain outside the camps rather than subject themselves to the will of the invading army.[417] Others took more direct action by helping those interned to escape by working covertly with British and Chinese espionage units.[418]

Since the Portuguese government had declared neutrality before the war, multiracial refugees who could demonstrate Portuguese ancestry as "Third Nationals" were allowed by the Japanese to travel to Macau. The classification was used by the army's "Civil Administration Bureau" in January 1942 to identify 8,834 third nationals left in the occupied colony, of which 2,646 were Portuguese.[419] This number did not include a few thousand more Macanese who had received British citizenship before the war, others who had already escaped to Macau through China, or those incarcerated in the Shamsuipo prisoner camp in Hong Kong among 10,000 British and Scottish soldiers.[420]

Refugees in Macau

Resettlement was a difficult experience for most Macanese. Many had relatives in Macau or were descendants of those who remained in the Portuguese colony a century before. Among the estimated four thousand Macanese with Portuguese citizenship who traveled to Macau from Hong Kong, and possibly up to ten thousand more with British citizenship who managed to escape, it is estimated that about half stayed with grandparents, elderly aunts, distant cousins, and friends, who generously opened their homes to those displaced by the war.[421] Other exiles, many who left all their property and valuables behind, were housed in refugee centers set up by the Macau government and the Catholic Church in requisitioned clubs, hotels, schools, military barracks, and even on an abandoned ship in the harbor.[422]

The Bela Vista Hotel - Macau housed several hundred

Refugee operations were organized through the Santa Casa da Misericordia (The Holy House of Mercy), an institution founded by the Church and local elites in 1569. But essential services for the entire colony, including the provision of food and shelter, were provided by a private company under contract with the government called the "Macau Cooperative Company Limited". The MCC was the largest company in Macau, but in the midst of the conflict it took on a more complicated role, which began with its ownership by three partners: Pedro Jose Lobo, a leading Macau businessman and a key broker with the Japanese, an unidentified second group representing the colony's wealthiest families, and the Japanese army.[423]

Although not born in Macau, Pedro Lobo was inextricable linked to Macanese history even before the war. Lobo's family traced Macanese migrations throughout the Portuguese colonies. Born in Manatuto Timor in 1892, Lobo was adopted at birth by Belarmino Lobo, a Goan of Portuguese and Indian descent. In 1920 Pedro married Branca Helena Hyndman, a Macan-

ese woman from a prominent Hong Kong family, whose roots were Portuguese, Dutch, and Chinese. Shortly after the wedding, the Lobos returned briefly to Timor for the birth of their first child in November 1920, then settled in Lourenço Macau in 1921 to raise five more children through the early 1930s. Pedro Lobo's central role as the director of Macau's Central Bureau of Economic Services and his success as the government's chief negotiator with the Japanese during the war resulted in his being named an "Honorary Citizen of Macau" in 1946.[424]

Lobo's young secretary was Stanley Ho, another mixed-race descendent of a Dutch-Chinese family from Hong Kong, and the grandnephew of Sir Robert Ho Tung, an investor in the MCC. Stanley Ho was later granted a monopoly for gaming in post-war Macau, which he parlayed into a casino and real estate empire. In an interview about his war-time experience, Ho explained MCC's unusual relationship with the Japanese in this way:

> *The Portuguese government supplied us (MCC) with all the surplus they could afford to give away – tug boats, launches, telephone equipment, anything they could part with – and I exchanged all that with the Japanese authorities, in the name of the company, for food from the Mainland. We supplied flour and rice, beans, oil, sugar, all the necessities to support Macao because the Portuguese government wasn't very wealthy, and they had to get all these supplies from the Mainland.*[34]

Such partnerships were not unusual for the "neutral" Portuguese regime, and extended to unoccupied Macau.[425] According to U.S. government records, during the war Portugal bargained extensively for rice, supplied tungsten and gasoline to the Japanese army in exchange for allowing Macau to remain unoccupied, then was permitted to allow Allied use of the Azores, and was involved in the laundering of German gold through Lisbon and Macau.[426] The conflicted interests those associations suggest not only Portugal's pragmatic war-time policies, but also concessions made in light of the conditions that were about to unfold in Macau.[427]

A significant issue was that the services offered by the MCC were selective, and had little effect on the mass of people who were seeking asylum. The flow of refugees actually began a few years before the war. Following the outbreak of the Sino-Japanese war in 1937, Hong Kong's population swelled from about 400,000 to 1.6 million by 1941.[428] In those years, it is estimated that 650,000 refugees fled the mainland. The great majority were Chinese escaping the Japanese army, many fearing atrocities that had occurred earlier in Nanking (Nanjing) and then in Hong Kong during the occupation. As a result, Macau's pre-war population of about 160,000 increased to over 600,000 during the war, which included many refugees who arrived from Hong Kong, Shanghai, and other regions of China.

Chinese refugees who managed to escape the onslaught of the Japanese army, largely unsupported by the Allies and forced to live in the close confines of Macau, were met with a series of calamities. A U.S. Naval embargo in early 1942 blocked supplies from the sea, and created a flourishing black market, especially for rice and other scarce resources. Under these conditions, the MCC in partnership with the Japanese army was delegated the authority to distribute most commodities. The arrangement was ripe for abuse. Journalist-historian Chan Tai-pak observed:

> *In this period of shortages of grain and other necessities, a small number of collaborators seized the opportunity to buy up and hoard food, making the situation even worse. This caused a scenario unprecedented in Macao – famine: an uncountable number of people crying piteously for food.*[429]

Supply shortages, cold weather, inadequate shelter, and a lack of medicine soon overwhelmed the colony, leading to mounting death tolls. There are some accounts of people selling their children to survive, and even cannibalism.[430] Macau's streets were reported to be littered with bodies during the early years of the war, and regularly sprayed with chemicals in an attempt to control the spread of disease. Reports of mass burials on Taipa, a neighboring island, of up to 400 bodies a day began to surface, leading to post-war estimates of 50,000 deaths during the war years.[431] The Macau police sequestered many of the survivors in camps, which Chan described as "… like prisons – poorly equipped, with low-quality food and stern discipline." Many more died there. By the summer of 1942, thanks to funds donated by overseas Chinese, 17,000 refugees were repatriated to Free China.[432]

The Routines of Life during the War

Despite the tragic circumstances, the Macanese refugee centers proved to be havens from the war, offering simple, and at times tedious, routines. But everything had a price. The nearly bankrupt government of Macau provided a meager $25,000 MOP ($3,130 USD) for the entire resettlement of refugees.[433] Macanese refugees were given a small monthly allotment and a line of credit equaling $4,500 MOP ($563

USD) while in Macau, which they could use for food and other living expenses.[434] Britain provided stipends directly to their refugees ranging from $30 to $120 MOP ($3.76 to $15 USD) monthly. Many American companies based in Hong Kong provided additional funds to maintain their employees in Macau. Most Macanese families pooled their rations and handed over the monthly allotments to center chiefs who organized menus to supplement their meager diets of rice, and occasionally vegetables, fruit, and powered milk.[435]

The Bela Vista Hotel, with about 300 refugees, became the leading center because of its well equipped kitchen. As a young refugee, Armando da Silva recalled that many meals were distributed from the Bela Vista to some of the smaller centers, including Armacao and the Escola Luso-Chinesa. Other centers, like the Caixa Escolar, received their rations from the Salesian Brothers in Macau.[436] Arnaldo de Oliveira Sales noted that "Once a month, each of the families went along to the collection point and was given a ration of so much flour, so much rice, so many catties of sugar, and so forth, according to the size of the family. ..." Each refugee facility elected a "Center Chief", the majority of whom were men, with the exception of Mrs. Alzira Alvares Xavier, chief of the center housed on the Tung Hui ship.[437] Each center was in charge of organizing meals and resolving disputes, and collectively decided where and when to allocate the scarce resources, often of poor quality, provided by the MCC.[438]

Besides food and shelter, a major priority was the education of young people, which had been cut short by the invasion. In late 1942, the Macau government, with the financial support of Pedro Lobo, requested the transport of several Irish Jesuits from Wah Yan College in Hong Kong to establish the St. Luis Gonzaga College for Boys in Macau. Soon after Italian Canossian nuns from St. Rosa de Lima high school in Hong Kong arrived to teach the girls.[439] The Japanese approved both requests because of Ireland's neutral status and Italy's membership in the Axis troika. The first classes began in January 1943, housed in buildings set aside by Lobo, and were open to Macanese, Chinese, Indian, and Eurasian students, as well as adults. The curriculum included mathematics, science, and the classics, and instruction in accounting, bookkeeping, and Chinese language studies. Each year through June 1945 about 200 boys and girls attended classes, and several more adults learned new skills.[440]

The Jesuits and Canossians were also instrumental in creating diversions for the refugees. Several priests and nuns organized lectures, one act plays, musical comedies, and more elaborate theatrical productions. One of the largest, called "The Path of the King", involved several acts and a large choir singing in Latin. Several other plays were written by individuals with professional training, and performed by dozens of performers. Playbills were produced on rough paper, printed on materials "liberated" from public toilets. Musical performances, dances and sporting events were also attractions, especially field hockey and softball among the Macanese.

Many activities provided opportunities for young men and women who were usually segregated before the war to mix under the "communal" conditions in Macau.[441] Such conditions led to romances with resident Macanese, who had little contact with those outside Macau. According to Armando da Silva, several refugee women married local men during the war. Since the Macanese from Hong Kong spoke little Portuguese, dating sometimes relied on both partners' knowledge of "Maquista", the Macanese patois, which was banned in Macau's schools, but was still spoken in Macau on the street and among expatriates in Hong Kong.[442] Two of da Silva's older sisters, Elsa and Delia, married local Macanese men, communicating during their courtships in Maquista. Da Silva, considered a "curator" of the patois within the community, suggests that the language may have been preserved and enhanced by the blending of Hong Kong and Macau "Maquista" during this period.[443]

Generally, for those who were not Chinese in Macau during the war, life under these conditions seemed almost normal.

People from different locations and cultural backgrounds were virtually thrown together in the Portuguese enclave as they waited out the conflict.[444] Restaurants, cafes, casinos, brothels, and opium dens remained open, in many cases flourishing because of the cash being spent by Japanese soldiers, gangsters, government officials, and opportunists who were involved in black market trade. Local radio stations offered daily news, and newspapers in Portuguese, Chinese, English and Japanese continued to print. Journalists and reporters, themselves refugees from Hong Kong and China, published stories that were heavily censored by the military police. Even the international cable, the only link to Europe and America, continued to operate. Despite the obvious dangers, the close of proximity of ethnic communities inside Macau required that they had to work together as a matter of survival.[445] As an observer wrote later:

> We lived pretty much in isolation from the outside world. Life went on, the civil service worked, and the machinery of government went on under beneficent leadership in difficult conditions. But we never forgot that the Japanese were just outside Macao, occupying China.[446]

The War Comes to Macau

The war often intruded in unexpected ways. In January 1945, Allied intelligence received reports from local operatives that the Japanese were storing fuel and other supplies at Macau's airport in a pre-war PAN-AM hangar. This proved technically inaccurate, since most of the supplies belonged to Pedro Lobo, the director of the MCC. During the first raid, Roger Lobo, his twenty-one year old son, hurried to the facility to check on a large stockpile of surplus goods he and his father had set aside for sale on the black market. After the planes made their first pass, the younger Lobo recounted:

> *I rushed down to see what was going on and the planes turned round and came back. I had my motorbike right at the door of the hangar and my father zoomed up behind me in his car. They (the planes) didn't just shoot at the hangar, they shot at the cars, the motorbike, everything. We started running all over the place, we hadn't bargained on that happening. Then the whole thing went up in flames. I saw my father running away ... but his car was shot out. Amazingly, neither of us was wounded.*[447]

The Lobos had extensive relations with both Allied and Axis sources, often negotiating to trade goods for rice, the most coveted and rationed commodity in Macau. They also obtained rice on their own. The Lobos originally acquired the raw grain from suppliers over Chinese border, then processed it using an old generator and a diesel engine the younger Lobo had found in the naval dockyard. Their surplus was stored in the large hangars at the PAN-AM depot. Everything else they could find, trade, barter, or obtain by other means was also secured there. The goods included gasoline, church bells, metal frames, wire, nails ... "anything we could get our hands on", the younger Lobo explained to the interviewer years later.

The Lobos' relationship with both sides in the war was not unusual. The younger Lobo and other members of the family worked periodically with British intelligence, even while his father exchanged goods with the Japanese.[448] The senior Lobo, even while apparently profiting from the sale of surplus goods on the black market, was heavily involved in Macanese education, including as noted earlier, helping to set up schools for refugees. Other Eurasians had similar seemingly conflicting relations, a historical legacy as colonial "intermediaries".[449] Stanley Ho, the future casino king of Macau, described how as the English instructor to Japanese *Kempeitai* (military police) chief, Colonel Sawa, he was able to barter brass shells for three ship loads of rice.[450] As the war was coming to a close, Ho used his contacts to start a trading company that earned him over a million Hong Kong dollars (by his own estimate), with which he purchased his first Macau casino after hostilities ended.[451] During the greatest conflict of the twentieth century, the opportunities to some seemed too good to pass up. As Ho recounted:

> *In those days, if you had money, you could enjoy the best kind of cigarettes, American, British, right up to the end of the war. If you had money, you could carry on using motorcars and motorbikes all through the war – gasoline was available. And you could have excellent food – if you had the money. I had big parties almost every night. ...* [452]

The demands of survival led others to improvise as best as they could. Some refugees interviewed recount selling family jewelry and furniture for food.[453] Felicia Yap writes that many who remained in Hong Kong during the occupation often collected scrap iron and other metals that they sold to the Japanese to make ends meet.[454] Others were more seriously involved, helping the Japanese purchase ships from the Dutch, or working directly with the Japanese secret police or the Chief Censor in Macau.[455]

Many Macanese, however, played important roles in support of the Allied war effort. Several young refugees, including Guido Sequeira (photo), worked as bodyguards for British Consul John Reeves and his family in Macau during a period when assassinations of Japanese, Portuguese, and Macanese officials were frequent.[456] But despite the best intentions, Sequeira and others received little training and had to rely on inferior equipment. As he recalled during an interview:

> *The day I was hired, the Japanese Consul, Yasumitsu Fukui, had just been assassinated (February 1945). We were on alert and spent the night on the roof of the British Consul to protect him. The next morning, I remember the chief guard saw (one of the*

bodyguards) with a gun, and asked: "Where did you get those guns from? They don't have any firing pins." We were stunned. None of us knew anything about firing a gun, or anything about the guns themselves. We later learned that the ammunition was also defective.[457]

Sequeira also drove Mr. Reeves' American wife on errands, and ferried rescued American flyers between locations to avoid detection by Kempeitai spies.

Other Hong Kong-based Macanese offered support to an underground group called the "East River Column" (ERC) that was led by Chinese Communists. The ERC also operated radio stations in Hong Kong's New Territories, and on Lantau Island. Separately, a clandestine radio operating out of the Salesian School in Macau relayed messages to British Intelligence (M19) and the Nationalist Chinese.[458]

M19 was shorthand for the "British Army Aid Group" (BAAG), an organization started by Lindsay Ride, an Australian physiologist who taught at the University of Hong Kong before the war. Ride's group, which included Alberto Ozorio, Dr. Horacio Ozario, and Dr. Eduardo Gosano (photo), was instrumental in collecting information from sources in China, Hong Kong, and inside Macau, as well as maintaining contacts with Chinese operatives in Hong Kong and the mainland. Gosano eventually replaced Ride as head of the unit when the latter escaped to unoccupied China in 1944, and operated BAAG using his extensive knowledge of the region and his contacts with local partisans.[459] Macanese operatives also organized prisoner escapes from Japanese camps and rescued British and American flyers shot down in China. Other Macanese worked with the American Office of Strategic Services (OSS)

gathering intelligence in Macau.[460]

As the war began to wind down, the unique character displayed by the Macanese seemed to overcome many pre-war prejudices, especially those existing in Hong Kong. Despite a history of segregation and mistrust of the colonial government, ethnic divisions still did not prevent Macanese collaboration with the British and many other national groups that worked closely with the Allies in Macau. Questions of loyalty to the Allied cause were also diminished by the large numbers of Macanese who fought and died during the invasion, and many more who were interned.

To some extent, Winston Churchill signaled the shift in attitudes on both sides of the racial divide by appointing Leonardo d'Almada y Castro, the only Macanese on Hong Kong's Legislative Council, to a postwar planning committee following his escape to London in June 1945.[461] Most BAAG operatives also returned to Hong Kong and Macau to rebuild, some appointed to positions in government. Others, with some notable exceptions, moved almost seamlessly back into their lives in banking, trade, and the casino business.[462] But the war brought some changes among the Macanese that cannot be easily attributed to the Allied victory. For it is clear from personal accounts that the end of the war brought about a change in social attitudes and ethnic identities that would largely define the future of the Macanese community in the post-war years.

Conclusion: The Re-emergence of Macanese Identity

The end of World War II was in many ways a defining moment for the Macanese, especially for those who were refugees in Macau. As we saw previously, pre-war hierarchies that separated the Macanese from their colonial "superiors" in Hong Kong seemed less relevant in neutral Macau during the war. Despite living under hostile conditions, many Macanese played important roles in the war effort, including Alberto Ozorio, Dr. Horacio Ozario, and Dr. Eduardo Gosano, who were intensely involved with the British and Chinese undergrounds, while others used their contacts and language skills to circumvent Japanese embargos, the military police, and the Axis network of collaborators.

Even those straddling ethical lines as black market profiteers, such as Pedro Lobo and Stanley Ho, could help support the feeding and education of refugees while also flaunting their new status as "entrepreneurs" in local cafes for all to see. Under less pressure than in occupied Hong Kong, the Macanese exercised a high degree of autonomy in their ancestral home, many exhibiting purpose and resolve to defeat the common enemy, while redefining pre-war identities as colonial underlings by reverted to traditional roles as "intermediaries" between antagonists, who in some instances were forced to deal with them.

A similar kind of upheaval was occurring in other pre-war colonies. Throughout Southeast Asia during the war years, especially in Malaya, Singapore, the Philippines, and in Macau's sister colony Timor, the Allies depended on local populations for intelligence and armed resistance to prepare for their return in the future. Like the Macanese, many Eurasians asserted themselves in guerrilla groups and other clandestine efforts, undermining the occupying army, and holding fast until liberation. In the process, their sense of purpose (for who had more to lose?), sustained a new outlook on the world after the war.

If as historian Felicia Yap writes, the war highlighted the "tensions of empire" in Asia, the assertion of new roles and identities among racial minorities that occurred as a result may have been the final step in destabilizing Britain's and Portugal's already weak colonial systems. [463] The rise of "liberation" movements in former colonies in Asia, Africa, and Latin America through the end of the 20th century provide ample evidence that such changes in ideology have as much force as the deployment of weapons. The challenge to the Macanese during the period was best captured in an observation by Fr. Henry

O'Brien, the wartime head of the Jesuit community in Macau. Reggie Pires, one of O'Brien's students, recalls:

> ... I remember his words to this day. "You Portuguese boys have the best of both worlds. You have the minds of the Asian and the stamina of the Europeans. The problem with you is that you have accepted your place in this world. You are happy to spend your lives subservient to the British in Hong Kong.[464]

Many Macanese took the essence of Fr. O'Brien's reproach to heart. Most in the youngest generation were not content to be subservient any longer, especially after taking prominent roles in helping the Allies win the war. Many believed that they deserved to reap the benefits of the victory that they had achieved. Similar sentiments were shared by other minorities around the globe. Indeed, accounts of Japanese-American, African-American, and Latino-American soldiers who served with distinction were similar to the Macanese experience.[465]

Our vantage from many decades removed should not diminish the fact that, rather than exhibiting a sense of entitlement, such sentiments suggest deeply felt emotions and "debts" that were thought to be "owed" to those who reconsidered their own priorities during the war. As with other cultural minorities, many Macanese re-imagined their value to society, given their roles in the recent global crisis, and employed such attitudes to support perceptions of their own identity after the war.

Those reassessments led many returning to Hong Kong, Shanghai, and other regions to begin the process of leaving behind a painful past and looking to the future. As a result, many families eventually left Southeast Asia seeking new lives as immigrants in unfamiliar countries. Their ability to "break" from the past, however, proved more difficult, and followed the experiences of other exiled groups. For example, in research on the aftermath of the Armenian genocide, survivors similarly sought to move quickly beyond the pain of personal loss as a mechanism of individual survival. This led, in later generations, to a collective loss of confidence and optimism. Like them, the Macanese diaspora has had similar and often conflicting repercussions on survivors and their descendants. [466]

In my own research involving Macanese immigrants born before and after World War II, there is an acknowledgement that older relatives often avoided discussions of their past lives in order to accommodate themselves in new societies to which they migrated. The underlying and unspoken reality, however, may have been their collective "shame" of being traditionally slighted as racially-mixed colonials, often referred to as "inferior" or "subaltern" in historical accounts, with little knowledge of their own history to define themselves. (A contemporary explanation for the lack of information is included in the "Epilogue".)

This may be understandable if we consider that ecclesiastic and colonial administrations over five centuries elevated European values to high culture, while often diminishing Asian traditions as "pagan" and "barbaric". As a people somewhere "between" Europe and Asia with ancestors from both continents, there have been few attempts to understand Luso-Asians and other racially-mixed groups who occupy such cultural spaces.[467] In the case of the Macanese who survived World War II, many carried this cultural baggage for decades, in addition to suffering the personal loss of loved ones, property, social status, and dignity in the aftermath of a foreign invasion and diminished circumstances as refugees.

In many cases, it was only years later that children, grandchildren, and great-grandchildren born in the Post-war period who were interested in family histories began gathering documents, conducting informal interviews, creating genealogies, and obtaining DNA summaries. Only then did Macanese elders still living reluctantly begin to recount their war-time experiences in more detail. As in the case of other exiled groups, younger Macanese often discovered meticulously written accounts, photos, and other documentation that had been hidden by relatives, whose reluctance to acknowledge their heritage as "mestizos" underpinned deeply troubling memories of the war that were uncomfortable to recall, and often too painful to recount, even to members of their own families. [468]

Beginning in late 1945, many Macanese who were unwilling to live and work in the confines of the old colonies started a four decade long migration to western countries, including to the United States, Canada, Australia, Brazil, and Portugal.[469] Their exodus in the post-war period and their reconnection to Macau in the 21st century is the subject of the final section.

Epilogue
The Last Migration

The end of World War II in September 1945, and the return of many Macanese from exile in Macau, led to a resumption of conflicts in mainland China between the Nationalists under Chiang Kai-shek and the Communists directed by Mao Zedong. The civil war resulted in one of the largest movement of people ever into Hong Kong. According to researchers at the University of Hong Kong and the United Nations, the colony's population grew from 600,000 in 1945, to 1.8 million in 1947, to 3 million by 1961, to over 4 million in 1974, over a six fold increase since the war.[470]

Although these movements were attempts to flee the conflict in China, many migrants also provided cheap labor and changed the post-war economy in Asia.[471] In Hong Kong the surge of humanity placed great pressure on the government to find refugee housing, while safeguarding the health of the local population and continue to provide services to the young and elderly.[472] In the absence of a timely response, a massive resettlement program was organized in the 1950s by international relief agencies and local organizations to provide food, shelter, and medical aid to thousands who resettled on Hong Kong Island, the Kowloon peninsula, and on 200 outer islands that made up the colony.[473] The inability to meet the demand in the first years resulted in numerous protests, while makeshift shanty towns suffered from fires, landslides during the rainy season, cholera outbreaks, and increased crime.[474]

The influx of Chinese only added to the fears of the Macanese and others who survived the war. The Japanese invasion and the evacuation to Macau caused many young members of the community to question their futures in Asia, especially whether the benefits enjoyed by their parents would continue for them and their children after the war.[475] That seemed unlikely due to the erosion of trust among non-British citizens in the Hong Kong government since the early 20th century.[476] As a result, many Luso-Asians prepared to leave the colony for the Americas, the British Commonwealth, and Western Europe, enticed by films, the promise of political freedom, and new opportunities offered by the expanding post-war economy. Continued instability in Hong Kong, Shanghai, and Macau marked the beginning of the next movement of Macanese.

The migration focused on the United States, Canada, Australia, Brazil, and Portugal beginning in late 1945. It continued as social unrest following the Communist revolution of 1949 pushed China's development, then settled after a normalization of relations with the west began with Richard Nixon's talks with Mao in 1974. The last phase began in early 1982 when Deng Xiaoping attempted to clarify the future relation of Hong Kong and Macau to China by suggesting the concept of "one country, two systems", in which both territories would be designated as "Special Administrative Regions" (SAR) to take advantage of their traditional contacts with the west, and were granted relative autonomy until 2049.[477] As a result, Hong Kong, territories on the Kowloon peninsula, and several local islands were returned to China in June 1997. Macau and the islands of Taipa and Coloane were transferred in December 1999.

Macanese Diaspora in the 21st Century

Since the "handovers" of Hong Kong and Macau to China, a significant reorganization of resources has taken place in both SARs. Shortly after the two-system strategy was fully implemented in early 2000, China began using Hong Kong as a commercial conduit to English speaking countries, due to its previous ties to England. International banking corporations, many with offices already in Hong Kong, were invited to begin new relations with their Chinese counterparts.[478] Following its own history, Macau was projected by China to be an international gaming center and as the gateway to Latin countries, specifically among Portuguese and Spanish speaking countries. In 2003 a new organization designed for this purpose was created called "The Forum for Economic and Trade Co-operation between China and Portuguese-speaking Countries", also known as the "Macao Forum". As of 2018, China has invested over $147 billion in the organization. [479]

Over the next two decades, Hong Kong grew into the third largest financial center in the world (behind London and New York) and an international model of stability and commerce, despite a series of protests in 2014 and 2019 that began slowing the local economy.[480] In Macau, following the expiration of gaming concessions in 2002 for Stanley Ho and others, China invited American, Australian, and Chinese companies to build new casinos on the islands of Taipa and Macau.[481] Six lavish gaming and entertainment venues opened between 2004 and 2010, and the construction of more than thirty others continues to this day.[482] Gaming revenues in Macau have since overtaken traditional venues in the United States, with current proceeds reported as five times greater than Las Vegas.[483] While corruption scandals in 2014-5 in Macau and the Covid-19 virus delayed growth, China also added Macau and Hong Kong to a new project called "The Greater Bay Area (GBA)", a large economic zone that currently includes Macau, Hong Kong, the cities of Shenzhen and Guangzhou, and the provinces of Guangdong, Hengquin, and Zhuhai, focusing on technology, environmental industries, research, and higher education.[484]

Institutionalizing the Macanese Diaspora

As gaming dominated Macau's economy and pressures from Beijing increased to diversify into other industries, a different kind of dynamic has begun to take shape: a search for cultural identity among the dwindling Macanese community.[485] A key organization in this search led by local "Maquistas" (Luso-Asians named for the patois), which works closely with cultural institutions, is the *Conselho das Communicades Macaenses*.[486] The CCM was created in 2001 to fund and advise several international associations called "Casas de Macau".[487] These associations are part of the CCM's mission to cultivate relations with Macanese who migrated to other countries, and to bring them and other relatives back to Macau for tourism, and potentially for professional exchanges.

The roots of the CCM's mission go back over a decade before Macau's 1999 handover to China. Several interviews with observers and participants conducted in Macau and the United States indicate the organization's role.[488] During early negotiations in 1986 the Portuguese heads of Macau's government, who were prominent members of the Maquista minority, negotiated "golden parachute" deals with the Chinese government to insure an easier transition between governments in exchange for preserving Macanese culture and maintaining the employment of local Portuguese after the handover.

The means to achieve these goals were a portion of gaming revenues, which were intended to preserve the cultural history of the territory through the restoration of old buildings, ancient architectural and religious sites, historical materials, and archival media, as well as to support pet projects which the former government leaders would manage going forward.[489]

The preservation activities included greater Maquista involvement in Macau's *Instituto Cultural de Macau*, founded in September 1982 and since renamed "The Cultural Affairs Bureau", which became the centerpiece of a large program. Since then, multiple buildings and squares have been restored, an archive and a modern central library opened in 1993, and a local museum was built in 1998. These efforts culminated in the designation of Macau's Historic Centre as a world heritage site by UNESCO in 2005.[490]

The Maquistas also convinced the Chinese government to retain Portuguese as one of two "official languages" (along with Mandarin) so that Macau's administration would continue functioning after the transition to Chinese rule, as well as to retain the employment and pensions of Portuguese staff. The retention of Portuguese strengthened ties to continental Portugal by maintaining local language schools and college programs previously supported by the government. Another initiative was continued funding of benevolent, educational, and research associations headed by Macanese, of which CCM is the most prominent, and the support of the expatriate "Casas" in other countries.[491]

Thus the "Macanese Diaspora" was officially recognized by the Chinese government through CCM's support of *"Casas de Macau"* (Houses of Macau) in several cities in which large numbers of Macanese families settled. Each association began receiving annual funding in 2002 and is governed by the CCM board of directors in Macau. Overseeing this council is a government foundation through which a percentage of gaming revenue is distributed as regular subsidies, called the *"Fundacao Macau"*. Also based in Macau, and staffed by locals and mainland Chinese, the foundation distributes funds in the form of grants to local associations and annual payments to "permanent" and "non-permanent" Macau residents.[492] The foundation's annual budget is estimated to be 1% to 3% of Macau's gaming revenues to support activities in Macau.[493]

Quid Pro Quo

In exchange for the institutionalization of Macau's legacy through preservation, language, and funded associations, local leaders pledged their political support to Chinese officials after the handover and their influence among the Portuguese population in Macau. They also offered to maintain and cultivate ongoing relations with international Macanese who migrated to other countries. This fit nicely with China's outreach efforts begun under Deng Xiao Ping through his "One country, Two systems" approach, continued under Hu Jin Toa from 2002 through 2012, and was later expanded by Xi Jing Ping in 2013 through an initiative called "One Belt, One Road".[494]

Unreported during the 1999 handover ceremonies, however, is an important issue that was apparently understood by the Chinese, but never plainly stated in the protocols negotiated in 1986. This was a tacit agreement that CCM's external relations would continue among succeeding generations of international Macanese to explore commercial linkages to Macau, especially in the United States and Europe where multinational corporations are headquartered.[495] The expectation among the Chinese was that the *Conselho das Communicades Macaense* would assist the new Macau government, through their management of the *Casas de Macau*, in diversifying and expanding the regional economy through international outreach in preparation for Beijing's 21st century programs, including the "Greater Bay Area" project.

Despite the apparatus and financial resources that could connect Macau to this bright future, Macanese leaders in Macau have struggled to define their own historical legacy, while attempting to identify the community's role in China's geo-political agenda. The CCM, the Cultural Affairs Bureau, and the Macao Government Tourism Office, have together implemented and supported a well-funded program to preserve a version of local history that securely ties Macau's economy to cultural tourism as the principal alternative to gaming, without addressing future business development. This has been achieved by maintaining historical appearances through the renovation of colonial buildings and historic sites, the preservation of archives and materials, the publication of reviews and books, and investment in research institutions through regular grants.

Notably absent is research being conducted by the Cultural Affairs Bureau that is kept private and not available to the public. The accumulated material and historical data would likely contribute to a better understanding of Macau's history, culture, and colonial legacy, and would be welcomed by local and international scholars.[496] Surprisingly, the details of Macau's history are neither shared nor taught in local schools. In fact, a review of curricula in Macau from 2013 through 2019 determined that very few courses were offered in Macanese history, anthropology, or ethnic diversity by local colleges and universities.[497] Few peer-reviewed articles or books in these subject areas have been published inside Macau, nor has much historical research been available to academic or general audiences since 2009.[498] As a result, periodic cultural events and the physical presence of local Maquistas have become little more than the "window dressing" of the government's preservation program, which offers only an outline of Macau's significant role in world history to tourists and the general public.

The outreach component of CCM's mission, which again was intended to support China's international initiatives, is also beginning to suffer. This involves the organization of *"Encontros"* (meetings) funded by the *Fundacao Macau* since 2001 directed toward international *"Casa de Macau"* members who have been encouraged to visit Macau every three years.[499] These meetings often involve elaborate dinners, receptions, lectures, visits to historical sites, photo opportunities and interviews with the local press, side travel to mainland China, and stipends to Casa presidents to encourage attendance. Older expatriates, many who left Macau, Hong Kong, and Shanghai between 1945 and 1980, have been the principal targets of these nostalgic campaigns, receiving small discounts for travel and accommodations.

The flaw in this strategy has been the *Encontros'* promotion to elder *Casa* members and an emphasis on "reconnecting" with Macau, rather than also utilizing familial ties to leverage professional connections among younger relatives in other countries. The issue apparently involves an unchecked abundance of funding. The budgets for the governing *Conselho* (CCM), which support annual salaries, international travel, staffing, building maintenance, and logistics between *Encontro* meetings, have grown steadily along with Macau's gaming revenue.[500] The target audience of the *Encontros*, however, has gradually declined as *Casa de Macau* members in the diaspora are typically over 60 years of age, retired and no longer working, and travel less frequently due to declining health.[501]

While *Conselho* leaders in Macau and international Casa de Macau directors enthusiastically promote the week long *Encontro* events, some now admit to an inability to involve second and third generation members in the cultural visits. There apparently is an awareness that young descendants are important, but no one seems to accept responsibility for the falling numbers. As Leonel Alves, President of CCM's General Council stated in 2019:

> *The Macanese of the so-called new generation will be able to discover Macau as a lever for the Mainland of China and for this region of the world ... ."* As for the inclusion of younger members, Alves continues: *"I think it's very difficult. It is not an easy task, ... It is the function of the Macau Houses (the Casas) ... to transmit the Macanese culture and this feeling of connection ... ."* [502]

There are also reports from attendees that *Encontro* organizers often disregard inquiries from international members who seek information about regional commerce or business opportunities.[503] This apathy is borne out by the lack of *Encontro* invitations to Macanese currently working in technology companies, finance, banking, healthcare, manufacturing, higher education, pharmaceuticals, bio-tech, and venture capital, who may be interested in both cultural and commercial exchanges. Virtually no effort, moreover, has been made to involve local Macanese professionals, a target of China's "Greater Bay Area" initiative, who speak multiple languages and are likely to be interested in these contacts.

Missing the Big Picture

The inability of Macanese leaders to include business professionals in tourism suggests a narrow focus on nostalgic visits at the expense of long term commercial development. Just as authentic sites in Macau, such the ruins of St. Paul's Cathedral, attract more tourists than the casinos or other "fake historical" venues, professional audiences will likely be attracted to the potential opportunities that cultural tourism offers in the much larger "Greater Bay Area".[504] This may become more significant as Hong Kong, China's other Special Administrative Region, slowly recovers from the "Umbrella" protests and the Covid-19 virus.[505] Macau, seemingly immune to political strife and also emerging from the pandemic, may be the best hope to keep at least one of the "Western Gateways" to China functioning as expected.

The indifference to new business in Macau may also undermine the Macanese relationship to China in general. For as long as China looks to Macau for cultural and commercial connections, the Macanese, now under a new Chief Executive, Ho Iat Seng, soon may be forced to demonstrate adherence to China's larger agenda or suffer the consequences. In a worst case scenario, the inability of locals to learn their own history and to involve new generations in Macau's recovery through tourism and professional connections may ultimately lead to their own cultural marginalization, and hasten their incorporation into the Chinese mainstream.

As Antonio Jose' de Freitas, an association leader suggested, there is concern that because local history is not taught in schools, Macanese identity is in danger of evaporating.[506] Local scholars also have not been silent. Professor George Wei, the former Director of the Department of History at the University of Macau, commenting on a general lack of professionalism in Macau, suggested that the skill of 19th century Macanese traders to connect international partners in a new global economy could well provide a model for the future.[507] After two decades since the handover, a lack of action may no longer be acceptable, and a new strategy may be necessary.

Rediscovering New Generations

Such a strategy should begin with better information about Macanese who will likely be participants in future cultural and commercial exchanges. A study to gather this data is currently being conducted by my research group at the University of California, Berkeley. We began the process by attempting to determine who they are demographically, where they live, to estimate the size of the international population through familial connections, and learn how they identify themselves culturally. We are also learning how international Macanese reconnect with Macau in the present. Clearly, occasional visits to China may be impractical for some. There may be other ways to remain in contact with the culture, including using social and visual media or joining an international association, that draw new generations and allow them to overcome logistical and generational barriers.

The Survey

The vehicle for gathering this data is named the "Far East Currents Macanese Survey", which was introduced in April 2019 and **remains active**. The purpose is to represent within statistical parameters the current status of the Portuguese from Macau, including those who live in and outside Asia. Due to the nature of their migrations, an effort was made to gather responses from many countries and across several digital media platforms.

The 2019 edition is based on others distributed in 2012, 2013, and 2017, which were conducted with the assistance of ten "Casa de Macau" organizations in different countries that provided access to their membership lists. The latest survey utilizes social media more extensively and is refined into 10 key questions to gather demographic information (age, location, family size), evidence of cultural identity, and determine family ties to specific locations based on past research. The new survey also asks about methods of staying connected using digital media, the interest of respondents in international business and cultural travel, and their willingness to share personal histories with researchers.

Who are they?

Past research based on interviews and e-mail contact found that many Portuguese descendants around the world are working professionals in business, technology, medicine, finance, law, bio-medical research, venture capital, and education. Other respondents in the generation born after WWII are now retired, while many of their grandchildren and great-grandchildren are students in higher education. In contrast to the 2012 and 2013 surveys, however, the 2019 survey found over 65% are working age adults (19-64), as compared to 70% of respondents in previous years who were retired (65 or older). This may be related to the distribution of previous surveys by e-mail, while the latest survey used both e-mail and social media, the latter of which was not widely used by Macanese before. The recent results may also mean that younger generations are becoming more aware of their cultural and familial ties to Macau. The chart below illustrates the generational divide.

THE MACANESE CHRONICLES

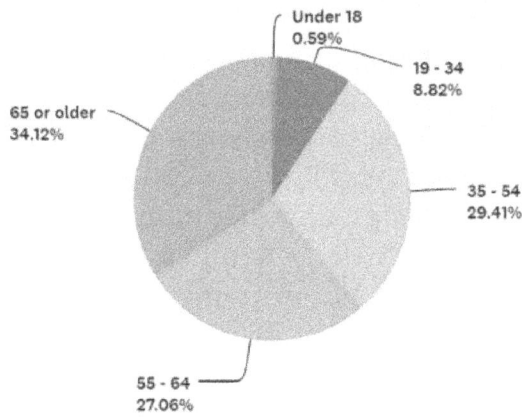

Where are they now?

Another recent finding is that while almost 66% live in the United States, over 24% live in Canada, Australia, and Europe (mostly Portugal), and 9% live in Southeast Asia, including Japan, the Philippines, Macau, and Hong Kong. As the map below illustrates, the dispersion of descendants suggests that the "Macanese Diaspora" remains truly global.

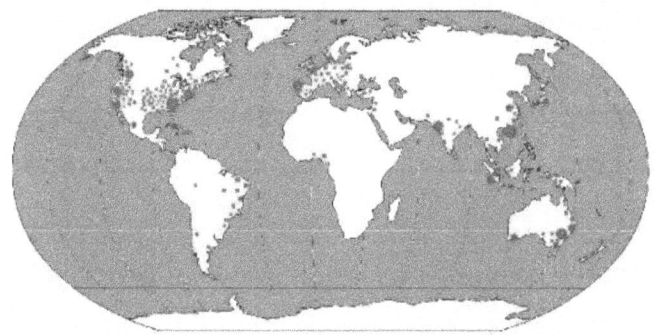

How do they identify themselves culturally?

The cultural identity of this community seems to be predominantly Macanese and Eurasian, that is, a racially mixed culture of Portuguese, Macanese, and mixed Europeans. When asked the question: "To Which Cultural Group do You Identify Most?" choosing only one response, 59% answered "Macanese",

23% stated "Eurasian", 15% responded "Portuguese", while an equal number of respondents answered "Chinese" (7%) and "European" (7%). One explanation for the wide dispersal of identities may be that while many respondents identify with the culture of Macau, a significant group also acknowledge present adopted nationalities. This may be an admission of multiculturalism that exists in many families, which closely follows the historic openness of Macau to many ethnic groups, some who arrived as traders, clerics, and merchants in its earliest days, while others were servants, soldiers, escaped slaves, and domestics in later years. Despite being second, third, and in a few cases fourth generation expatriates, the strong identification as Macanese from Macau seems to have been transferred to a majority of the community despite their migration to over 35 countries around the world.

Where have they been, in terms of migratory history?

A related question about the countries and regions from which ancestors originated was asked to determine the migratory paths of individual families. Based on the results, 73% stated they had family ties to Macau, 63% were linked to Hong Kong, 54% had ancestors from Portugal, and 32% had family from Shanghai. Significantly, more than 27% also had ancestors from Goa, Canton, Japan, Malaysia, Singapore, and Timor. These results suggest that a majority have ancestors that followed distinct migratory routes, which corroborates past research that the Portuguese from Asia traveled over a 500 year period from Portugal and settled in western India, Southeast Asia, and most recently in western countries.

How many are they?

This is a key question of the survey. Rather than simply ask for the total number of people in a household, based on past research we theorized that family size and extended connections are important features of this culture. So, we asked: "How many living relatives do you estimate are in your immediate and extended family?" This question allows us to estimate the total population of the Portuguese from Macau based on Genealogist Jorge Forjaz's 1996 and 2017 studies of 60,000 Macanese divided among 500 families.[508] We thus sought to determine the size of family groups in order to estimate the total population of the global community by blending the survey data with Forjaz's research from several archives in Portugal, Macau, Goa, Malaysia, and Timor.

Again, we found some surprising results. The average size of family groups from the survey is 56.5 people, while 14.2% of families counted more than 150 relatives in which they were in contact. We then adjusted for the statistical deviation and controlled for multiple responses from the same family. Joining the survey with the genealogical data resulted in an estimate of 1.687 million Portuguese from Macau in the "Macanese Diaspora". While this is only an estimate, it follows other population estimates from multi-generational populations, including the descendants of 17th century Mayflower settlers (1620) in the United States.[509]

How do they remain in contact today?

Another question is how such a far-flung population not only continues to share a common culture, but asked about the methods they use to stay connected. This is another development that contrasts with responses from surveys in 2012 and 2013 when social media was not widely used. In the early studies, the means of contact were through e-mail, visits to websites, telephone, and in-person meetings. In the 2019 survey nearly all respondents used social media, many on multiple platforms for different purposes. For example, over 89% use Facebook accounts for personal connections. More than 67% also use digital messaging services such as WeChat, WhatsApp, and Viber, and almost 34% have LinkedIn accounts for professional and personal communications. Almost 62% also use Snap, Instagram, and Twitter for leisure and entertainment.

The importance of social media usage by this community cannot be overstated. Due to the ubiquity of smartphones and other mobile internet devices, social media connections have proliferated over the last decade. Among Portuguese descendants from Asia, a number of Facebook sites, for example, are dedicated to different cultural elements, such as food, history, language, social commentary, nostalgic photographs, personal family histories, religion, music, and popular theatre. The number social media sites dedicated to the Portuguese from Asia increased from three (3) in 2013 to twenty-five (25) 2019. Many have a few hundred members, while some have a few thousand.

The actual number social media connections can be lost if not fully understood. Following current industry measures, if a member on any one social site "likes" or "shares" any single post, the original post will appear on the timelines of each of that member's "friends" or contacts. According to recent studies, the average Facebook user has 338 contacts.[510] The number of connections increases exponentially each time any of these users "likes", "shares", comments, or otherwise responds to a post, increasing the number of connections by the second or third tier into the millions. While this is probably a generational phenomenon for younger respondents, the use of social media among 65% of working adults (19-64) to stay culturally connected to relatives and friends may be a major reason why descendants of Portuguese from Asia can remain in close contact across national borders.

International Contact and Personal Histories

We also asked about the interest of respondents in international relations and cultural travel. We learned that about 38% had relatives who work in companies that do business with China. In a follow up question, however, 57% expressed an interest in learning about international business opportunities and cultural travel related to Macau. This may be suggestive of how working adults (19-64) in the community now view their roles, by seeking opportunities to learn and interact with other cultures. Their responses also suggest that younger generations may have adopted a global perspective on their current and past relations with Asia given their family histories. This is in contrast to responses of earlier generations who expressed much less interest in these forms of contact.

The survey concluded by asking respondents their interest in contributing materials and documentation to the present research study conducted at U.C. Berkeley. A majority (54%) not only expressed interest in contributing family documents and materials, but many added their e-mail addresses for future contact. This is no doubt an important step in insuring that others in their families, given the trend toward large connected groups, will contribute their personal stories, materials, and data in the future.

Final Thoughts on the End of a Journey

This contemporary profile provides a fitting conclusion to our study on the history of the Macanese community. We will recall that our narrative journey began with a discussion of the origins in Goa, and followed succeeding migrations over 500 years through India, Southeast Asia, Australia, Europe, and the Americas. Along the way we discussed how early Luso-Asians and their Macanese descendants maintained relations and expanded trade to new regions, taking on intermediary roles as colonial empires in Asia and Europe rose and eventually retreated.

We also discussed Macanese contributions to the distribution of information and knowledge about China through printing enterprises, which became a focal point for international commerce in the early 19th century. In a period before telegraphy, telephony, and wireless radio reached Asia, printing became an important pillar of the global economy well into the 20th century. As relations between Asian and western countries evolve in the 21st century, we may also see that this history and Macau's cultural legacy are recognized as attractive additions to a regional economy beginning to recover from a global pandemic.

In the end, by presenting the multiple sides of Luso-Asian history and cultural development, my hope is that this study will lead to others in the field. Contributing to that legacy is ultimately the purpose and the promise of any research in this area. However that research proceeds, it is likely that stories about the "Portuguese from Asia" will continue to be told and passed on to new generations. There are few narratives, in all the diverse elements of ethnic studies, that have fascinated me more for so many years.

Notes and Bibliography

[1] Some information was adopted from local legends and from a study by Cathryn H. Clayton, Sovereignty at the Edge: Macau & the Question of Chineseness, Harvard University Press, 2009:41.

[2] Louise Levathes, When China Ruled the Seas: The Treasure Fleets of the Dragon Throne, 1405 – 1433, Oxford University Press, 1994.

[3] John E. Wills, Jr. China and Maritime Europe, 1500–1800: Trade, Settlement, Diplomacy, and Missions. Cambridge University Press, 2010.

[4] J.M. Braga, The Western Pioneers and Their Discovery of Macao, Instituto Portugues de Hongkong, Macau, 1949: 109-110. See also CA Montalto, Historic Macau, University of Macau, 1906:25

[5] The settlement at Macau came after a forty year break in relations with China, dating roughly from Jorge Alvares' landing on Lin Tin island in the Pearl River Delta in 1513 to the piracy incident in 1553. The hiatus was the result cultural misunderstanding and the actions of a rouge captain, Simão Peres de Andrade, who violated Chinese laws. In 1554 Leonel de Sousa, Captain-Major of the Japan Voyages, finally negotiated trading rights in exchange for paying duties. The permanent settlement built on Macau in 1557 is now considered the "official" date of founding.

[6] Studies of Portuguese India and Asia written from the 16th through the

early 20th centuries are summarized by Luís Madureira, "Tropical Sex Fantasies and the Ambassador's Other Death: The Difference in Portuguese Colonialism", Cultural Critique, No. 28 (Autumn, 1994:149-173. See also Rebecca D. Catz, The Travels of Mendes Pinto, University of Chicago Press, 1989.

[7] A.J.R. Russell-Wood makes this point by emphasizing "historical fragmentation" that fails to place the Portuguese overseas empire within a larger context as the first European nation to establish the boundaries of the modern world. A. J. R. Russell-Wood, The Portuguese Empire: 1415-1808, Johns Hopkins Press, 1998: xx-xxi.

[8] Anders Ljungstedt, A Historical sketch of the Portuguese settlements in China: and of the Roman Catholic Church, James Monroe and Co., Boston, 1836. For a biographic sketch of Ljungstedt (1759-1835), see Projekt Runeberg at http://runeberg.org/authors/ljungand.html.

[9] C.A. Montalto de Jesus, Historic Macau, Kelly and Walsh, Hong Kong, 1902.

[10] See Stuart Braga, Appendix 4 – A Book Burning in Macau: The suppression of C.A. Montalto de Jesus' Historic Macao, in 1929, p. 513-524, in his doctoral dissertation: Making Impressions: The adaptation of a Portuguese family to Hong Kong, 1700-1950, The Australian National University, October 2012.

[11] During World War II, Portugal's "neutrality" was never fully accepted by the Allied powers, which classified Salazar's regime as "non-belligerent" due to its willingness to trade in war materials with both sides and benefit as an intermediary. See "U.S. and Allied Efforts to Recover and Restore Gold and Other Assets Stolen or Hidden by Germany During World War", William Z. Slany, U.S. Department of State, May 1997, p. 12.

[12] For an overview of this debate, see Diogo Ramada Curto, "The Debate on Race Relations in the Portuguese Empire and Charles R. Boxer's Position": e-JPH, Vol. 11, Number 1, Summer 2013.

[13] The Times of London Literary Supplement provided a general criticism in 1952 in "Portugal's Present Generation", TLS, August 29, 1952:38.

[14] Much of Portugal's history was not translated into English until the 19th century. Recent studies in English, especially concerning Luso-Asians, at times romanticize ethnic origins in India and China. See Alfredo Gomes Dias, "The Origins of Macao's Community in Shanghai, Hong Kong's Emigration (1850-1909)"? Bulletin of Portuguese - Japanese Studies, vol. 17, 2008, pp. 197-224. Other examples include two pamphlets by Fredric James Silva, All

Our Yesterdays, UMA, Inc. of California, 1979, and Reminiscences of a Wartime Refugee, Instituto Internacional Macau, 2013.

[15] In addition to Russell-Wood's, The Portuguese Empire, op. cit., see the work of Ângela Barreto Xavier on Goa, including "Power, Religion and Violence in Sixteenth-Century Goa", Portuguese Literary and Cultural Studies, 19, University of Massachusetts, Center for English Studies and Culture, 2010.

[16] See George Bryan Sousa, The Survival of Empires: Portuguese Trade and Society in China and the South China Sea 1630 – 1754, Cambridge Un. Press, 1986, and James C. Boyajian, Portuguese Trade in Asia under the Hapsburgs, 1580 – 1640, Johns Hopkins Un. Press, 1993.

[17] A noteworthy and well received exception is the two-volume anthology, The Making of the Luso-Asian World: Intricacies of Engagement, Laura Jarnagin (ed.), Institute of Southeast Asian Studies, Singapore, 2011.

[18] In addition to The Making of the Luso-Asian World, op. cit. 2011, see the many works of C.R. Boxer, including The Portuguese Seaborne Empire, 1415 - 1825, New York, 1969, Diffie, Bailey (1977), Foundations of the Portuguese Empire, 1415–1580, University of Minnesota Press. 1977, Mark Meuwese, Brothers in Arms, Partners in Trade: Dutch-Indigenous Alliances in the Atlantic World, 1595-1647, the Netherlands, 2012, p. 129; Stefan Halikowski Smith, Creolization and diaspora in the Portuguese Indies: the social world of Ayutthaya, 1640-1720, Leiden, Boston, 2011; and Genevieve Escure and Amir Schwegler, Creoles, Contact and Language Change: Linguistic Interpretations, Philadelphia, 2004, 5-6.

[19] The cultural identification of Macanese developed from roughly 1553 through the "handover" to China in 1999. At present, it is estimated that there are currently 1.6 million are now living in over thirty-five (35) countries around the world, as indicated in on-going surveys begun in 2019, which will be discussed in the conclusion.

[20] See A. J. R. Russell-Wood, The Portuguese Empire: 1415-1808, Johns Hopkins Press, 1998, James C. Boyajian, Portuguese Trade in Asia under the Hapsburgs, 1580-1640, Johns Hopkins Un. Press, 1993; and George Bryan Sousa, The Survival of Empires: Portuguese Trade and Society in China and the South China Sea 1630-1754, Cambridge Un. Press, 1986.

[21] The history of Portuguese and Macanese printing will be discussed more fully in Chapter 9.

[22] A recent survey conducted by the "Portuguese and Macanese Studies Project" at U.C. Berkeley indicates that 16% of Macanese still identify themselves culturally as "Portuguese". The results will be discussed in the conclusion.

[23] C.R. Boxer, The Portuguese Seaborne Empire, Knopf, 1969: 249-272.

[24] C.R. Boxer, ibid, 249.

[25] Sheyla S. Zandonai makes this point throughout her study, Global Diversity, Local Identity: Multicultural Practice in Macau, Intercultural Communication Studies XVIII: 1 2009: 19-32.

[26] Angela Xavier Barretto, "Power, Religion and Violence in Sixteenth-Century Goa", Portuguese Literary and Cultural Studies, 19, University of Massachusetts, 2010.

[27] Some of the earliest examples were provided in The Travels of Pietro Della Valle in India, The Hakluyt Society, 1889, Translation into English in 1663, from a work completed in Goa in 1623, and the Travels of Peter Mundy in India and Asia, 1608-1667, The Hakluyt Society, 1907, based on his chronicle of 1637.

[28] China under the influence of Confucianism effectively closed its society to foreigners around 1485. Japan after unification under the Tokagawa Shogunate expelled foreigners around 1639. See also Lucio Sousa, "The Legal and Clandestine Trade in the History of Early Macao: Captain Landeiro, the Jewish "King of the Portuguese from Macao", Kanagawa Prefectural Institute of Language and Culture, 2009.

[29] The first Portuguese settlement in Western India was founded by Pedro Alvares Cabral in Cochin in 1500. Afonso de Albuquerque was sent to build its first fort and military garrison in 1503. Diffie, Bailey W.; Winius, George D., Foundations of the Portuguese empire, 1415–1580. Europe and the World in the Age of Expansion, Minneapolis: University of Minneapolis Press, 1977.

[30] "Standing orders from Dom Manoel, King of Portugal to Diogo Lopes de Sequeira, sent to discover the town of Malacca", Translation by Manuel Pintado, Portuguese Documents on Malacca, Vol. 1, Kuala Lumpur, 1993: 15-17.

[31] Pires, ibid, Vol. 2: 254-255.

[32] Pires' observations are taken from his two-volume work: The Suma Oriental of Tome Pires: An account of the East from the Red Sea to China, written in Malacca and India in 1512-1515, Vol. 1 of 2, Armando Cortesao (ed.), New

Delhi, 2005. Biographical information on Pires can be found in Cortesao's introduction in Vol. 1.

[33] Armando Cortesao, Introduction, Tome Pires, The Suma Oriental of Tome Pires, op. cit. 2005: p. lxii.

[34] Louise Levathes, When China Ruled the Seas: The Treasure Fleets of the Dragon Throne, 1405 – 1433, Oxford University Press, 1994.

[35] See Cheah Boon Kheng, Ming China's Support for Sultan Mahmud of Melaka and Its Hostility towards the Portuguese after the Fall of Melaka in 1511, *Journal of the Malaysian Branch of the Royal Asiatic Society, Vol. 85, No. 2 (303), December 2012: 55-77*

[36] Boxer noted that the most striking feature of the Portuguese empire was its dispersion over such a vast territory touching the Middle East, Latin America, Africa, and Asia. See Boxer, The Portuguese Seaborne Empire: op cit.:51.

[37] James Boyajian, Portuguese Trade in Asia under the Hapsburgs, 1580 – 1640, Johns Hopkins Un. Press, 1993:41.

[38] This estimate is based on the following variables: one silver 16th century Portuguese cruzado weighed just under one ounce (.80953). A cargo worth 5.1 million cruzados would then equal 4.128 million silver ounces. At the current (2020) price of silver ($15.46 p/oz), each cargo would be worth about $64 million (USD).

[39] It is likely that Boyajian's estimates included Japan, but we separated Japanese economist Kotaba Atsushi's estimate for the sake of illustration. Both Russell-Wood and George Bryan Souza cite Atsushi's estimate of up to 1.537 million kilograms of silver in these years, which would be calculated as 877.2 million ounces of silver, multiplied by the current price of silver ($15.46 p/oz) or $838,453,257, divided by 92 years, equaling about $9.113 million USD each year. A. J. R. Russell-Wood, The Portuguese Empire: 1415-1808, Johns Hopkins Press, 1998:144. George Bryan Sousa, The Survival of Empires: Portuguese Trade and Society in China and the South China Sea 1630–1754, Cambridge Un. Press, 1986:57.

[40] Kotaba Atsushi, "The Production and Uses of Gold and Silver in Sixteenth and Seventeenth Century Japan", Economic History Review, 2nd Series, 18, 1965.

[41] See Boyajian, Portuguese Trade in Asia under the Hapsburgs, op. cit., Appendix B, 254-257, in which he lists New Christian families who were investors.

[42] C.R. Boxer, Fidalgos in the Far East: 1550-1770, Oxford University Press Hong Kong,1968:6-7 and C.A. Montalto de Jesus, Historic Macau, 1902, Chapter IX. See also John E. Willis, Jr., China and Maritime Europe, 1500–1800: Trade, Settlement, Diplomacy, and Missions, Cambridge Un., 2011:44.

[43] Boyajian, Portuguese Trade in Asia under the Hapsburgs, op. cit.: 65.

[44] Boxer noted the inability of the Portuguese to close the Red Sea to the Venetian spice route. Portuguese Seaborne Empire, op. cit. p. 47.

[45] A.J.S. Russell-Wood, The Portuguese Empire, op. cit., xiv.

[46] Boyajian, Portuguese Trade in Asia under the Hapsburgs, op. cit. p. 5-6.

[47] Tome Pires, The Suma Oriental of Tome Pires, op. cit. p. 269-277.

[48] One cruzado equaled .80953 oz of silver. A cargo worth 15,000 cruzados would be 12,143 oz of silver, worth about $187,730 USD in 2019. 30,000 cruzados would equal $375,461 USD. 80,000 would equal $1,001,227. Note that the value of cruzados in Portugal and Goa fluctuated throughout the 16th century. The examples used here and those previously are only for illustration. See also Niels Steensgard's values in, The Asian Trade Revolution of the Seventeenth Century, University of Chicago Press, 1973: 418.

[49] The Luso-Dutch conflict is well documented by C.R. Boxer, The Portuguese Seaborne Empire, op. cit. 1969: 106-127.

[50] George Boyajian, op. cit., 1993: 7-11

[51] Tome Pires, The Suma Oriental, op. cit. 2005: 277-78

[52] James Boyajian, op. cit., 1986: 8-9.

[53] James Boyajian, op. cit., 1986: 9.

[54] Quoted by C.R. Boxer from Couto's Sixth Decada (1612), in the former's study, The Portuguese Seaborne Empire, 1415-1825, Knopf, New York, 1969: 228.

[55] Boxer, The Portuguese Seaborne Empire, op. cit. p. 74.

[56] Boxer, ibid, p. 66.

[57] The persecution of Hindus began in Goa in 1540 with a series of laws instigated by the Crown and the Church. See Boxer, The Portuguese Seaborne Empire, op. cit.: 66-68, and Angela Barretto Xavier in "Power, Religion and Violence in Sixteenth-Century Goa", Portuguese Literary and Cultural Studies (201) 17/18:250-5.

[58] James Boyajian, Portuguese Trade in Asia under the Hapsburgs, p. 30.

[59] Couto writes that in the first sixty-two years New Christians made up 71% of those tried by the Goan Inquisition and handed over to authorities for punishment. Dejanirah Silva Couto, "Some Observations on Portuguese Renegades in Asia in the Sixteenth Century", in Vasco da Gama and the linking of Europe and Asia, Anthony Disney and Emily Booth (eds.), New Delhi: Oxford University Press, 2000: 179.

[60] Hannah Chapelle Wojceihowski, Group Identity in the Renaissance World, Cambridge University Press, 2011, p.215-216.

[61] James Boyajian, ibid, p. 71-72, and C.R. Boxer, Fidalgos in the Far East, op. cit.

[62] James C. Boyajian, ibid, p. 71-75.

[63] James Boyajian, ibid, p. 72.

[64] Journal of Indian history, 1980, Volume 58. p. 57.

[65] Boxer, The Portuguese Seaborne Empire, op. cit.:53.

[66] Boxer, ibid, p. 77.

[67] One was Galeote Pereira, who accompanied the India Fleet on trading voyages to the China coast between 1539 and 1547. South China in the Sixteenth Century (1550-1575), Being the narratives of Galeote Pereira, Fr. Gaspar da Cruz, O.P., Fr. Martin de Rada, O.E.S.A., (1550-1575), ed. Charles Ralph Boxer, Routledge, London 1953 (2010 version). P. 35-38.

[68] A. J. R. Russell-Wood, The Portuguese Empire: 1415-1808, Johns Hopkins

Press, 1998, p. 33, 75-78.

[69] Although there is inadequate documentation, both Boxer (op. cit. p. 51) and Boyajian (op. cit. p. 71) seem to agree with this estimate.

[70] Boxer, op. cit.:249.

[71] Edgar Prestage, The Portuguese Pioneers, London, Oxford University, 1933, pp. 299-300.

[72] Jose Nicolau da Fonseca, A Historical Sketch of Goa, Bombay, 1878:143.

[73] Teotonio R. De Souza, "The Portuguese in Goa", in Acompanhando a Lusofonia em Goa: Preocupações e experiências pessoais. Lisbon: Grupo Lusofona, 2016, P. 26.

[74] Edgar Prestage wrote "... After his conquest of Goa, he married some hundreds of his men to natives, ... and is said to have conducted the ceremony himself." The Portuguese Pioneers, op. cit. p. 299.

[75] Prestage added: "He could not keep his officers in the East, but he was anxious to maintain there a body of artisans, soldiers, and especially gunners, for his power depended, next to personal valour, on artillery." ibid, p. 300.

[76] Boxer, The Portuguese Seaborne Empire, op. cit., p. 297.

[77] Boxer, The Portuguese Seaborne Empire, op. cit., p. 53.

[78] Quoted by Boxer, op. cit., p. 305.

[79] Boxer, op. cit.:307.

[80] Boxer, The Portuguese Seaborne Empire, op. cit.:306.

[81] Genevieve Escure and Amir Schwegler, Creoles, Contact and Language Change: Linguistic Interpretations, Philadelphia, 2004, 5-6.

[82] Paulo Teodoro de Matos, 'The Population of the Portuguese Estado da India, 1750–1820: Sources and
Demographic Trends', in Laura Jarnagin, ed. Portuguese and Luso-Asian Legacies in Southeast Asia, 1511– 2011,

Vol. 1, p. 162.

[83] Boxer, The Portuguese Seaborne Empire, op. cit.: 66-67.

[84] Stefan Halikowski-Smith, "Languages of Subalternity and Collaboration: Portuguese in English settlements across the Bay of Bengal, 1620-1800", International Journal of Maritime History, 2016, Vol 28, Issue 2: p.2.

[85] The Travels of Pietro Della Valle in India, London: The Hakluyt Society, 1892: p. 427. Della Valle traveled to Goa in 1620.

[86] Lucio Sousa, 'Legal and Clandestine Trade in the History of Early Macao: Captain Landeiro, the Jewish "King of the Portuguese" from Macao', Kanagawa Prefectural International Language and Culture Academia Bulletin 2, 2013: p. 52.

[87] Lucio Sousa, ibid.

[88] Tomé Pires, The Suma Oriental: an account of the east, from de Red Sea to Japan written in Malacca and India in 1512-1515, Translated by Armando Cortesao, 1948.

[89] Fernao Lopes de Castanheda, History of the discoveries and conquests in India by the Portuguese: Ch.CXII: translation by Manuel Pintado, Portuguese Documents on Malacca, Vol. 1, Kuala Lumpur, 1993: 87

[90] M.C. Ricklefs, (1969). A History of Modern Indonesia Since c. 1300, 2nd Ed. London, 1969: 23-24.

[91] M.C. Ricklefs, op. cit. 24.

[92] M.C. Ricklefs, op.cit. 25-26.

[93] Antonio Pinto da Franca, Portuguese Influence in Indonesia, Gunung Agung Ltd. Singapore, 1970: 103-108.

[94] Antonio Pinto da Franca, Portuguese Influence in Indonesia, op. cit. p. 103.

[95] Om Prakash, "Opium Monopoly in India and Indonesia in the Eighteenth Century", in India and Indonesia during the Ancien Regime, E. J. Brill, Leiden, New York, 1989: 74

[96] Pintado, ibid, 171-173.

[97] Joao de Barros, Decadas da Asia (Decades in Asia) : translation by Pintado, ibid: 171-173.

[98] Pintado described the gifts as "cuirasses (amour) covered in satin and crimson cloth, a lance, a dagger and an ornamented helmet". Ibid.

[99] Pintado, ibid, 395.

[100] Pintado, ibid, 273.

[101] Letter dated October 22, 1552, reproduced by Jorge Morbey, in Aux Portes de la Chine, Tientzin, 1933, p. 49. Morbey conducted research in the Historical Archives of Macao when was the director of the Instituto do Cultural in the 1980's. He generously provided his research notes for this project in March 2016.

[102] Letter dated December 1, 1555, Brother Luís Fróis, S. J. to the brothers in Goa, reproduced by Jorge Morbey from the National Malacca Archives, B.A., 49-IV-51, 91v - 94v

[103] Letter dated December 2, 1561, - Father Jerónimo Fernandes, reproduced by Jorge Morbey, in which he states: *"the door to the most glorious missions and enterprises that there are in India* (B.A., 49-IV-50, 401v- 403).

[104] Pintado, ibid, 405-409.

[105] John Byrne, "The Luso-Asians and other Eurasians", in The Making of the Luso-Asian World, Vol. 1, Laura Jarnagin (ed.), Institute of Southeast Asian Studies, Singapore, 2011: 136.

[106] C.R. Boxer, The Portuguese Seaborne Empire: 1415-1825, New York, 1969: 106-07.

[107] Boxer, ibid, 114-15.

[108] Boxer, ibid, 115 – 117. The Dutch also employed mercenaries from Germany, France, Scandinavia, and some English to support their own soldiers. Many were better fed and provisioned, in contrast to Portuguese soldiers, who were often slightly built underfed mestizos recruited from occupied territories.

[109] The narrow emphasis of many Portuguese scholars on their history of exploration and the neglect of local descendants, for example, remained virtually unchallenged until the publication of C.A. Montalto's book Historic Macau, in 1902, which focused on the diverse origins of Macau's history and culture.

[110] Pires, The Suma Oriental, ibid, 277-78.

[111] Diffie and Winius, Foundations of the Portuguese Empire: 1415 – 1580, University of Minnesota Press, 1985: 419-422.

[112] George Bryan Souza, The Survival of Empire: Portuguese Trade and Society in China and the South China Sea 1630-1754, Cambridge University Press, London, 2004:87

[113] Ronald Daus, Portuguese Eurasian Communities in Southeast Asia, Institute of Southeast Asian Studies, Singapore, 1989:7-8.

[114] Antonio Pinto da Franca, Portuguese Influence in Indonesia, Gunung Agung LTD, 1970:18

[115] Souza, ibid, pgs. 94-95, Table 5.1.

[116] Souza, p. 101.

[117] Souza, ibid, p. 34, valued today at approximately $6,768 USD.

[118] The equivalent value would be about $198,000. The merchandise was worth much more if sold in Europe.

[119] Letter from Father Francisco Telles, in Siam, to the Loyal Senate of Macao, 1721, June 28 – Siam. The Portuguese Viceroy of India had named Telles acting Captain-Major in the absence of a new appointee. Jorge Morbey, citation from the Macau Archives, AH/LS/319, fl. 127; AM: I: 3: Agosto 1929: 153-165; AM: 3.ª série: VI: 1: Julho 1966: 36-37. Translation and references provided by Jorge Morbey, March 2016.

[120] In a letter dated 1723, March 18 - Macao: The King of Siam stipulated to the Loyal Senate of Macao several rugs, indicating the length he wished them to be. Jorge Morbey, citation from the Macau Archives, AH/LS/331, fl.110; AM: 3.ª série: II: 6: Dezembro 1964: 377. Translation and references provided by Jorge Morbey, March 2016.

[121] J.M. Braga, "The First Sino-Portuguese Treaty made by Leonel de Souza in

1554", Review of Culture, Cultural Institute of Macau, March 1987. See also C. Willies, (Ed.) China and Macau, Ashgate, Hampshire, UK: 2002. The dates of the encounters with pirates in the South China Sea are noted by C.R. Boxer, Fidalgos in the Far East, 1969, op. cit., and C.A. Montalto, Historic Macau, 1902.

[122] See Chapter 1 for an estimate of colonial revenue coming through Macau to Goa, Japan, and Portugal based on trading silver, gold, silk, and porcelain.

[123] My purpose here is to suggest the role the Macanese played in the early years of a global economy later discussed by Emanuel Wallerstein and others, including Paul Van Dyke in his work on the 18th century Canton and Macau Trade System, and Carlo Trochi in his research on Britain's introduction of opium as the foundation of the 19th China Trade.

[124] Dorothy Carrington, The Traveler's Eye, Pilot Press, London, 1949, p. 178-79. See also Peter Mundy, Merchant Adventurer, ed. R.E. Pritchard, Bodleian Library Press, Oxford, 2011.

[125] Peter Mundy's quotes were taken from The Travels of Peter Mundy, London, 1919, Volume III. Mundy was hired as a "factor" or a commercial agent. See also C.R. Boxer, Fidalgos in the Far East, London, 1968, p. 123.

[126] Carlos Augusto Montalto de Jesus, Historic Macao, Kelly and Walsh, Hong Kong, 1902: p. 41.

[127] Precise population numbers are not available. Both Anders Ljungstedt, in An Historical Sketch of the Portuguese Settlement in China, James Monroe, Boston, 1835: p. 27; and John Byrne, op. cit., include this estimate. Citing Dutch sources, Boxer estimates between "700 to 800 Portuguese and Eurasians" in Macau. C.R. Boxer, Fidalgos in the Far East, 1550 – 1770, Oxford University Press, London, 1968: p. 75.

[128] John Byrne, "The Luso-Asians and other Eurasians: Their Domestic and Diasporic Identities", The Making of the Luso-Asian World, ed. Laura Jarnagin, Institute of Southeast Asian Studies, Singapore, 2011:133-134.

[129] John Byrne, ibid, 137.

[130] Sheyla S. Zandonai, "Global Diversity, Local Identity: Multicultural Practice in Macau", Intercultural Communication Studies, XVIII:19-32, 2009.

[131] Malyn Newitt, A History of Portuguese Expansion, 1400 – 1668, Routledge, London, 2005:2.

[132] See C.R. Boxer's chapter V, "Midsummer Day in Macao, Anno 1622 Fidalgos in the Far East, 1550 – 1770, Oxford University Press, London, 1968: p. 71-92.

[133] Boxer noted that prior to the invasion two English ships joined two Dutch ships in a blockade of Macau, but the Dutch were under orders not to include the English or share any booty. Fidalgos in the Far East, ibid,73.

[134] The presence of what Portuguese historian Jaime Courtesao called "a purely democratic foundation" in Macau may have been exaggerated, but as Boxer suggests, different people from diverse ethnic backgrounds contributed to the victory. Jaime Courtesao, Historia de Portugal, Barcelos, 1933.

[135] Slavery in Portuguese territories was prohibited in 1761 under the Marquis of Pombal (1749-1777), C.R. Boxer, The Portuguese Seaborne Empire, 1415 – 1825, Knopf, New York, 1969:192. Chinese and Japanese slaves became illegal in Macau after 1758.

[136] George Elison, Deus Destroyed: The Image of Christianity in Early Modern Japan, Harvard University Press, Cambridge, 1973:54. Ikuo Higashibaba, Christianity in Early Modern Japan: Kirishitan Belief and Practice. Brill Academic Publishers, 2001:139.

[137] Rui D'Avila Lourido, "The Impact of the Macao-Manila Silk Trade from the Beginnings to 1640", in Vadime Elisseeff (ed.), The Silk Roads: Highways of Culture and Commerce, Berghahn Books, 1998:211. See also, Lucio de Sousa, "Legal and Clandestine Trade in the History of Early Macau: Captain Landeiro, The Jewish 'King of the Portuguese' from Macao", Bulletin of Kanagawa Prefectural, Institute of Language and Culture Studies, Vol. 2, 2013:49-63.

[138] Rogerio Miguel Puga, The British Presence in Macau: 1635 – 1739, Hong Kong University Press, 2013:49.

[139] Robert J. Anthony, Elusive Pirates, Pervasive Smugglers: Violence and Clandestine Trade in the Greater China Seas, Hong Kong University Press, 2010:107-08.

[140] Rogerio Miguel Puga, ibid, 2013:67.

[141] Puga, ibid, 67.

[142] Information about the origins of Portuguese and Macanese printing was taken from Jose Maria Braga's article, "The Beginnings of Printing in Macao", English translation printed by the University of Hong Kong Library from the original published in Portuguese in Studia (Revista Semestral), No. 12, July 1962:29-137.

[143] Olyphant was an elected member of the American Board of Commission-

ers for Foreign Missions (ABCFM). Gregory Adam Scott, Bridgette C. Kamsler, "Missionary Research Library Archives: D.W.C. Olyphant Papers, 1827-1851", Columbia University Library Archives, May, 2014.

[144] Peter Perring Thomas, originally hired by the EIC as a printer to assist Morrison in 1813 and departed in 1825; William Milne, an English missionary and printer, accompanied by his wife, was initially hired by the EIC as Morrison's assistant in 1814. Milne was later expelled from both Canton and Macau because he did not have official clearances. He and his wife were eventually posted to Malacca in 1817. There was also the American William W. Wood, hired by the Alexander Matheson to print and edit the Canton Register in 1827, who left China in 1834. In addition to Braga, see Alain Le Pichon, <u>China Trade and Empire: Jardine, Matheson & Co. and the Origins of British Rule in Hong Kong</u>, 1827-1843, British Academy, 2006:68, note 46 on W.W. Wood.

[145] Hoi-to Wong, "Interport Printing Enterprise: Macanese Printing Networks in Chinese Trading Ports", p.141, in <u>Treaty Ports in Modern China: Law, Land and Power</u>, edited by Robert Bickers and Isabella Jackson, Routledge, 2016.

[146] As observed by two of Morrison's contemporaries, Dr. W. W. Cadbury and Miss M. H. Jones writing at Canton, printing and the information provided by the EIC allowed Macau to become a bridge into the sealed city of Canton and a "backdoor" to the mainland. Braga, op. cit. p.64.

[147] Hoi-to Wong, "Interport Printing Enterprise: Macanese Printing Networks in Chinese Treaty Ports", <u>Treaty Ports in Modern China</u>, (eds.) Robert Bickers, Isabella Jackson, Routledge, New York, 2016:139-157.

[148] Macau's latest stagnation effectively lasted from the conclusion of the Opium Wars in 1860 to its marginalization as a refugee destination during World War II, until the deregulation of gambling and its rise as an entertainment and gaming resort in 2003.

[149] Luis Cunha, "Macau Between Republics: Neither War nor Peace (1914-1918)", e-JPH, Vol. 15, number 1, June 2017:106.

[150] The story was reported in the Macau newspaper "Comercio" on March 1, 1990, as related by the historian Fr. Manual Teixeira, who consulted the parish records of Sao Lourenco Church. Cunha noted governmental disarray at the time: "(The) Local administration was divided up between two constituencies ..., that is, the municipality of Macau, with four parishes, and the Military Command of Taipa and Coloane, ...", 107. Cunha also describes the "impunity in which pirates and opium smugglers operated in the waters and islands adjacent to Macau, ..." Cunha, ibid: 106-107.

[151] Carlos Augusto Montalto de Jesus, "Macao's Deeds of Arms". <u>The China Review</u>, Hong Kong: 1894:21(3): 156.

[152] Austin Coates, <u>A Macao Narrative</u>, Hong Kong University Press, 2009: p. 133-35.

[153] Portugal had been going through a financial crisis of its own since the late 1890s and was forced to seek loans from Britain and Germany. Britain agreed to support the loans and protect Portuguese colonies from all enemies in exchange for colonial revenues (i.e. opium profits) if Portugal defaulted. Teresa Pinto Coelho, "Lord Salisbury's 1890 Ultimatum to Portugal and Anglo-Portuguese Relations", p.7, Oxford University paper, (undated): http://www.modlangs.ox.ac.uk/files/windsor/6_pintocoelho.pdf.

[154] Cunha, ibid, 107.

[155] Teresa Pinto Coelho, ibid.

[156] While the collection of Macau's historical data remains sporadic, an indication of low population growth may be evidence of economic stagnation. At least one researcher indicates that Macau's population grew very little during the period, from 71,700 in 1868 to 74,900 in 1915. See Jan Lahmeyer's distillation of data from Chinese government sources, "Macau: Historical Demographic Data", http://www.populstat.info/Asia/macauc.htm.

[157] Macau's recovery, in could be argued, did not resume until the loss of Stanley Ho's gambling monopoly in 2000, and agreements to build several American and Australian owned casinos and entertainment resorts beginning in 2003.

[158] See Alain Le Pichon, <u>China Trade and Empire</u>: Jardine, Matheson & Co. and the Origins of British Rule in Hong Kong, 1827-1843 (Records of Social and Economic History), Oxford University Press, 2006.

[159] Austin Coates, <u>Macau and the British, 1637 – 1842: Prelude to Hong Kong</u>, Hong Kong University Press, 1966: 36-37. See also, Zhidong Hoa, <u>Macau: History and Society</u>, Hong Kong University Press, 2011:22, 211.

[160] Canton Register, April 25, 1836, as quoted by Ernest John Eitel, <u>Europe in China, A History of Hong Kong</u> from the beginning to the year 1882, Hong Kong, Kelly and Walsh, 1895: 127.

[161] John M. Carroll, A Concise History of Hong Kong, 34.

[162] Richard J. Grace, Opium and Empire: The Lives and Careers of William Jardine and James Matheson, McGill-Queen's University Press, Montreal, 2014: 223, 228-229.

[163] Xiao Weiyun. (2001), *One country, two systems. An account of the drafting of the Hong Kong Basic Law.*
Peking University Press, Peking, 2001:65-66.

[164] Richard J. Grace, op. cit.

[165] John M. Carroll, A Concise History of Hong Kong, Rowman & Littlefield, 2007:12.

[166] Xiao Weiyun, One country, two systems, op. cit. p. 66.

[167] Peter Ward Fay, The Opium War, op. cit.: p. 326.

[168] Frank Welsh points out that other populations were not counted, including 800 "immigrant merchants", who could be Indian-Parsee, and 300 itinerant "labourers from Kowloon", probably Chinese mainlanders. Frank Welsh, A History of Hong Kong, HarperCollins, 1997, 137.

[169] Peter Ward Fay, The Opium War, UNC Press, 1975, 322.

[170] Frank Welsh, A History of Hong Kong, 214.

[171] Frank Welsh, A History of Hong Kong, 215.

[172] Frank Welsh, A History of Hong Kong, 215.

[173] Frank Welsh, A History of Hong Kong, 214.

[174] The Hongkong Government Gazette, Feb. 23, 1856, March 28, 1857, April 25, 1857, Sept. 6, 1858, and March 17, 1859.

[175] R. E. Park, (1924). The Concept of Social Distance as Applied to the Study of Racial Attitudes and Racial Relations, Journal of Applied Sociology 8

(1924):, 339-344.

[176] For example, see Georg Simmel, (1908/1976) *The Stranger,* The Sociology of Georg Simmel' New York: Free Press, and Nedim Karakayali, (2006). "The Uses of the Stranger: Circulation, Arbitration, Secrecy, and Dirt". *Sociological Theory.* 24 (4): 312.

[177] In India, as a response to anxiety about the effects of colonization on the English character, Sudipta Sen describes the segregation of Indian subjects as "… a distance that was made formal as the company-state (referring to the East India Company) became more firmly entrenched in the Indian soil." Sudipta Sen, A Distant Sovereignty, op. cit., 2016: XXV and p.140.

[178] Robert E. Park, The Concept of Social Distance, 342.

[179] Welsh mentions that the structure of Hong Kong society included Portuguese and Eurasians who fulfilled "essential clerical and minor administrative roles", as well as being "habitually slighted (by racial attitudes), and confined to the lower ranks" of government service. Frank Welsh, A History of Hong Kong, 380 and 382.

[180] In 1885, 10 year old Annie Oakes Huntington, the daughter of an American executive working for Russell & Co., described her residence at Brockhurst on the Peak. She wrote "… the house is very large, with a wide veranda on three sides of it and at the back, is called a bungle [sic] because there is no upstairs. We keep 9 servants, a butler and Amah, a boy, house Coolie, cook and four chair coolies." Hong Kong, July 11th, 1885. https://gwulo.com/node/31235. See also Hong Kong's "Peak District Reservation Ordinance 1904".

[181] For a discussion of "Institutional Racism" in Hong Kong, see Barnabas H.M. Koo The Portuguese in Hong Kong and China, Their Beginning, Settlement, and Progress to 1949, Vol. 2, Macau and Hongkong, International Institute of Macau, 2013: 76-79 (based on Jose Pedro Braga's original research and manuscript published in 1944).

[182] In 1853 the government counted 32,800 inhabitants. Britons and Americans totaled only 467 (1.4%). The Portuguese numbered 459 (1.3%). The Chinese made up the bulk of the population at 31,865 (97%). By 1881, the population in Hong Kong swelled to 160,402, broken down as: British – 785 (.005%); Portuguese – 1,869 (1.1%); and Chinese – 150,690 (94%). Hongkong Government Gazette, 22 August, 1891, Government Notification No. 361, Report of the Registrar, J.H. Stewart Lockhart, Dated 15 August, 1891, 745-746.

[183] *Hong Kong and Shanghai Banking Corporation, Protocols for New Employees,*

1886, excepted in Gwulo: Old Hong Kong, https://gwulo.com/node/8912.

[184] Frank Welsh, A History of Hong Kong, HarperCollins, London, 1993:385.

[185] These alliances did not lead to the representation of Chinese on Hong Kong's Legislative Council until an appointment in 1880. A Macanese, Jose' Pedro Braga, was not appointed until 1929. Both were "Non-Voting" members. For more information, see John Carroll, "Chinese Collaboration in the Making of British Hong Kong", p. 13-29, in Tak-Wing Ngo (ed.), Hong Kong's History: State and Society under Colonial Rule, Routledge, 1999.

[186] Social attitudes toward ethnic communities appeared early on. A Royal Navy officer visiting Hong Kong in 1855 described his compatriots as "all more or less rowing the same boat ... striving to amass as many dollars as opportunity would admit ..." but "absurdly snobbish", displaying "much nonsensical narrow-mindedness and unsociability." Frank Welsh, A History of Hong Kong, op. cit., p.216.

[187] The fear apparently originated from the potential for racial mixing between Britons and Indians in the 18th century, creating an aversion toward Eurasians in colonial India. Sudipta Sen, A Distant Sovereignty: National Imperialism and the Origins British India, Routledge, 2016: XXV and p.140.

[188] Tak-Wing Ngo, Hong Kong's History,128.

[189] The primacy of the opium trade to the British economy is described in some detail by Richard Grace to the point that the East India Company by the 1820s was highly dependent on drug sales to support its governing of India and looked to China as its principal market. Richard J. Grace, Opium and Empire, 86-87.

[190] Richard J. Grace, Opium and Empire, 301-302. Appropriately, among the first landmarks in Hong Kong were James Matheson's opium store in Victoria and separate British, Portuguese, and Chinese cemeteries. Austin Coates, Macau and the British, 1637 – 1842: Prelude to Hong Kong, Hong Kong University Press, 1966, 214.

[191] The origins of banking crises in Southeast Asia is analyzed by W.E. Cheong, The Beginnings of Credit Finance on the China Coast: The Canton Financial Crisis of 1812–1815, Journal of Business History, Vol 13, Issue 2, 1971:87-103.

[192] Tak-Wing Ngo, "Industrial History and the Artifice of Laissez-faire Coloni-

alism", p. 128-129, in Tak-Wing Ngo (ed.), Hong Kong's History: State and Society under Colonial Rule, London, 1999.

[193] Alain Pichon's research includes correspondence between Jardine and Matheson that mentions Barretto and his family and provides insight into the early relations between the British and the Portuguese in Macau. Alain Pichon (ed.), China Trade and Empire: op. cit.: p.84, Note 26.

[194] Bartolomeu's brother, Joao Antonio Gonsalves Barretto and his nephew, Bartolomeu Antonio Barretto, also worked for Jardines. The nephew was one of two bookkeepers in the firm's early days and William Jardine's trusted aide who oversaw accounts in Canton, Hong Kong, and Manila. Like his uncle, Bartolomeu Antonio Barretto used his knowledge of Portuguese and Chinese to settle disputes for the company, including those between ship captains and Chinese officials just prior to the Opium War. Pichon, op. cit., p. 84, Letter 20, and p. 404-405, Letter 188.

[195] This strict separation of groups within businesses and government institutions was a consistent theme throughout many of the interviews conducted by the author with Macanese immigrants from post-World War II Hong Kong.

[196] Fredric "Jim" Silva, a member of the community born in Hong Kong now living in the United States, stated during an interview that the Macanese often served as political intermediaries to Chinese business owners during civil protests in Hong Kong from November 1966 through January 1967. Interview with Silva, September 2011, San Francisco. Video and transcript in author's files.

[197] The conditions in the Macanese community are described in Jose Pedro Braga's book, The Portuguese in Hong Kong and China, Their Beginning, Settlement, and Progress to 1949, Vol. 1, p. 141.Macau and Hongkong, 2013: 114, edited by Barnabas H.M. Koo (based on Braga's original manuscript completed in 1944)

[198] The literal meaning in the Macanese creole (Maquista) was "Kill the dark skinned ones.", a remnant of an old antagonism with the Moors who invaded Portugal in the 8th century. The fact that such references still existed suggests that Macanese ties to Europe in the 19th century, including racial biases, remained intact after more than a millennium.

[199] Koo, Vol. 2, op. cit. p. 50-58.

[200] Roy Eric Xavier, "Family Networks, Diasporas, and the Origins of the

Macanese in Asia", Review of Culture, Instituto Cultural do Governo da R.A.E.M. in Macau, No. 48, 2015.

[201] This information is based on interviews conducted for the following research paper: "Portuguese Community Life in Hong Kong: 1841 – 1941", Roy Eric Xavier, 2011, published in an edited version in the UMA News Bulletin, July-September 2011, Vol. 34, No. 3 under the title: "Hong Kong Stories – Life before the War", p. 1-6.

[202] A biographical sketch and interview of Fr. Gosano published as "The Life and Times of Father Jose "Zinho" Gosano", UMA News Bulletin, Vol. 34, No. 2, April-June 2011, p. 1-5.

[203] Horatio F. Ozorio, http://www.diasporamacaense.org/thewayitwas, "Were Amahs Charitably Treated by Us?" March 12, 2008.

[204] According to the Hong Kong Census of 1931, the Macanese population grew from 2,558 in 1911 to 3,198 in 1931. 90% originated from Hong Kong, Macau, or other parts of China, and lived in Kowloon. Report on the Census of the Colony of Hong Kong, 1931, Government of Hong Kong, p. 112.

[205] Gosano interview, UMA News Bulletin, op. cit.

[206] Information on Leonardo d'Almada y Castro was found in the Jorge Pereira Forjaz Collection (JPF), Old China Hands Archive, Oviatt Library, California State University, Northridge, under JPF files 2,4,5,14,15,16,22,26,and 27. Braga, op. cit. 2013:125 mentions that d'Almada served in the Office of the Superintendency of British Trade in China in 1836. A younger brother, Jose Maria, served as Second Clerk in the same office during the same period.

[207] D'Almada was particularly active in 1860, during which he sold fifteen (15) lots in Showkewan and seven (7) more in Aberdeen in 1861. From 1864 through 1866 d'Almada placed advertisements for at least eight (8) different houses, some with "a detached two story granite Godwin" to facilitate access to the docks and shipping. Reflecting the times, d'Almada also owned homes in Macau, but had difficulty renting them. In 1867 several ads by him appeared in local papers listing properties with reduced rents, suggesting that there was lower demand due to a dwindling number of traders who had yet to move to Hong Kong. JPF, op. cit.

[208] Jose Pedro Braga writes that in the 1870s d'Almada deeded land and a building on Caine Road on Hong Kong Island to the Italian Canossian sisters for an orphanage and a school. Other members of the d'Almada family made contributions as well. His brother, Jose d'Almada y Castro, private secretary to Governor Sir John Pope Hennessey, added to the land in the 1880s, allowing

the sisters to maintain a presence in Hong Kong throughout the 20th century. Leonardo's oldest daughter, Ana, took the veil of the Canossian Sisters in 1878 and remained in the order until her death at age 90 in 1938. JPF files, op. cit. See also Braga, op. cit. 2013: 125-128.

[209] Accounts and Papers, Session, 24 January – 28 August 1860, British Parliamentary Papers and House of Commons and Command, Volume 48, p. 101, and J.P. Braga, p. 202.

[210] "NATURALIZATION OF JANUARIO ANTONIO DE CARVALHO ORDINANCE," *Historical Laws of Hong Kong Online*, http://oelawhk.lib.hku.hk/items/show/440.

[211] For example, see Braga's acknowledgement in the "Preface" of his pamphlet: "The Rights of Aliens in Hongkong", Noronha Press, Hong Kong, 1895.

[212] Hoi-to Wong, "Macanese Printing Networks in Chinese Treaty Ports", 139-157. op. cit.

[213] Braga, op. cit., p.148-149.

[214] Eduardo M.S. Xavier, "The Portuguese in Business", <u>Hong Kong Business Symposium</u>, Hong Kong Chamber of Commerce, 1956, pg. 302.

[215] Leonardo d'Almada y Castro files, JPF Collection, CSUN, op. cit.

[216] Just before leaving his post in 1882, Governor John Pope Hennessey disclosed that one of Pope's predecessors, Sir John Bowring, had ignored an order from the Colonial Office in London to appoint Leonardo d'Almada as Colonial Secretary of Hong Kong, the second highest position in the colony. Bowring refused to make the appointment due to local objections that d'Almada, a Portuguese citizen of Macau, was not a British subject, and should not be in a position of authority over "native-born" Englishmen. Braga, op. cit. 127, and JPF Collection, CSUN, op. cit.

[217] Braga, Vol. 1, op. cit., p. 208.

[218] Braga, Vol. 1, op. cit., p. 130.

[219] Braga, Vol. 1, op. cit., p. 129-130.

[220] H.J. Lethridge, "Hong Kong Cadets: 1862-1941", <u>Journal of the Royal Asi-</u>

atic Society, Vol. 10, 1970:36.

[221] Joao Hyndman, for example, was succeed by Superintendent of Police, Francis Henry May, a former cadet officer who was appointed governor in 1912. HJL, op. cit.

[222] "Salaries of Public Officers", Report of the Commission appointed by Governor Sir. G. William Des Voeux, 13December, 1889, Appendix I, 321-323 (SPO)

[223] "Budget Notices for 1906" by A.M. Thomson, Colonial Treasurer, HK Legislative Council Minutes, 13 September 1906 (BN).

[224] SPO, op. cit.

[225] Relations between Macanese families and Chinese domestic workers, who shared different ties to British colonialists, were especially close among children. Many years after leaving Hong Kong, some former residents, then retired adults, returned to China in search of "amahs" who raised them. See Horatio F. Ozorio, op. cit.

[226] Barnabas Koo, op. cit., Vol. 2: 48.

[227] The smaller community in Shanghai founded in 1860 is described by Alfredo Gomes Dias in THE ORIGINS OF MACAO'S COMMUNITY IN SHANGHAI. HONG KONG'S EMIGRATION (1850-1909), Bulletin of Portuguese - Japanese Studies, Universidade Nova de Lisboa, Lisboa, Portugal, Vol. 17, 2008: 197-224. See also Wang Zhieheng, Portuguese Shanghai, R. Edward Glatfelter (ed.), Fundacao Macau, 1996.

[228] The development of these cultural elements are themselves subject to different emphasizes by different writers. For example, Jorge Morbey, an author and former head of the Instituto Cultural in Macau suggests the "polyhybrid" origins of the Macanese produced an identity suspended between Europe and Asia. Jorge Morbey, "Aspects of the Ethnic Identities of the Macanese", Review of Culture, Instituto Cultural do Macao, 1994: 203-212. Joao de Pina-Cabral argues that identity touches on three points: language, religion, and degrees of Eurasian appearance. Joao de Pina-Cabral , Between China and Europe: Person, Culture and Emotion in Macao, Continuum, New York, 2002: 39. This "otherness" is also reflected in the poems of Cecilia Jorge and the novels of Henrique de Senna Fernandes.

[229] Information about Macanese clubs and associations is taken from two principal sources: Luis Andrade de Sa, The Boys from Macau, including his chapter, "Clubes e organizacoes da comunidade", Fundacao Oriente : Instituto

Cultural de Macau, 1999, (translation provided by Francisco A. Da Roza, Feb. 2017), and Barnabas H.M. Koo, Vol. 2, op. cit., especially the chapter "Some Key Portuguese Institutions in Hong Kong", p. 25-46.

[230] These developments were originally described in Jose Pedro Braga, The Portuguese in Hongkong and China, Vol. 1, Hong Kong, 1895: 132 – 200. See also, Koo, Vol. 2, op. cit., 50-58. Hong Kong's history of development is also provided in the research of Professor Cecilia Chu at the University of Hong Kong: **CCHU9048 The City: Histories of Urbanism and the Built Environment.**

[231] Always looking to expand his interests, Noronha also purchased Shanghai's "Celestial Empire Press" from Antonio H. Carvalho around 1875, and installed one of his sons, Leonardo, as the manager. Following his father's example, Noronha's oldest son, Henrique, later served as the Superintendent of Printing for the Government of Singapore and was a leader of the Macanese community there. Koo, op. cit., Vol. 2, p. 106.

[232] Braga, op. cit. Vol. 1: 133.

[233] R. Edward Glatfelter, Introduction to Wang, Shicheng, Portuguese in Shanghai, Fundacao Macau, 1997, citing the research of Linda Cooke Johnson, Shanghai: From Market Town to Port City: 1074-1858. Stanford University Press, 1995:155-75.

[234] In 1843 the English horticulturist, Robert Fortune, described walking through the streets of Shanghai, found shops selling merchandise such as silk and embroidery, cotton goods, porcelain, ready-made clothes, and numerous curiosity shops offering carved bamboo ornaments. Robert Fortune, Three Year's Wanderings Among the Northern Provinces of China, London, 1847: 109-110.

[235] Data and information cited here can be found in Wang Zhicheng, Portuguese Shanghai, edited by R. Edward Glatfelter, Fundacao Macau, 1997:18.

[236] North China Herald, August 3, 1850; The Chinese Repository, 1851,141-49.

[237] The 1887 "Treaty of Friendship and Commerce" between Portugal and China resulted in limited recognition of Macau's permanence and "dual jurisdiction" so long as local policies remained acceptable to China's Imperial government. Austin Coates, A Macao Narrative, Hong Kong University Press, 2009:133-35.

[238] Shanghai's Public Bureau of Municipal Government census of 1945 later listed 110,868 foreign residents, of which 2,043 were Portuguese. Shanghai's Public Security Bureau from early 1950 indicated there were over 4,000 Portuguese. Wang Zhicheng, op. cit., 1997:12,45,84-118.

[239] A review of recent genealogies of several individuals mentioned in this article suggest that several traveled directly from Macau to Shanghai in the period 1840 to 1860. See Jorge Forjaz, Familias Macaense, 1996 and 2017 editions., International Institute of Macau.

[240] Wang Zhisheng, Portuguese in Shanghai, 1997, op. cit.

[241] Hoi-to Wong, "Interport Printing Enterprise: Macanese Printing Networks in Chinese Treaty Ports", in Bickers, Robert, and Isabella Jackson, Treaty Ports in Modern China, Routledge, London, 2016:143.

[242] The following Information is included in Wang Shisheng, Portuguese in Shanghai, 1997, op. cit.

[243] Information about the Portuguese Company of the Shanghai Volunteer Corp is scattered among many obscure documents, some that have recently surfaced from private collections. The present article relies on a history of the Portuguese Company entitled "Twentieth Anniversary of the Portuguese Co. SVC " published in 1926.

[244] Jose Pedro Braga was granted the Ordem de Militar de Cristo de Portugal (Military Order of Christ of Portugal) in 1929, and the Order of the British Empire in 1935. He died in Macau as a refugee in 1944. Jorge Forjaz, Familias Macaense, Fundaco Macau, 1997:324.

[245] Information on Vicente Braga is from Stuart Braga, Making Impressions: A Portuguese Family in Macau and Hong Kong, 1700-1945, National Library of Australia, Sydney, International Institute of Macau, 2015:208-218. Additionaql background information on Vicente Braga is also found in Meiji Portraits, "Vicente Emílio Rosa Braga, (1834-1911)", http://www.meiji-portraits.de/meiji_portraits_b.html#20090527093402531_1_2_3_107_1

[246] He was later joined by his oldest son, Francisco. See "Vicente Emílio Rosa Braga, (1834-1911)", http://www.meiji-portraits.de/meiji_portraits_b.html#20090527093402531_1_2_3_107_1

[247] Stuart Braga, Making Impressions, op. cit., 209.

[248] "Annual Report of the Postmaster General of 1894", Hongkong Government Records, paragraph 19. Printed in the Hongkong Government Gazette, 17 August, 1895.

[249] J.P. Braga, The Rights of Aliens in Hongkong, Being a record of the discussion carried on through the medium of the public press as to the employment of aliens in the colony, Noronha & Co, Hong Kong, 1895.

[250] We can only estimate Braga's readership based on a later census. In 1897 there were 1,392 British residents, including administrators, civil servants, and employees of banks and trading houses, 2,263 Portuguese adults, and an unknown number of English speakers in the Chinese, Malaysian, Indian, Japanese, Jewish, and Parsee communities. The total population of Hong Kong was 241,762, not including the Chinese boat population. See "Report on the Census of the Colony for 1897", Hongkong, June 20, 1897.

[251] Braga, The Rights of Aliens in Hongkong, op. cit., *Preface, Xi*

[252] Circular, Downing Street, 25th, August 1862, published by the Colonial Secretary's Office, Hongkong, 28th October 1862.

[253]. J.P. Braga, op. cit., 3-8.

[254] J.P. Braga, op. cit., 84.

[255] J.P. Braga, Preface, The Rights of Aliens in Hongkong, op. cit., xxi

[256] Correspondence with author from Stuart Braga, April 20, 2013.

[257] J.P. Braga, Preface, The Rights of Aliens in Hongkong, op. cit., 77.

[258] The uniqueness of Macanese culture in Hong Kong was suggested to me in 2015 by Dr. Armando da Silva, a noted writer on the patois and a retired professor from Towson University, who remarked on the transition of language. He pointed to the use of certain terms in Hong Kong, such as "egual-egual" to replace the use of "misma" (the same) by Macanese in Macau, which seemed to blend English and Iberian dialects. Although it is plausible that such usage was adopted among the second generation, a more precise time frame has yet to be attempted.

[259] H.J. Lethbridge, "The Condition of the European Working Class in Nineteenth Century Hong Kong", Journal of the Hong Kong Branch of the Royal Asiatic Society, 15, 1975:107.

[260] Hong Kong Legislative Council Report for the Year 1918, IX General Observations, pp. 30–31.

[261] Hong Kong Report of the Director of Public Works for the Year 1918, Q19, No.34. The dry weather in Hong Kong during January and February was also mentioned in reference to the epidemic that year. Peter K. Olitsky , 'Report on the Investigations of the Outbreak of Epidemic Meningitis in Hong Kong', Rockefeller Institute for Medical Research, New York, October 17, 1918, p. 68.

[262] Alfred, Marquis de Moges, Recollections of Baron Gros's Embassy to China and Japan in 1857–58 (London, Richard Griffin, 1860).

[263] "Fifth Day of the Inquiry: Views as the Cause of the Collapse", The China Mail,16 March 1918, includes testimony from Swedish and Portuguese licensees.

[264] A requirement of the auction read aloud in Chinese and English stated: "Intending bidders are informed that the prohibition against gambling remains in force. "The Race Course Tragedy-Coroner's Court of Enquiry Opens",
The China Mail, 7 March 1918, p. 4.

[265] Ibid. The price of each license auctioned in 1918 varied greatly depending on the location and the bidding. For example, the most expensive was site No. 15 for HK$1,230 won by the Japanese Benevolent Society. The least expensive was site No. 18 for HK$100 won by Lo Chi Ngai, a salesman who also licensed No.17 and No. 19. The total licensing revenue reported in the press also differed from the figure reported by the Public Works Department in its 1918 annual report. (See Note 16 below.) We use the figure reported by the government. The cost of each shed is taken from the testimony of Ma Cheung Kee, a partner in the Taz Hop construction firm, which built most of the matsheds at the racecourse that year. See "Race Course Tragedy: Fifth Day of Inquiry", The China Mail, 12 March 1918, p. 4, which includes a list of all winning bidders for 1918.

[266] The China Mail, 7 March 1918, p. 4.

[267] The China Mail, 7 March 1918, p.4.

[268] Ibid.

[269] Ibid.

[270] Ibid.

[271] Ibid.

[272] "Race Course Tragedy: Eleventh Day of Inquiry", The China Mail. 23 March 1918, p.4.

[273] Hong Kong Public Works Report-1918, Q14, no.20, reported under 'Sites for Booths at Race Course' that the revenue from the licensing of matsheds that year was HK$13,420.50 (about $3.3 million USD). Construction costs were stated in the previously cited article in The China Mail, 12 March 1918, under "The HK Police and Fire Report, 1918", K22, Table 1, reported 20 structures, including the Hong Kong Jockey Club and the Golf Club House, were destroyed in the fire, valued at HK$30,000. See Hong Kong Public Works Report-1918, note 2: Q21, no.42.

[274] The average for each matshed license was HK$700. Adjusting for inflation and exchange rates, each winning bidder paid the equivalent of over US$172,000 (HK$1 = US$247.46). Calculating a 15% commission on an average of five ten dollar bets each (HK$ 50) for an average of 300 bettors in each stand, the net profit for a successful licensee would be over US$380,000. This is the equivalent of over HK$1,500 in 1918, or 60% more than the annual average wage (HK$900) of a mid-level English government worker at the time. Wages to Portuguese and Chinese workers were much less. For a reference, see H.J. Lethbridge, "The Condition of the European Working Class in Nineteenth Century Hong Kong", JHKBRAS,15 (1975) p. 106, and Marjorie Topley, 'The Role of Savings and Wealth amongHong Kong Chinese', in I.C. Jarvie, ed., Hong Kong: A Society in Transition, London: Routledge & Kegan Paul, 1969.

[275] The majority of the participants included representatives from the English, Swedish, Portuguese-Macanese, Chinese, and Japanese communities. " Fifth Day of the Inquiry: Views as the Cause of the Collapse", The China Mail, 16 March 1918,

[276] Marjorie Topley, op. cit.

[277] Aureliano Jorge was the father of eleven legitimate children and three illegitimate children from a Chinese concubine who lived in a separate apartment above his office. Family information is provided by his granddaughter, Doreen Jorge Cotton (DJC), on her blog at http://doreenjorgecotton.com

[278] The following information is from an unpublished account written by Bernardino de Senna Fernandes d'Assumpcao (BSFA), provided by his son, Henry d'Assumpcao through the genealogical website: Macanesefamilies.com.

[279] BSFA, p. 1.

[280] BSFA, ibid.

[281] Ibid, and MacaneseFamilies.com citations for Lisbello J. Xavier, who was Pedro, Vasco, Paulo, and Daria Xavier's father.

[282] "Race Course Tragedy Inquiry", The China Mail, 13 March 1918, p. 3.

[283] The China Mail, 13 March 1918, p.3.

[284] Ibid.

[285] "The Race Course Tragedy: Sixth Day of Inquiry, The China Mail, 15 March1918, p. 4.

[286] "The Race Course Tragedy: Sixth Day of Inquiry, The China Mail, 15 March 1918, p. 4.

[287] Ibid.

[288] Ibid.

[289] Ibid.

[290] "The Race Course Tragedy: Fifth Day of Inquiry", The China Mail, 12 March 1918, p. 4.

[291] "The Race Course Tragedy: Seventh Day -Evidence of the Booth Owners", The China Mail, 16 March 1918, and
"The Race Course Tragedy: Eighth Day of the Inquiry, The China Mail, 18 March 1918.

[292] "The Race Course Tragedy: Seventh Day -Evidence of the Booth Owners", The China Mail, 16 March 1918, and
"The Race Course Tragedy: Eighth Day of the Inquiry, The China Mail, 18 March 1918.

[293] Ibid. John Olson testified that he and his partners had owned their mat-sheds for 13 years. Francisco P. Xavier testified that his family had owned its matshed for 9 years.

[294] The Hong Kong Daily Press, Front Page, Wednesday, 27 February 1918.

[295] The Hong Kong Daily Press, Front Page, Wednesday, 27 February 1918.

[296] BSFA, p. 2.

[297] The Hong Kong Daily Press, Front Page, ibid.

[298] "The Race Course Tragedy: Sixth Day of Inquiry" The China Mail, 15 March 1918, p. 4.

[299] The China Mail, 15 March 1918, p. 4.

[300] Ibid.

[301] Ibid.

[302] The Hong Kong Daily Press, Front Page, Wednesday, 27 February 1918.

[303] "The Race Course Tragedy: Why the Sheds Collapsed", The China Mail, 21 March 1918, p. 1.

[304] BSFA. P.4.

[305] "The Race Course Tragedy: Sixth Day of Inquiry", The China Mail, 15

March 1918, p. 4.

[306] BSFA, p.4. Paulo's daughter, Jeannette Xavier Smith, also confirms her father's account and his attempts to save his sister. (Correspondence, 7 April 2012).

[307] The Hong Kong Daily Press, op. cit. Police Cadet Lopes was also injured during the rescue.

[308] BSFA, p. 2-3.

[309] "Race Course Tragedy Inquiry", The China Mail, 13 March 1918, p.3 (Testimony of F.P. Xavier) and BSFA, p. 4.

[310] "The Race Course Tragedy", The China Mail, 27 February 1918, p. 1, and "The Race Course Tragedy: Why the Sheds Collapsed", The China Mail, 21 March 1918, p. 1.

[311] DJC, "A Man on Fire", 31 March 2013.

[312] BSFA, p. 3. This account is confirmed by Jorge's granddaughter, Doreen Jorge Cotton (DJC op. cit.).

[313] Despite reports in The China Mail and other papers listing a smaller number of dead, "The Hong Kong Report of the Secretary of Chinese Affairs-1918, Appendix C, C13, no.81, noted the official tally was 670.

[314] The dead included: Eduardo Pereira, J.D. Barros, J. Rodrigues, F. Seto, Maria Ernestina Vieira Ribeiro, Jose Libanio Manuel Spencer do Rosario, his wife, a son, and two sisters-in-law, Gustavo Maria do Rosario, Carlota Isabel Vieira Ribeiro, Maria Amelia Vieira Ribeiro, Ludovino Leopoldo Xavier, Daria Maria Xavier, Aureliano Guterres Jorge, and Luis Gonzaga Baptista. The injured included:Mr and Mrs J. Remedios. There also are unconfirmed reports that members of the d'Aquino family were among the dead. (Correspondence to the author from Fredric J. Silva, 8 April 2012.)

[315] "The Portuguese Community and the Catastrophe", The China Mail, 6 March 1918.

[316] "Pontifical Requiem Mass at Shameen (Canton)", The China Mail, 12 March 1918.

[317] "The Race Course Tragedy: Why the Sheds Collapsed", The China Mail, 21 March 1918, p. 1.

[318] "The Race Course Tragedy Inquiry", The China Mail, 28 March 1918, p. 4.

[319] "Race Course Tragedy: Twentieth Day of Inquiry", The China Mail, 5 April 1918, p. 4.

[320] "Race Course Disaster Inquiry: Coroner's Questions to the Jury", The China Mail, 12 April 1918, p. 4.

[321] Ibid.

[322] Hong Kong Legislative Council Minutes, (HKLCM). Questions and Answers, 23 May 1918, Race Course Disaster, p. 16-17.

[323] Ibid. <u>Hong Kong Business Symposium</u>, South China Morning Post, 1957, p. 48.

[324] Ibid.

[325] Ibid.

[326] "The Race Course Tragedy", The China Mail, 27 February 1918, p. 1.

[327] The Legislative Council set aside a 7,319 sq. ft. plot on the slopes of Mount Caroline In Hong Kong as a burial ground for the unidentified victims, <u>Hongkong Government Gazette</u>, 23 June 1922.

[328] Jose Pedro Braga, <u>The Portuguese in Hongkong and China</u>, Their Beginning, Settlement, and Progress to 1949, Vol. 1, Macau and Hongkong, 2013:148-49, edited by Barnabas H.M. Koo (based on Braga's original manuscript completed in 1944.)

[329] Eduardo M.S. Xavier, "The Portuguese in Business", <u>Hong Kong Business Symposium</u>, Hong Kong Chamber of Commerce, 1956:302.

[330] <u>Hongkong Telegraph</u> newspaper, August 31, 1895. An editorial suggested that any foreigner coming to Hong Kong who was competent and willing work had the same right to government employment or elsewhere as those who were British born. As competition for lower wages increased, however, the solution for the Portuguese was to "turn to the trades and handicrafts". The editor concluded: "There is pride of race among them that is out of place in this Free Trade generation… they must not confine themselves to being clerks and bookkeepers."

[331] J.P.Braga, <u>The Rights of Aliens in Hong Kong</u>, Noronha & Co., 1895:45-50.

[332] Hoi To Wong, "Interport Printing Enterprise: Macanese Printing Networks in Chinese Trading Ports", <u>Treaty Ports in Modern China: Law, Land and Power</u>, Robert Bickers and Isabella Jackson, eds., Routledge, London, 2016:141.

[333] Geoffrey C. Gunn, <u>First Globalization</u>: The Eurasian Exchange 1500-1800, Rowman & Littlefield, 2003. Gunn argues that "…European hegemony was in many ways contingent on three centuries of intellectual negotiation and ideological contestation with the East." 19th century Macanese printing through its facility with multiple languages and the acquisition of abandoned English presses was one example.

[334] Wolfgang Keller, Ben Li, and Carol H. Shiue, "China's Foreign Trade:

Perspectives From the Past 150 Years," NBER Working Papers, 2010:23-24, 16550, National Bureau of Economic Research, Inc.

[335] The following information on Lisbello Xavier and his family was provided by Dr. Anita M. Xavier, including "A New Direction: the Hongkong Printing Press, Lithographers 1888 – 1929", and several other unpublished manuscripts on the Sarrazolla and Xavier families, Queensland, Aus. 2000.

[336] Stuart Braga, Making Impressions: A Portuguese Family in Macau and Hong Kong, 1700 – 1945, International Institute of Macau, July 2015:228-233. This is also supported by Anita Xavier's research, op. cit.

[337] Bye-Laws of the Club Lusitano, Limited, Hongkong, 1904:19

[338] Family members report this may have been a random act. No other corroboration was available.

[339] Helmut Kipphan, Handbook of Print Media: Technologies and Production Methods, Springer Science & Business Media, 2001

[340] Debin Ma "Money and Monetary System in China in the 19th-20th Century: An Overview", Working Paper 159, London School of Economics, January 2012:13.

[341] T. Rawski, Economic Growth in Prewar China, University of California, Berkeley Press, 1989:157

[342] German traders had been active in Canton since 1783, headquartered first to Macau, then moved to Hong Kong in 1859 during the last stages of the Opium Wars. See Carl Smith, "The German Speaking Community of Hong Kong, 1846-1918", Journal of the Royal Asiatic Society-Hong Kong, Vol. 34, 1994.

[343] The Portuguese press in Hong Kong often included accounts of immigrants traveling back and forth between Macau and Hong Kong for vacations and family visits. For example, Delfino Noronha's family, including his grandson Jose Pedro Braga who was born in Hong Kong, also lived in, or retreated periodically to Macau. Stuart Braga, Making Impressions: op. cit. 299-303.

[344] Francisco was identified as "Francis Paul Danenberg" in a jurors list in the Hongkong Government Gazette, 19th Feb. 1904. Francisco's brother, Antonio Maria Danenberg, was married to Glafira Antonia Xavier, the daughter of Lisbello de Jesus Xavier's older sister, Maria Francisca Xavier. Jorge Forjaz's Familias Macaense, Fundacao Macau, 1996 and 2017 editions.

[345] "A New Direction: the Hongkong Printing Press, Lithographers 1888 – 1929", unpublished manuscript, family histories of the Sarrazolla and Xavier families, compiled by Dr. Anita M. Xavier, Queensland, Aus. 2000:2.

[346] Ibid.

[347] York Lo, "The Needle, the Bible and "Our People": Chiuchow Christians and the Swatow Lace Industry in Hong Kong" , October 30, 2017, http://industrialhistoryhk.org/swatow-lace/#comment-33819

[348] As recorded by Dr. Anita M. Xavier, op. cit. in the "New Directions" manuscript:
1913: Chan Wai Seng Bank, Chewsang, (Kwangtung);
1914: Kwan Chin Chong Private Bank, Guo Hong Yu Private Bank, Tan Hua Loong Chong Bank, The Commercial Bank, The GWA Swarmwun Yiack Private Bank, Guandong Private Bank
1916: Lee Yick Cheong Bank
1918: Banco Nacional Ultramarino (Macau)
1922: Hon Tat Lung Kee Bank, Hung Tai Chong Bank, Chin Hong Local Bank, Yee Seng Chong Private Bank
1928: Zhi Fa Private Bank

[349] Letter written by Pedro Xavier, dated 2 August 1943, to the British Consul in Macau. Xavier family archive, compiled by Dr. Anita M. Xavier, 2000.

[350] The buyers were C. Burnett and V. Labrum, who agreed to payment in monthly installments of $700 at 7% interest. "A New Direction", Xavier family archive, Dr. Anita M. Xavier, 2000.

[351] Ibid

[352] See Fr. Zinho Gozano's account of his old Kowloon neighborhood in: THE LIFE AND TIMES OF FATHER JOSÉ "ZINHO" GOSANO, UNIAO MACAENSE AMERICANA Bulletin, Apr-Jun 2011 Vol 34 No 2.

[353] "A New Direction", Xavier family archive, Dr. Anita M. Xavier, 2000.

[354] A History of the Hongkong Electric Company Limited, http://www.fundinguniverse.com/company-histories/hongkong-electric-holdings-ltd-history/ See also Arnold Wright, Twentieth Century Impressions of Hongkong, Shanghai, and other Treaty Ports of China, Hong Kong, 1908:168.

[355] "A New Direction", Xavier family archive, op. cit.

[356] "A New Direction", Xavier family archive, op. cit.

[357] The shares included: Nanyang Brothers Tobacco Co., Ltd. 3,800 shares, and Chan Lim Pak 2,800 shares, "A New Direction", Xavier family archive, op. cit.

[358] Lou Kau arrived in Macau with his family from Guangdong in 1857 and

opened a private bank ten years later. He then invested in pork from his home province and sold the meat in Macau. In 1881 Lou was granted the first opium franchise, followed by the gambling concession for "Fan Tan", a Han Chinese game, in 1882. He spent the next two decades supporting charitable projects among the Chinese, including hospitals and schools. In 1906, however, under pressure from creditors in Guangdong Lou committed suicide, elevating his son Lou Lim-lok to the head of the family business. Mark O'Neill, "Macao Mansion Hides Story of Wealth and Tragedy", Macau Magazine, January 2010, Issue No. 2.

[359] "The History of Gambling in Hong Kong and Macau", in Chi Chuen Chan, et. al., Problem Gambling in Hong Kong and Macau, Singapore, 2016:13-14.

[360] "A New Direction", Xavier family archive, op. cit.

[361] Masato Shizume,"The Japanese Economy during the Interwar Period: Instability in the Financial System and the Impact of the World Depression", Institute for Monetary and Economic Studies, Bank of Japan Review, May 2009.

[362] "A New Direction", Xavier family archive, op. cit.

[363] "A New Direction", Xavier family archive, op. cit.

[364] Apparently weary of reports of conflict and brutality, a lead story announced in early 1938 that "The old year was swamped under the maddest and merriest reception a New Year has ever received.", Hong Kong Daily Press, January 1, 1938.

[365] Frank Welsh, A History of Hong Kong, HarperCollins, 1993:382-84.

[366] Henry Lethbridge, "Condition of the European Working Class in Nineteenth Century Hong Kong", Journal of the Royal Asiatic Society Hong Kong, Vol. 15, 1975:110-111.

[367] Frank Welsh, op. cit. p. 382.

[368] The following account was taken from several press reports: The China Mail, Dec. 29, 1930, "Mrs. Xavier Charged with Attempted Murder"; The Hongkong Telegraph, December 29, 1930, "Portuguese Woman Before Court. Charge of Attempted Murder"; The China Mail, Feb. 2, 1931, "Manton Shooting Affair"; The Hongkong Telegraph, Feb. 2, 1931, "Wanchai Shooting Incident. Manton Tells Story at Trial. Plea that Mrs. Xavier meant to Shoot Herself"; The China Mail, Feb. 3, 1931, "Mrs. Xavier Committed to Trial"; The Hongkong Telegraph, February 3, 1931, "Manton Shooting Affair"; The China Mail, Feb. 18, 1931, "Mrs. Xavier to Appear"; The China Mail, Feb. 24, 1931, "Wanchai Shooting Affair". Individual page citations are not included due to the errors

in reproduction.

[369] The China Mail, Dec. 29, 1930, "Mrs. Xavier Charged with Attempted Murder".

[370] Ibid.

[371] Lethbridge, op. cit. 108-7, 110.

[372] The following information can be found under each respective name in a genealogical study by Jorge Forjaz, Familias Macaense (Macanese Families), Fundacao Macau, 1996 and 2017 versions.

[373] In a study of prison time for "Non-British" residents of British colonies, two scholars observed: "I(i)n colonial contexts, prisons were part and parcel of the 'civilising mission' of colonisers, as existing penal practices, which were often based on physical punishment, were viewed as 'barbaric' and 'uncivilised'. Dikötter, F. and Brown, I. (Eds.) Culture of Confinement: A History of the Prisons in Africa, Asia and Latin America. New York, Cornell University Press:2007: Introduction,3-4.

[374] The China Mail, Feb. 24, 1931, "Wanchai Shooting Affair".

[375] Treatment was hampered by overcrowding and emphasized "physical restraint and temporary custodial care". Zhai Hailong and Gao Yan, "Early psychiatric services in Hong Kong from 1841 to 1947", Mental Health in Family Medicine, 2017, 13: 436-437. They write: "In 1938, (the Victoria Mental Hospital) had a bed complement of 23 but had to house more than 100 patients. "Services … at that time were provided by a part time European Medical Officer in-charge, a part-time Chinese Medical Officer in-charge, one Head Male Attendant, one Assistant Male Attendant, three Mental Nurses, three dressers and a group of 23 Amahs, ward-boys, laborers and coolies."

[376] Hong Kong Legislative Council Minutes, 25 July 1940: 100.

[377] Frank Welsh, A Borrowed Place: The History of Hong Kong, Kodansha, New York, 1993. See Chapter 13, "A Colonial Backwater", 378-385.

[378] Vivian Kong, 'Hong Kong is my Home': The 1940 Evacuation and Hong Kong Britons, The Journal of Imperial and Commonwealth History, 2018:3.

[379] Tony Banham, Reduced to a Symbolic Scale: The Evacuation of British Women and Children in 1940, Hong Kong University Press, 2017:57.

[380] Branham, ibid, p.75

[381] "Compulsory Evacuation", Hong Kong Volunteer and Ex-POW Association of New South Wales, Australia, Occasional Paper #20, August 2013.

[382] Kong, op. cit. p. 4.

[383] This position was related as late as October 1941, as related by W. V. Taylor to the Australian Minister for Home Affairs, 3 October 1941, A1608, B 39/1/3, National Archives of Australia, NAA. Citation provided by Vivian Kong, op. cit. p. 12.

[384] Hong Kong Legislative Council Minutes, 25 July 1940: 115-116.

[385] Both Banham, op. cit., p.33 and the writer of "Compulsory Evacuation", op. cit., p. 2 provide examples.

[386] The South China Morning Post, August 20, 1937, reported approximately 1,000 Macanese refugees from Shanghai arrived in Hong Kong on the French steamer The Aramis. Another writer claimed that 1,203 Portuguese refugees had fled Hong Kong by August 1941, followed by 950 people on January 6, 1942 and another 450 the next day. R. Pinto, 'War in Peace', Macau Magazine, No. 96, 1996:90.

[387] See also, Roy Eric Xavier, "Hong Kong and the Introduction of "Social Distance", Working Paper, The Portuguese-Macanese Studies Project, Institute for the Study of Societal Issues, University of California, Berkeley, 2019.

[388] See Henry Lethbridge's article, "19th Century Working Class Hong Kong, Journal of the Royal Asiatic Society, Hong Kong Branch, Vol. 15, 1975.

[389] See Chapter 7.

[390] See Chapter 8.

[391] See Chapter 9.

[392] See Chapter 10.

[393] The China Mail, front page, July 23, 1940.

[394] Kong, op. cit. p. 16.

[395] Hong Kong Legislative Council minutes, 25 July 1940: 113-114.

1 [396]Some of the information was found in the unpublished writings and oral histories of Macanese immigrants who recorded their impressions of life and conditions as they experienced them. Comparisons of their recollections with published historical analysis, and other unpublished ac-

counts, were used to determine accuracy.

² [397]As related in an interview with Stanley Ho, in "Dr. Stanley Ho: King of the Casinos", <u>Macao Remembers</u>, Jill McGivering, Oxford, 1999, p. 110. Also, see Fredric Jim Silva, "Reminiscences of a Wartime Refugee: Macau and Hong Kong during World War Two", International Institute of Macau, August 2013, p. 28.

[398] In Hong Kong, the estimated population in 1939 was 1.05 million: "Report on the Social and Economic
Progress of the People of the Colony of Hong Kong for the year 1939", Chapter III, *Population and Births and Deaths*, pgs. 1-3. The report also states that Hong Kong's population increased by an estimated 650,000 that year because of refugees fleeing the Sino-Japanese war. By 1940 there were approximately 1.07 million. Hong Kong "Blue Book" for the year 1940, *Population and Vital Statistics*, 1-2. By the middle of 1941 Hong Kong's population was 1.639 million, of which 1.615 million were Chinese. See Barnabas H.M. Koo, The Portuguese in Hongkong and China, Vol. 2, International Institute of Macau, pg. 12, based on G.B. Endacott's estimates in his History of Hong Kong, Oxford, 1973, 289.

[399] Frank Welsh, A History of Hong Kong, London, 1997 pg. 411, quoted from Churchill's book, The Second World War, (Vol.1) London, 1948, pg. 551.

[400] Add Geoffrey C. Gunn.... Macau during WWII.

[401] Rana Mitter makes the point succinctly in her book, Forgotten Ally. Mitter writes: "Japanese Pan-Asianism had metamorphosed in the decades between 1900 and the 1930s, and the Japanese were seized with a sincere, if deluded, belief that they had a duty to lead their Asian neighbors, including China, in a journey of liberation from Western imperialism. <u>Forgotten Ally</u>: China's World War II, 1937-1945, Houghton Mifflin Harcourt, 2013, p. 143.

[402] Add reference here about pre-war Hong Kong as refuge for spies and the Nationalist army

[403] Koo, Vol. 2, op. cit. p. 125, and note 21, based on interviews with eyewitnesses.

[404] One observer characterized the Macanese volunteers in this way: "Many joined more for the camaraderie of their friends, not even dreaming that one day they would be called upon to use their training to fight in an actual war defending our homeland." – Basil A. Xavier, "The Rising Sun", in "The World War II Years: Growing Up in Wartime Macao", 1996, unpublished, p. 2.

[405] Brian Castro, <u>Shanghai Dancing</u>, Giramondo Publishing, Australia, 2003, pg. 295.

[406] A remembrance written by Isabella Palmer for "Sapper Edward Filomeno Hyndman", pg.2, found under
"Other Links" at www.macanesefamilies.com, a web site listing Jorge Forjaz's genealogy of Macanese families.

[407] Basil Xavier, op. cit., pg. 1.

[408] Basil Xavier, op. cit., pg. 1.

[409] One of Brian Koo's interviewees reported 398 people were housed in Acting Consul Francisco Soares' residence, while many more were given sanctuary in neighboring houses. Brian Koo, op. cit. Vol. 2, p. 124-127.

[410] The tension of the evacuation and the bombings proved too much for Pedro Marques, who suffered a fatal heart attack one night. Interview by the author of Marques' daughter, Margarida Maria Marques Savant, San Francisco, October 2013.

[411] The following account was taken from an interview with Reginald Pires conducted by the author in Salinas California in September 2011.

[412] This account is taken from "Escape from Kowloon", Elaine de Souza and Vince de Souza Jr., <u>UMA News Bulletin</u>, Fall, 2011:19.

[413] The first group of approximately 900 Portuguese-Macanese refugees left Hong Kong on February 6, 1942. A second group of about 600 left in March. A third group of unknown number left for Macau on April 20, 1942. Brian Koo, Vol. 2, op. cit. pg. 123.

[414] As related by Margarida Marques Savant in an interview with the author in October 2013. Similar incidents appear in the personal accounts of Basil Xavier in his unpublished paper: "The World War II Years: Growing Up in Wartime Macao", in the author's files.

[415] Such was the case of Elisa Alvares Xavier and her daughters Claudette and Jacqueline, who had Portuguese passports, and their father, Paulo Xavier, who worked for the Hong Kong Police Department and held a British passport. Information provided by Jeannette Xavier Smith, April 2014.

[416] Brian Koo, Vol. 2, op. cit., pgs. 124-127.

[417] Brian Koo, Vol. 2, op. cit., p.133.

[418] Brian Koo, Vol. 2, op. cit., p. 136.

[419] "The Hong Kong News", published by the Japanese civil administration on December 25, 1942, Vol. IVXI, No. 466 (copy in author's files). Koo writes that among them were Macanese in the HKVDC and policemen holding British citizenship who fought the Japanese during the invasion, were captured, and tried to escape to Macau to join their families. Brian Koo, Vol. 2, op. cit., p. 133.

[420] The large number of Portuguese in Hong Kong with British papers may be accounted for by Macanese who were issued British citizenship beginning in the late 19th century. For example, Januario Antonio de Carvalho, the Chief Cashier of Hong Kong's Treasury, was granted British citizenship in 1883. "NATURALIZATION OF JANUARIO ANTONIO DE CARVALHO ORDINANCE," No. 14 of 1883, December 28, 1883, Historical Laws of Hong Kong Online, http://oelawhk.lib.hku.hk/items/show/440. The trend continued through the 1930s, and included Macanese members of the Legislative Council: Jose Pedro Braga (1929) and Leonardo D'Alamada e Castro, Jr. (1936). Both eventually escaped to Macau with the help of Portuguese consul Francisco P. Soares.

[421] The actual number of Macanese refugees has been elusive among observers. For example, Stuart Braga, a historian of the period, wrote in 2007 that "Hong Kong's Portuguese population fled by the "thousands" to Macau, and almost ten thousand of them were able to claim British nationality." Stuart Braga, "He Kept the Union Jack Flying in the Far East", Casa de Macau Australia newsletter, June 2007. The South China Morning Post of August 20, 1937 reported 1000 Macanese refugees arrived from Shanghai on the French steamer The Aramis. Another writer in 1996 claimed that 1,203 Portuguese refugees had fled Hong Kong in August 1941, followed by 950 people on January 6, 1942 and another 450 the next day. R. Pinto, 'War in peace', Macau Magazine, No. 96, p. 90.

[422] The ship was the Tung Hui, an abandoned river steamer nicknamed "The Hulk" by the Macanese who lived on it. The other refugee centers in Macau were the Bela Vista Hotel, the Armacao and the Escola Luso Chinesa, two Chinese schools abandoned during the war, Caixa Escolar and the Clube de Macau, a club with a theatre and a stage, the Club Sargento, a club for non-commissioned Portuguese officers, the Gremio Militar, a military barracks, and a number of smaller residences, including the San Paulo, located near the ruins of St. Paul's cathedral, two adjoining houses on the Rua Pria Grande, a group of small residential houses on Rua Formosa, and the Chacra Lietao, a rural farm house located outside the city center. Fredric Jim Silva, "Remin-

iscences of a Wartime Refugee", op. cit. p. 20-21.) Horatio Ozorio, "A WWII Refugee remembers Caixa Escolar Days in Macau", http://www.diasporama-caense.org/The%20Way%20It%20Was.htm.

[423] "Dr. Stanley Ho: King of the Casinos", op cit., p. 107

[424] Biographical information on Pedro Jose Lobo was taken from Jorge Forjaz, Familias Macaense, op. cit., Vol. II, p. 353. Additional information on Lobo's family can be found at www.macanesefamilies.com under "Lobo, Peter", which lists documentary materials from Forjaz's genealogy.

[425] The United States government made a distinction between "neutral" and "non-belligerent" countries. In a 1997 report on the shipment of Nazi gold during World War II, it stated: "Technically, only Switzerland and Sweden were "neutral" countries during the War according to generally-accepted definitions of neutrality. Spain, Portugal, Turkey and Argentina were "non-belligerent" but not neutral. However, ..., the neutral and non-belligerent countries are, for the sake of simplicity, referred to as "neutrals" when mention of them is made collectively." U.S. and Allied Efforts to Recover and Restore Gold and Other Assets Stolen or Hidden by Germany During World War", William Z. Slany, U.S. Department of State, May 1997, p. 12, note.

[426] Macau's need to bargain with the Japanese is illustrated in Geoffrey Gunn's study of Japan's efforts to monopolize rice distribution in Southeast Asia during the war. He writes: "... in early August 1944, Allied intelligence stated that the Japanese were shipping considerable rice from Saigon to occupied Java, Singapore, Hong Kong, Shanghai as well as Japan. In August 1944, Macau Governor Gabriel Teixeira gained Japanese agreement to send a vessel (the SS Portugal) to northern Vietnam to load coal and beans for shipment to Macau at a time when the Japanese choke on Portuguese-controlled Macau had reduced sections of the population to cannibalism." (http://www.japan-focus.org/-Geoffrey-Gunn/3483)

[427] See "U.S. and Allied Efforts To Recover and Restore Gold and Other Assets Stolen or Hidden by Germany During World War", William Z. Slany, U.S. Department of State, May 1997. The report states in part, "During the course of the war, Portugal was an important source of wolfram, tin, manganese, mica, chrome, and antimony for the Third Reich's war machine. Of these, wolfram (tungsten) was the most coveted by the Nazis. In February 1943 Germany concluded an agreement with Portugal to obtain 100 percent of the output of its German owned wolfram mines and 50 percent of all other mines with the exception of those owned by Allied interests. Portugal, wary of the long-term value of the Deutschmark, requested payment in gold. The Allies contended that most of this gold had been looted from occupied countries and peoples after 1942."

[428] See footnote 7 above.

[429] Interview of Chan Tai-pak in "Macao's Oldest WWII Journalist Hero Retells the Past", <u>Macao Magazine</u>, Living History, Issue 7, 2009.

[430] Geoffrey C. Gunn, <u>Encountering Macau</u>: A Portuguese City State on the Periphery of China, 1557-1999, Westview Press, Boulder, CO, 1996, p. 126.

[431] The estimate is provided by Chan Su-weng, Chairman of the Macao Historical Society, in "Scourge of the War", Mark O'Neill, <u>Macao Magazine</u>, Issue 8.

[432] "Macao's Oldest WWII Journalist Hero Retells the Past", ibid.

[433] The exchange rate for Macau pitacas (MOP) to United States dollars (USD) in 1942 is estimated at 1 MOP = 0.1252 USD. $25,000 Macau pitacas during the war was thus worth $3,130 (USD).

[434] Information provided by Daniel Gomes in "Wartime Macau", <u>UMA News Bulletin</u>, Spring 2011, p. 3.

[435] Fredric Jim Silva, "Reminiscences of a Wartime Refugee", op. cit. p. 24.

[436] Information obtained from a telephone interview with Armando da Silva in April 2014, and from personal correspondence from Reggie Pires, a refugee at Caixa Escolar during the war, dated May 2, 2014.

[437] As noted by Fredric Jim Silva, op. cit. p. 22. Alzira Alvares Xavier was from a well-known Macau family. Although living in Hong Kong since at least 1921, she was the granddaughter of Dr João Jacques Floriano Álvares (1819-1899), surgeon-general of the Macau's militia who was knighted by the Portugal crown in 1849 for helping to stop a cholera epidemic in Asia. Jorge Forjaz, <u>Famílias Macaenses</u>, Vol., 1996, 177, 640.

[438] Silva described the rice as "… of the poorest quality, with a high percentage of broken grains and lots of impurities such as sand and dirt. The rice had to be 'picked ' over laboriously and slowly cleansed of impurities, before it could be turned back to the main kitchen to be cooked. Other food rations were generally of poor quality and scarce. As a result, many people would fall prey to malnutrition and diseases." Fredric Jim Silva, "Reminiscences of a Wartime Refugee", op. cit., pg. 22.

[439] Silva, op. cit. pgs. 40-43. According to other interviewees, elementary school children were taught at Escola Central (boys), and in a separate section at St. Rosa de Lima School for younger girls. Pires and Savant interviews, op. cit.

[440] Fredric Jim Silva, op. cit. p. 40-42. Student rosters from that period also illustrate the size and ethnic composition of the classes. "Complete List: St. Luis Gonzaga College, Macau, January 1943 to June 1945", copy in the author's files.

[441] Silva, ibid, p. 43.

[442] Another refugee also noted the lack of Portuguese spoken among Macanese in the Caixa Escolar center, and by extension, among most members of the Hong Kong community. Reggie Pires correspondence, May 2, 2014.

[443] The patois of Macau, "Maquista", is currently spoken or understood by about 500 Macanese expatriates and is used by theatre companies and other performance artists in Macau. Surveys were conducted by the author in 2012 and 2013 as part of his current research, summaries of which can be found at: www.macstudies.net.

[444] The diversity of refugees in Macau was impressive, including Jews, Persians, British, Germans, Irish, and Italians. Threats to some nationals who fraternized with "undesirables" also occurred, including Nazi threats to Germans living in Macau. See "A Nazi Threat to a Macau resident", Macau Closer, March 2011.

[445] Arnaldo de Oliveira Sales: "A Gentle War", in Macao Remembers, Jill McGivering, Oxford University Press, 1999, p. 65-66.

[446] "A Gentle War", McGivering, ibid, p. 66.

[447] "Sir Roger Lobo: Wartime Resistance", in McGivering, 1999, op. cit., p. 77.

[448] "Sir Roger Lobo: Wartime Resistance", in McGivering, 1999, p. 75. See also Felicia Yap, "Portuguese Communities in East and Southeast Asia during the Japanese Occupation", in The Making of the Luso-Asian World, Laura Jarnagin (ed.), Singapore, 2011, p. 215-216.

[449] Felicia Yap, ibid, p. 212.

[450] "Dr. Stanley Ho: King of the Casinos", McGivering, 1999, ibid, p. 108.

[451] "Dr. Stanley Ho: King of the Casinos", McGivering, 1999, ibid, p. 109-110.

[452] "Dr. Stanley Ho: King of the Casinos", McGivering, 1999, ibid, p. 108.

[453] Fredric Silva, Reggie Pires, and Guida Savant each described such incidents during interviews with the author, (August 2011 - October 2013).

[454] Felicia Yap, op. cit. p. 212.

[455] Felicia Yap, op. cit. p. 211 and note 48 in the same article.

[456] Guido Sequeira interview with the author in April 2012.

[457] Guido Sequeira interview, ibid.

[458] Daniel Gomes, "Wartime Macau", UMA News Bulletin, Spring, 2011, p. 4. Yap also mentions Gosano and other Macanese who worked for the resistance. Felicia Yap, op. cit. p. 215.

[459] See Gosano's autobiography and Lindsey Ride's biography

[460] Daniel Gomes, ibid, p. 5, mentions the work of medical student Alberto Ozorio. Yap writes about Bernard Xavier, an OSS agent in Macau during the war. Felicia Yap, op. cit. p. 215., citing "Bernard Felix Xavier, interview by the Imperial War Museum, 21 December 1999: interview 19226, reel 2, transcript, IWM".

[461] Yap, op. cit. p. 215.

[462] Some Macanese professionals like Dr. Eduardo L. Gosano, however, were not immune to discrimination in post-war Hong Kong. Despite his service to the Allies at grave risk to his life as an intelligence operative in Macau, Gosano, a noted surgeon, was not granted surgical privileges at Hong Kong's Queen Mary Hospital for several years after his arrival after the war. This situation led to his migration to San Francisco in the 1960s. Eddie Gosano, Hong Kong Farewell, Greg England Publications, June 1997.

[463] Felicia Yap, "Eurasians in British Asia during the Second World War", Journal of the Royal Asiatic Society, 2011, Series 3, 21, 4, pgs. 485.

[464] Reggie Pires correspondence with the author, May 2, 2014.

[465] For example, see Linda Tamua, <u>Nisei Soldiers Break Their Silence</u>: Coming Home to Hood River, University of Washington Press, 2012, Neil A. Wynn, <u>The African-American Experience during World War II</u>, Rowman and Littlefield, 2010, and Rogelio Saenz and Aurelia Lorena Murga, <u>Latino Issues</u>, Santa Barbara, 2011.

[466] My point is that the aftermath of upheavals such as mass migrations or genocide have effects on later generations in unexpected ways. As Rouben Adalian wrote: "When the struggle for survival is so individuated as during genocide, the confidence in the strengths of the collectivity is sapped. For the Armenians, the sapping of their societal confidence and their cultural optimism was perpetuated by the fact that they did not return to their former spaces". Rouben R. Adalian,"A Conceptual Method for Examining the Consequences of the Armenian Genocide", <u>Studies in Comparative Genocide</u>, eds. Levon Chorbajian and George Shirinian, St. Martin's Press, New York:1999:54.

[467] See the writings of Jorge Morbey, "Aspects of 'Ethnic of Identities' of the Macanese", <u>Review of Culture</u>, 1994, Instituto Cultural do Governo da R.E.M. de Macau, and Joao de Pina y Cabral, <u>Between China and Europe</u>, Person, Culture and Emotion in Macao, Continuum, London, 2002.

[468] I am deeply indebted to those community members and scholars who continue to gather historical materials, and to many who have shared their family accounts and stories for this study so that the world can appreciate the extent of their contributions.

[469] One example is the experience of Rafael Alfonso Duarte, a Spaniard married to a Macanese woman, who survived the war in Manila, and migrated to Southern California in May 1945. Based on Correspondence with his granddaughter, August 2016.

[470] Fan Shan Ching, "The Population of Hong Kong", The Committee for International Coordination of National Research in Demography, Joint Study by the University of Hong Kong and the United Nations, 1974:2-3.

[471] Glen Peterson, "The Uneven Development of the International Refugee Regime in Postwar Asia: Evidence from China, Hong Kong and Indonesia", <u>Journal of Refugee Studies</u>, Vol. 25, No. 3, Oxford University Press, 2011:335. Peterson observed that the major effort to absorb the refugees seemed to be "conditioned by earlier colonial strategies involving the use of contract labour and the transnational relocation of 'surplus populations' for the development of plantation agriculture and frontier territories."

[472] Tai-Loc Lui, Stephen W.K. Chiu, Ray Yep, Routledge Handbook of Contemporary Hong Kong, New York, 2019.

[473] See Ke-Che Yip, "The Transition to Decolonization: The Search for a Health Policy in Post-War Hong Kong: 1945-1985", Chapter 2, Public Health and National Reconstruction in Post-War Asia, Liping Bu and Ke Che Yip (eds.): 2015.

[474] The 1953 Shek Kip Mei Fire, for example, left more than 50,000 refugees homeless.
https://www.youtube.com/watch?v=Dt8USmzvKbo . See also Ke-Che Yip, "The Transition to Decolonization: The Search for a Health Policy in Post-War Hong Kong: 1945-1985", op. cit.

[475] Such fears were mentioned repeatedly during several interviews by the author with Macanese immigrants in San Francisco and Los Angeles from 2012 through 2017.

[476] Roy Eric Xavier, "J.P. Braga and 'The Rights of Aliens' in Colonial Hong Kong", Working Paper, the Portuguese and Macanese Studies Project, ISSI, U.C. Berkeley, 2018. Roy Eric Xavier, "The Sum of All Fears: The Evacuation of British Subjects from Pre-War Hong Kong", Working Paper, the Portuguese and Macanese Studies Project, ISSI, U.C. Berkeley, 2019.

[477] Arnaldo M.A. Gonçalves, "Hong Kong and Macau Special Administrative Regions: The Downfall of the "One Country, Two Systems" Policy, International Journal of Humanities and Social Science, Vol. 9 • No. 10 • October 2019:11-25.

[478] These relationships have become an important part of global finance and commerce. The German broadcasting company, Deutsche Welle reported in May 2019 that "Foreign companies need Hong Kong too. The territory is a base for over 1,500 multinational companies who use it as an easy way into the China market — 60% of foreign investment comes through Hong Kong." Hong Kong critical to China but uncertainty reigns, https://www.dw.com/en/hong-kong-critical-to-china-but-uncertainty-reigns/a-50041265.

[479] The countries served are Angola, Brazil, Cape Verde, Guinea-Bissau, Mozambique, Portugal, and East Timor, as well as the islands of São Tomé and Príncipe. The purpose is to reach over 200 million Portuguese speakers, mostly in Brazil and Portugal, for "co-operation — including intergovernmental co-operation — in trade; investment and entrepreneurship …" The Forum's mission currently does not include an estimated 45 million cultural Portuguese in many other countries that are not part of the current strategy.

[480] Mark Yeandle, Mike Wardle, The Global Financial Centres, Index 26, <u>Long Finance & Global Financial Centres</u>, September 2019.

[481] James Fallows, "Macau's Big Gamble", <u>The Atlantic</u>, September 2007. https://www.theatlantic.com/magazine/archive/2007/09/macau-s-big-gamble/306131/ The Lui family of Hong Kong was able to gain controlling interest in 2005 of Galaxy Entertainment, which currently operates six casinos in the territory.

[482] Mingjie Sheng and Chaolin Gu, "Economic growth and development in Macau (1999–2016): The role of the booming gaming industry", <u>Cities</u>, Volume 75, May 2018: 72-80.

[483] "Las Vegas vs. Macau: Which Is the Capital of Casino Gambling?", <u>Business Matters</u>, 16 May 2019. https://www.bmmagazine.co.uk/business/las-vegas-vs-macau-which-is-the-capital-of-casino-gambling/
The Covid-19 virus has led to a 88% drop in Macau's gaming revenues in comparison to 2018, but is expected to recover by 2021. https://asiatimes.com/2020/03/macau-casino-takings-plunge-a-record-88/.
https://www.usnews.com/news/cities/articles/2020-03-24/macau-how-a-densely-populated-chinese-territory-is-keeping-coronavirus-at-bay

[484] According to Colliers International, the GBA is aimed at young tech workers as well as research and development activities, distinguishing itself from competing regions around a regional hi-tech productivity cluster. The GBA also includes the new Hengquin campus of the University of Macau, a $2 billion teaching and research institution opened in 2013. Rosanna Tang and Sean Ellison, Colliers International, <u>Greater Bay Area: A 2030 Outlook</u>, 2019.

[485] According to the latest United Nations data, the Macanese community in Macau is estimated to be 11,688, or 1.8% of the total population of 649,335. Gaming in Macau currently accounts for 86% of total government revenue. "Macau Gaming Industry Responsible for 86 Percent of Enclave Government Tax Revenue", Devin O'Connor - December 19, 2019.

[486] The Maquistas, who are Luso-Asian or colloquially "Portuguese from Asia", are named after the local patois, a blend of Portuguese, Chinese, and Malaysian vocabularies that has existed since the 16th century. Data collected by Portuguese scholars and independent surveys conducted by the Portuguese and Macanese Studies Project at U.C. Berkeley suggest that there may be more than 1.6 million Macanese and related Luso-Asians in at least 35 countries. See Jorge Forjaz, <u>Familias Macaenses</u>, Fundacao Oriente, Macau, 1996, revised 2017.

[487] There are currently 13 Casas are located in the United States (three in the San Francisco Bay Area), Canada (near Vancouver and Toronto), Australia (Brisbane and Melbourne), Portugal (Lisbon), Brazil (Rio de Janeiro and Sao Paulo), Britain (London), and Hong Kong. The total membership is estimated to be about 7,000 members.

[488] The interviews were conducted by the author in Macau between 2013 and 2017 with former legislators, newspaper editors, association leaders, attorneys, businesspeople, and educators during research visits. Other interviews were conducted by telephone in the United States through the end of 2019 with Casa de Macau officials who attended meetings when the protocols were discussed and signed. All of the participants have asked to remain anonymous.

[489] The destruction of Macau's ancient architecture by Hong Kong Chinese investors in the late 1970s gave additional impetus to preservation advocates. See the New York Times, April 22, 1981 and March 31, 1988.

[490] The earliest activities began in 1953 with a list of colonial sites in the national archives of Portugal. For a review of the history see: Hilary du Cros, "Emerging Issues for Cultural Tourism in Macau", Journal of Current Chinese Affairs, 1/2009: 76-78.

[491] The other associations include: Associacao dos Macaenses (ADM), a cultural association, The International Institute of Macau (IIM), a publishing association, APOMAC – an Association of Pensioners and Retirees of Macau, The Institute of European Studies of Macau (IEEM), research facility, and Associação Promotora da Instrução dos Macaenses (APIM), for the promotion of education in Macau.

[492] The distinction is based on birth and long-term residency. Permanent residents are identified as those who were born in Macau or have lived and worked there for at least seven years. Non-permanent residents are expatriates who no longer live in Macau but retain citizenship through birth or ties to first or second generation family members who were residents.

[493] Macau casino gaming revenue in 2019 was $36.5 Billion. If the estimates of those interviewed are accurate, the Fundacao Macau's revenues in that year would have been between $365 million to $1.095 billion.

[494] China Daily, "Xi proposes a 'new Silk Road' with Central Asia", September 8, 2013.

[495] This understanding was confirmed to me by an official in the Liaison office

of the Central People's Government in Macau during an interview in 2017. The expectation of more business connections remains unfulfilled. No formal or informal gatherings between local and international businesspeople have been organized by the *Conselho das Communicades Macaenses* since its founding in 2001.

[496] The only publishing outlet appears to be The Cultural Bureau's "Review of Culture", which accepts international work, but is not widely distributed outside Macau. Other local research groups, including the Jesuit-run Macau Ricci Institute, are not granted access to the government's archives. In 2016, noting the lack of public access to Macau's 80 special libraries and 34 university collections, the institute began a 10 year project to build its own digital library.

[497] The review was conducted during research visits from 2013 through 2017, including one when I was a Fulbright scholar at the University of Macau in 2015. I was informed then by faculty members that most government schools and universities did not offer Macau history courses to their students.

[498] The University of Macau's "Research Centre for Luso-Asian Studies", another potential source of information, is now focused on Portuguese linguistics. RCLAS has not produced historical research since a 2009 study of 16th Macau by Professor Isabel Lenoir da Silva de Seabra on *Muitsai* women (racially diverse girls sold by their parents as servants and concubines to Portuguese settlers, an important basis of Luso-Asian kinship in Macau).

[499] The meetings began in 1993 under the colonial government and continued after the handover to China in 1999.

[500] CCM's budgets are not made public. Estimates by those interviewed, place annual CCM grants from the Fundacao Macau at approximately $5-$6 million USD. This does not include separate funds allocated every three years for the *Encontros*, nor the value of real property in Macau purchased by the foundation for daily use by the Conselho.

[501] Although attendance data is not publicized, personal observation, journalist interviews, and reports from attendees indicated that participation declined from 1800 in 2013, to 1250 in 2016, to "less than 1000" in 2019. Attendance in 2019 was reportedly supplemented by local Macanese who were charged admission to the events.

[502] Jornal Tribuna de Macau, "Meeting of Macaenses as "Roagem de Saudade", November 22, 2019.

[503] These occurrences were considered "common practice" in interviews with international Macanese who regularly attend the meetings, or asked questions during tours and at cultural events in Macau.

[504] Du Cros notes a Macao tourism study that found historical sites attracted 45% more visitors than faux attractions with historical themes. Hilary du Cros, "Emerging Issues for Cultural Tourism in Macau". op. cit., pg. 88. The attraction of the combined cultural and commercial resources of Macau, Zhuhai, Hong Kong, and Guangdong should not be overlooked for long.

[505] In 2016, as Beijing again ordered "adequate diversification" in Macau, a leading newspaper warned of an economic recession. "Recessao Ainda em 2016 e 2017?", Jan. 8, 2016, Jornal Tribuna de Macau. This prediction came true in 2020 as a result of the pandemic. Casino revenue is currently down over 80% for the year.

[506] Opinion, Jornal Tribuna de Macau, Feb. 26, 2016.

[507] Hoje Macau, Front Page, Dec. 7, 2015.

[508] Jorge Forjaz, Familias Macaenses, Fundacao Oriente, Macau, 1996, revised 2017.

[509] The Mayflower Society of the United States claims over 35 million descendants based on 102 pilgrims who landed in Plymouth Massachusetts in 1620, sixty-three years after Macau was founded. Based on discussions with other scholars studying the Portuguese in Asia, including Jorge Forjaz in 2016, our most recent estimate may actually be low.

[510] "53 Incredible Facebook Statistics and Facts", Kit Smith, Brandwatch.com, June 1, 2019. https://www.brandwatch.com/blog/facebook-statistics/

---

[1]

[2]

www.ingramcontent.com/pod-product-compliance
Lightning Source LLC
Chambersburg PA
CBHW022111150426

43195CB00008B/358